Tommy (Flash) Fowler

QUITE SIMPLY A FLASH OF GENIUS
THE LIFE AND TIMES OF NORTHAMPTON
TOWN LEGEND TOMMY FOWLER

IBSN 0 954151305

First published in 2001 by
FRANK GRANDE

Printed and Bound in the United Kingdom
by Woolnough Bookbinding Ltd,
Irthlingborough, Northants.

Those responsible for the launch of the book
Back Row: (Left to Right) Roger Clarke (Committee member, White Hart), Graham Page
(graphic designer), Dave Herbert (Committee member, White Hart), Ian Turnock
(photographer), Dave Walden (sponsor), Frank Grande (Author);
Front Row: (Left to Right) Bill Graver (Committee member, White Hart), Tina Grande
(treasurer), Tommy Fowler, Joyce Fowler, Tom Fowler (grandson).

This book would not be possible if it was not for the help of the following people; Dave Walden, the long time Cobblers supporter who has sponsored the project, Ian Turnock who took the up-to-date photographs, Graham Page, the computer 'Whiz Kid' who cleaned up the old photographs, and designed the cover. The Committee of the 'White Hart Social Club' – especially Bill Graver, Dave Herbert and Roger Clarke. Jenny Parker of the Sixfields Travel Club and Brian Webster of the Trust Travel Club.

Northampton Town F.C., *The Chronicle and Echo*, the *Kettering Evening Telegraph*, Radio Northampton, Rob Marshall and WALOC for their publicity and Roy Walton for his old Stand Tickets and also ex-players Ben Collins, Stan Frost, Arthur Dixon, Ron Patterson, Frank Upton, Don Hazeldine, Derek Danks, Ken Leek, Alan Woan, Larry Canning, Barry Hawkings, Frank Griffin, Bela Olah, Norman Coe, Terry Branston, Ron Spelman, Alex Carson, Theo Foley, Tommy Robson, Garry Knibbs, Peter Pickering and Jim Hall.

To John English, son of Jack, for lending me his father's memorabilia, and to my wife Tina, who once again has given me all her support in another one of my 'projects'. Also to Mark Beesley, for 'proofing' the text.

Not forgetting Tommy, Joyce and other members of the Fowler family.

FRANK GRANDE

PREFACE

Whatever the language and nationality, football supporters around the world are very passionate of their own football team and their own individual stars.

There are not many advantages of growing old, with the aches and pains you never had in your younger days, but one great advantage is memory.

It was a great pleasure as a Cobblers supporter of over 50 years to see the finest left winger Northampton Town ever had, in Tommy Fowler.

He was a great club man, liked by all the players, and he contributed towards many goals in his playing days

Councillor J. J. Gardner, B.E.M., F. R. S. A
Mayor of Northampton 1975-1976
Chairman of Northamptonshire County Council 1998

AUTHOR'S NOTES

My introduction to Northampton Town was in the mid 1950s, when the club competed in the Division Three South. Ron Patterson, a qualified F.A. Coach would come to the primary school I attended at Hackleton and teach us the finer arts of the game.

My father had no interest in football at all, luckily a neighbour did, and it was he who used to chaperone me to the old County ground.

A lasting memory of those early days was the crowd's reaction to Tommy.

If ever Northampton were behind or struggling, there would be shouts of, 'Give the ball to Flash' or 'let Flash loose on them'.

When he did go on one of his left wing runs, he would leave defenders trailing behind him, much to the pleasure and amusement of the fans

'You'll never catch him' or 'need to get yourself some skates' were such comments directed at the struggling defender who was on a loser from the word, Go.

Anyone who saw Tommy play will always remember, those runs, those crosses, and those short shorts !

For those who never had the pleasure, I hope this book will enlighten you.

FRANK GRANDE

EARLY DAYS

Engand beat Belgium 4-0 in an International at the Hawthorns, the home of West Bromwich Albion, with a brace of goals apiece from the Aston Villa players, Billy Walker and Arthur Dorrell.

There was controversy at Burnden Park, in Bolton Wanderers home match against Nottingham Forest. The away side were awarded a spot kick, but their penalty taker, Harry Martin, had been carried off earlier. With no one wanting to assume the responsibility of taking the penalty, they carried Martin back on again. From a standing position, he pivoted on his good leg, swung at the ball with his bad one, scored, collapsed in a heap, and was carried off again.

Bolton followed up with an official complaint, but the Football Association rejected their appeal on the grounds that Nottingham Forest had done nothing wrong. However, the 1-1 draw that Forest managed, did them no good, they were still relegated from Division One at the end of the season.

In the Division Three North Durham beat Grimsby 6-1 with Billy Bertram netting four goals, a third of his season's total. St. Johnstone played their first ever game at Muirton Park, against Queens Park, while a ground record was set at Sandeys Park, home of New Brighton, for their game against Tranmere Rovers, where 15,173 attended.

On a sadder note, the Burnley manager, John Haworth, died of pneumonia, he was only 48. He had been at Turf Moor for 14 years and was one of the club's most successful managers. All this happened in December 1924.

Little or no interest was being shown of the new arrival of Enoch and May Fowler, in Prescot. But then no one would know what an influence the new arrival would have on the game, in a small town over 100 miles away, in the years to come.

Thomas Fowler, was the youngest of five children. He had two brothers Joe and Harry, and two sisters Ada and Annie. The gap between Ada and Tommy was 19 years.

Enoch worked at the Prescot cable factory, although he did start his working life down the pits. With seven mouths to feed money was tight and to supplement the household finances May took in washing, but the continual working in a damp atmosphere took its toll, and she died of double pneumonia when Tommy was only two years old.

Ada, the eldest sister decided to marry her boy friend Walter earlier than they planned, they took over as head of the household. Their first chore was to find a bigger house, but father did not want to leave, so the family had to find a four bedroom house and move while Enoch was at work, and worry about the consequences afterwards. Even then, one of Tommy's brothers had to be farmed out to his grandmother's.

Prescot was a small town, filled with neat streets of terraced houses, where front doors were left unlocked, and Women prided themselves on having the cleanest doorstep. Everybody was family orientated a classic example of

1920s/30s northern, working class environment

Opposite the new home was a gospel hall, Tommy would spend hours kicking a tennis ball against its wall, often being chased away by the caretaker. Even at that early age, he realised he was in love with the game.

Leather balls with bladders, were expensive and scarce, with just one boy in the street owning one. If he did not come out to play, or his mother would not let him bring the ball out, the lads in the street were reduced to kicking rags, tied up in a ball shape. It is easy to imagine the lad who owned the ball may not have been the best footballer, but no one argued with him in case he went home and took his ball with him.

Tommy hated school !

There was no real reason why he should, but given any chance of bunking off he did just that. In later life he put it down to the fact he had lost his mother at such an early age. Seeing his class mates with their mothers must have had a subconscious effect, the only lesson he ever enjoyed was football.

However, every Sunday he attended Victoria Place Methodist Chapel, in Prescot with his father. Enoch always wore his best suit with a starched collar, and was always brushed down by a member of the family. Young Tom felt so proud walking alongside him. All the children attended Sunday school, and then joined the adults to sing hymns and listen to the last part of the service.

Sometimes he was called on to 'blow the organ'. He would sit behind a curtain, next to the organist, and push and pull a pair of long handles. They pumped like bellows, and the object was to keep a lead weight above a certain marker, if they failed, the music stopped coming from the organ. 'I often wonder how some lads did not take cat naps',

Tommy reminisced, 'Using up all that energy, and then listening to a sermon that could be boring and last between 30-45 minutes.'

From the chapel they would walk to Tommy's grandmother's house, Here he would always get an orange and a penny, which bought him a decent bar of chocolate from the paper shop on the corner. The country was in deep recession. There was so much unemployment and the council put up Nissen huts where the unemployed could play cards, or sit and talk. The younger ones played football and Tommy, on his lesson dodging jaunts, would join in. Playing against older and bigger opponents perhaps played a large part in making him quicker and sharper, something he would learn to use later on..

He seemed to spend so much time off school that once a teacher remarked to one of his cousins 'When is Tommy coming back? We need him for the football team'.

Ada tried to be a mother to him, but after all she was just his eldest sister, she had a tendency to protect and cover for him, but that was not the case with Tommy's new brother in law. It all came to a head one morning, while Walter was returning from a night shift. He saw some men playing football, with Tommy among them when he should have been at school. There were no questions asked and no quarters given. Walter grabbed his younger brother in law by the scruff of the neck, pulled him all the way down to the school, and did not stop until they were both in the headmaster's study. It was an experience the young Tommy would never forget, and maybe one of the reasons he learned to run so fast in his later life.

It was agreed that if the youngest member of the Fowler family would attend school on a regular basis, they would drop him down a year to give him the chance to catch up on his education. It was something of a relief to the youngster, for his biggest fear was not the cane or any other kind of physical punishment, but being dropped from the school team. It was never mentioned, so Tommy quietly returned to his studies and carried on doing what he loved the most. Playing football.

Walter also made sure the rest of the family pulled their weight. He had a smallholding with greenhouses, growing flowers and tomatoes. Every Saturday morning they would fill a barrow with these, and Tommy would push it around the street selling the tomatoes at 3d or 4d a pound. It brought in a little extra revenue as well as giving Tommy a sense of responsibility.

Whenever possible the young Fowler liked to go and watch Liverpool. He would catch a tram from Prescot to Liverpool centre, then walk to Anfield.

There he would be ushered into the 'boys pen', an enclosure where just schoolboys were allowed. The Liverpool team of the time were an average first division side, but they had some excellent players such as the South African Berry Nieuwenhuys and full back Tom Cooper, who was to die in a motorcycle accident while serving with the military police during the war. There was the tall commanding goalkeeper, Arthur Riley, another South African, and a Scottish wing half named Matt Busby. Of all these, Tommy's favourite was Alf Hanson, the outside left.

'I modelled myself on him', Tommy confessed. 'He was fast, direct, and a wonderful crosser of the ball, and like myself he was left footed. It's fair to say when I was running down the wing during those school day football matches I was Alf Hanson'.

Bootle born Hanson scored 52 goals in 177 appearances for Liverpool, during his six seasons there. He moved on to Chelsea but hardly had time to hang up his coat before war broke out and prematurely ended his career. He was also a very good cricketer and baseball player.

Football is full of ironies and superstitions and cases of *deja vu*. Someone who was to benefit greatly from Alf Hanson's crosses was centre forward Sam English. Some fifteen years later the man who scored over 100 goals for Northampton, mostly from Tommy's crosses, was Jack English. They were though, unrelated. . .

Prescot was a small town, but as far as football went it came under the auspices of St. Helens, though that town was not much bigger. Football was a secondary sport in the area. It was a strong rugby area.

Tommy's continued good form on the wing for his school at Whiston soon caught the eye of the St. Helens' school selection committee. Along with another boy he was invited play for St. Helens' boys, against school teams from other towns in the Lancashire area. 'I was overjoyed at being selected, but it was a little disappointing to find out there were no training sessions, no get-togethers, not even a pre-match team-talk. We just received a card, telling us where and when we should be. We arrived, changed, played the game, and went home.' Tommy's father Enoch was a great supporter of his youngest son, and whenever possible made a point of watching him play, along with some of Tommy's uncles, always there to cheer him on.

Most successful people in life will tell you at some stage they made a supreme sacrifice somewhere along the way. Tommy made his in 1938. He enjoyed turning out for St. Helens, So strong was the pull of football he agreed to stay on at school just to keep playing. It was to be one of the best decisions he ever made, for despite the problems, and the fact that often he would turn up for a game and find someone else as his inside forward partner, or a fresh face at left half, Tommy found he could fit in with most players and they soon realised his strengths, and played to them.

For the first and only time in their history, St. Helens had a season to remember; 'It was a cracking side' Tommy recalled. 'We just seemed to knit together, we somehow knew what the next man was going to do, and anticipated the move'.

St Helens boys never had a side like it before, or one since. Despite being limited from the small amount of schools to choose from, they made their way through the rounds of the English schools shield, before falling to the all-powerful Manchester side, who had won the competition four times in the previous seven seasons. Despite a brave fight by the underdogs the Manchester team were superior in every department, and had the added advantage of playing the game at Maine Road.

The Northern clubs had a stranglehold on the competition, having won it for the previous 16 years with the exception of a sole Islington success in 1931. On top of that, a Lancashire side had won it six times in a row.

There was some sugar to coat the bitter pill of defeat, St. Helens went on to win the Lancashire Schools Cup, beating Blackburn in the final, and Enoch and other members of the Fowler dynasty proudly watched the youngest member of their family collect his first ever gold medal.

With an ambition achieved, Tommy left school, joining his father and uncles in the cable factory. It was probably not what he wanted to do, but in those days 'beggars could not be choosers'. You had to take whatever was on offer. He later joined his brother working in a warehouse for a haulage company. At least he knew it was bringing money into the house.

Tommy was also turning out regularly for Prescot Rangers, and later Prescot Rovers, with whom he won the Prescot League. Jack Lyon was a team mate in the successful St. Helens side, and he was also training with Everton. It was Jack who recommended Tommy to Everton, and they invited the young winger along to training sessions. It was eight miles to Goodison Park, and Tommy would attend two evenings a week, travelling by tram, train or bus before returning home, grateful at the chance of receiving coaching from professionals.

It was August 1941, after an evening training session, when the players were all getting changed that one of the trainers came in, walked up to Tommy and said; 'Mr. Kelly wants to see you'.

His heart skipped a beat.

Theo Kelly was the manager of Everton. They had been one of the last clubs to appoint such a position, relying on a secretary to arrange travel and accommodation, a trainer to keep the players fit and a committee to select the side. But in 1939, they conformed to tradition, and made Theo Kelly their Secretary/Manager, having previously held simply the secretary role.

Legend has it that Mr. Kelly was a good organiser and had a good business brain, but was a little too aloof with the players. He tended to keep too great a distance between himself and the players, upsetting some of them in the process. The supporters were also angered when he allowed Tommy Lawton and Joe Mercer to leave, although Lawton made it quite clear that he wanted to move south for the sake of his wife's health. In Mercer's case they just did not get on. Supporters were also annoyed at the fact these stars were never replaced with other big names. Instead the manager relied on youngsters, like Tommy, coming through the ranks

The young outside left made his way to the manager's office with a certain amount of nervousness and anxiety, taking the lift up to the second floor where Mr Kelly's office was situated. He knocked on the door.

'Come in'.

Tommy stood face to face with the Everton manager for the first time. He saw the amateur forms pushed in front of him and remembered little of the conversation they had, except for one sentence: 'You remind me of Cliff Bastin'.

There could be no better compliment paid At the time. Bastin was the 'child prodigy', who made his debut for Exeter City at 16, was signed by Arsenal for a near record fee, was capped for England at 19, and went on to win 21 further international honours. His collection included five league championships, two F.A.Cup medals among the 23 he acquired while a 'Gunner',and he also amassed 283 goals in 700 appearances.

Tommy was 16 when he signed those forms, and as he left the ground that evening, he felt seven feet tall.

The Second World War was raging in Europe, all professional footballers had their contracts cancelled and many were either in the forces or in auxiliary work like firemen or policemen. Clubs were having to make do with what players were left in the area, professionals with other clubs who were stationed locally, or homespun talent such as Tommy.

For the season 1941-42, Tommy would play regularly for the reserves or 'A' team, mainly depending on who was available at the time. He would receive his postcard in the middle of the week, telling him which team he was in, and where and when to be on Saturday. He would still turn up for his training twice a week.

Even at this stage of his career he was catching the eye, and some newspaper reports were giving him good reviews. 'Everton's up and coming right winger' or 'another fine display by Fowler, of St. Helens boys', were typical of the comments made.

Patience paid off, and in October 1942, Tommy made his first team debut, in a home match v Bury. It was ironic that the player he replaced was Jack Lyon, the very man who had introduced him to Everton.

The team that day was made up of goalkeeper George Bennett, who would later play for Oldham, full back Billy Cook, who used to stuff his boots with cotton wool before a game. He later coached all over the world including Norway, Peru . . . and Wigan! Norman Greenhaulgh was his partner, the man Stanley Matthews liked playing against least. 'I can understand why', Tommy recalled, 'He took no prisoners. If he tackled you, you stayed tackled'. Stan Bentham, later to coach Luton Town, and Gordon Watson, were the half backs. Legend was that Watson spent so much time as 12th man at Everton, the other players bought him a cushion to sit on. A local lad H. Jones was the centre half. The forward line was mainly made up of guests. Outside right Ron Dellow played for a host of clubs.

later marrying a Dutch girl and moving to Holland as a coach. George Mutch was his inside partner, famed for taking the penalty for Preston in the 1938 Cup Final v Huddersfield. The forward line was led by Frank Curran, another much travelled player, from a footballing family. He played for nine clubs, and guested for another four during the war. At inside left was Alex Stevenson. Alex was capped for both Eire and Northern Ireland, and was a ball playing schemer.

Records show that the youngest player to play for Everton was Joe Royle. He made his first team debut aged 16 years and 233 days in January 1966, but did not score his first goal for the club until April 1967, which made him 17 years and 354 days. Although Tommy was older when he made his first team appearance, he also scored, meaning he was just 17 years 304 days when he first found the net. Although war time appearances and goals are 'unofficial', one wonders if he was not the youngest player ever to score for Everton.

The club were in a war time league with many of the opponents a lot weaker, so the 9-1 scoreline was not too much of a shock. Tommy grabbed one for himself, the third, in sequence, when he netted just two minutes from half time.

It was true that the Bury keeper was injured at half time, and replaced by an outfield player but nothing could be taken from this rampaging, yet skilful, Everton side.

Match reports gave Tommy a glowing write up, some claiming he was Stevenson's best partner for some time and well worth his first team spot. He in fact ousted Jack Lyon, who's Everton career spanned just two war time seasons, scoring 11 goals in 39 games, from either inside or outside left.

Tommy was to make 17 appearances that season and score eight goals. He would also be joined during the season by Walter Boyes, the schoolteacher, who had one leg shorter than the other. Walter was an outside left, but was moved to the right wing to accommodate Tommy, although nothing was said at the time, later reports indicating that Boyes may have been 'upset' by this transfer. Centre half Tommy Jones, also made a few appearances, he could have been one of the first players to be 'lured by the lira', when Roma made a bid for him in 1948, but there was a breakdown over the currency exchange, and the deal fell through. There were also the two big names at the club,

Tommy Lawton, and Joe Mercer, both appearing in the same side as Tommy at stages during the season. 'It was incredible, I would look at the pegs in the dressing room in awe. At centre forward there was Tommy Lawton, at inside left Alex Stevenson, and at outside left Tommy Fowler! At no time did anyone ever make me feel anything but welcome, I was part of the team and made to feel such.'

Because of the unevenness of the competition, and because of the fact it was never possible to put out the same eleven players two games running, there were some strange results. Otherwise how could Everton beat Southport 10-2 in a game and a month later lose 1-4 to the same team. War time football had a two-pronged effect. It gave the people in the country one of their few chances of entertainment, and it kept footballers fit, as well as giving youngsters like Tommy a chance.

The young winger from Prescot netted four goals in his first five games, and in one match at Tranmere, the chairman of the home club, Bob Trueman, a noted 'spotter of talent', remarked on the performance of Everton's new winger. It

Tommy proudly wearing the St. Helens Boys' strip. Then just 15 years old.

Tommy's first medal, won in 1939, by winning the Lancashire Schools Shield

seemed the stage was set for a career in top flight football, but fate wielded its heavy hand. Midway through his one and only season in the 'Toffeemen's' first team, Tommy Fowler got his call-up papers.

FROM PRESCOT TO ROSS ON WYE – VIA FRANCE

Tommy wanted to join the Navy.

It was his father who pointed out that his football would be restricted if he was to serve most of his time on board a ship or even worse in a submarine. So after a rethink he decided on the Army.

Signing up was done in Formby in Lancashire, before he was drafted into a Scottish regiment, followed by a border regiment at Carlisle where Tommy spent three months on weapon training. It was fair to say in the first six months of National service the Prescot lad had done more travelling than in his previous 18 years.

Next stop was Hythe in Kent, where he was attached to the South Stafford-shire regiment. More training followed and a move again, this time to Dimchurch.

It did not take long for Tommy to start playing football again. He appeared for his regimental side, playing against other service sides, mainly at the ground of Folkestone Town.

The club, who still kept going through the war, invited him to turn out for them whenever possible, and he made several appearances on the left wing at Cheriton Road. On one such occasion, not only did he assist his adoptive side to an 11-0 victory over the R.A.F., but notched four second half goals in the process.

Once again it was a case of football being a tight knit community Although no one knew it at the time, some of the players who 'guested' for Folkestone, along with Tommy, would have connections with his previous and future clubs.

Henry Wright was a goalkeeper on Derby County's books He would later go into coaching, and hold such a post at Everton as well as Walsall and Luton, before widening his field and coaching the national Lebanese side and becoming a member of the Institute of Sport in Patiala.

Harry Ware of Norwich, would also turn out for Northampton Town during hostilities. He was to receive chest wounds at Normandy which led to his premature retirement from the game. Dudley Law, also of Norwich, was Welling-borough born, and also turned out regularly, for the Cobblers reserves.

It was July 1944, when the 2/6th battalion of the South Staffs regiment were called into active duty and sent to Normandy, along with many other regiments.

The company, made up of 18- and 19-year-old boys saw their first action after a week. The instructions were to take a chateau, near the town of Epron, that was being used by the German Army as a base.

The regiment were informed they were going over the top at 4.10 a.m the next morning. At the time a lot of the lads thought they were in a Western, with comments such as 'Let me at them' or 'just give me a gun, I'll show them'.

Tommy sat back and watched, saying nothing, and only speaking when spoken to . . . a policy he would adopt for the rest of his life.

'I knew a lot of it was bravado, for in the cold light of day when they lay, waiting for the order to go over the top, there were a lot of frightened lads', Tommy remarked.

There was a more than even chance that many of these teenagers had never left their home town or village, yet here they were in a foreign country, with a gun in their hand fighting someone they never knew, not knowing if they would ever return to see their families again.

Tommy remembers laying in the field, his gun in his hand, and his head kept down low, waiting for the order. Then at 4.00 am the skies lit up, like a giant bonfire. The battleships on the coast sent a barrage of shells inland towards the German lines This gave the soldiers of the South Staffs a two-pronged disadvantage. It could give away their positions to German snipers if the sky remained brighter than daylight. After all, the reason they were attacking in the dark was to do so under cover. There was also the chance that some soldiers could be caught by the barrage, something that was later termed 'friendly fire'.

All these thoughts raced through Tommy's mind, until he heard the order, and with his fellow soldiers went over the top.

He found himself in a cornfield, holding an Anti Tank gun, remembering his instructions to 'keep low at all times'. His concentration was broken when he felt a hand grab his ankle, he quickly turned to see one of his fellow soldiers laying on the floor, his hand grasping Tommy's ankle tightly.

'What are you doing ?', Tommy asked in shocked surprise.

'Don't go without me', he pleaded.

'All right but for goodness sake, keep your head down, or you'll get us both killed.'

The soldiers stayed there until daylight. Then the order came to regroup, and the soldiers took over the German trenches in the orchard of the chateau, before returning to the coast.

Back at base the bravado returned as the lads told tales of what they had achieved and what they had done, until an instruction came from the commanding officer - 'volunteers wanted - to bury the dead'.

Boasting and laughter stopped, with worse news to follow, some 120 of the soldiers were missing, presumed dead. Most were simply inexperienced teenagers who had naively stood up, before being picked off by German snipers. Later it became apparent they should never have been on the front line in the first place. Clearly more experienced soldiers would have minimised casualties, leaving the rookie soldiers for the clearing up operations.

The dead were later buried in Canbes-En-Plaine. Tommy often makes the pilgrimage, together with other survivors, to lay wreaths on the graves.

After a week's rest the regiment was back in action. By this time, Tommy had won a 'promotion in the field', and he was now a lance corporal. 'I can never remember if I got paid more, but at the time money did not seem so important', Tommy said.

They advanced and found small pockets of foreign troops in hiding. They were mainly White Russians, who were taken prisoner, often wondering if they were going to be shot?.

Tommy came across a brand new belt, and a short bayonet that the Germans used. He decided to keep these as 'spoils of war' and show them to his family on his return home.

Within firing distance of the enemy, they dug in and spent a lot of time in the trenches, exchanging fire with the Germans. It was here Tommy found it was not just the Germans who caused problems, sometimes they came from within.

He turned to find a fellow soldier, the same one who had grabbed his ankle in the cornfield, dropping his trousers to answer a call of nature.

'Hey!' spat Tommy. 'You can't do that in here '

'I'm most certainly not going out there to do it', came the reply.

One soldier volunteered to go out and wipe out a sniper who was causing the troops a lot of problems, but he was shot in the stomach, and packed off to the field hospital. Tommy decided to take things into his own hands and went out next.

'I crawled along, slowly, crouching every time I reached something that would give me cover, trying to locate the sniper' Tommy remembered. 'Suddenly, there was a crack of a rifle, and something hit my helmet and spun me around. I felt a trickle of blood running down my face, but did not take a lot of notice, despite being in some pain. I was still alive and had all my senses. Anyway, I wanted to finish the job I had started, even more so now'.

Despite this, he was despatched back to the field hospital, together with the soldier who had suffered the stomach wounds, it was while being carried on a stretcher, with his helmet resting on his chest that he actually saw the two bullet holes in his headgear. It was then he realised a bullet must have gone straight through the helmet, catching his forehead at the same time.

He wondered just how bad his injuries were as he was laid on a makeshift bed. A doctor came to examine him, but recoiled away in shock. Tommy was relieved to find this had nothing to do with his wounds, but the hand grenades still strapped to his tunic.

Another disappointment was that his 'finds', the belt and bayonet had been confiscated, although later he realised why. For as he was given a bed in the hospital, he found himself alongside wounded German soldiers as well. Tommy well understood that the war had to stop somewhere . . .

It was decided that the wound was bad enough for him to be sent back home So for Lance Corporal Thomas Fowler 14550764 of the 2/6th battalion of the South Staffs regiment, the war was over. He spent another two days in the field hospital and then it was back to England in a ship used for landing tanks. The floor was covered in wounded soldiers on stretchers, some without limbs, some blinded, some badly burned, and others like Tommy himself, the walking wounded. It was the most depressing sight that Tommy ever saw in his life.

As they arrived at Southampton docks they were put onto a train and returned to Aldershot barracks, Here those who were active were kitted out with essentials, such as shaving kits. From there it became a merry go round of military hospitals for the young Prescot lad.

First it was off to Blackburn Royal Infirmary, then on to Southport, where all wounded soldiers were dressed out in blue uniforms. Another one of those ironies, as Southport would play a part in his Cobblers career.

Warrington was the next stop. Here he had a minor operation, at least there was the consolation that it gave him the the chance to visit his family in Prescot. Here he met Don Welch. He was a Colour Sergeant Major Instructor in the army, but a professional footballer in civvie street, who would play for Charlton Athletic in the 1947 F.A. Cup final against Burnley.

It was here Tommy befriended another young, wounded soldier, who had spent some time in a German prisoner of war camp, He would take him home with him if he had a day, or half day's leave, but the youngster suffered from fits because of his experiences, and often lay on his bed, shouting, sometimes in German, More upsetting was the fact he knew when a fit was about to come on. He would lay on his bed and wait for it to happen.

With constant medical treatment and square meals, Tommy became stronger and it was not long before he started to regain full fitness and his mind turned again to football, although he was still under the supervision of the Army medics.

The chance came at his next stop, Kempston near Bedford. It was a convalescent centre for soldiers, where injured servicemen regained full fitness. Tommy met up with two men who were to change his life, Their names were Jack Jennings and Harold Shepherdson Both men helped out at the centre, and both men were to leave their mark in football in years to come.

Jack Jennings was a wing half, playing for Wigan Borough, Cardiff Middlesbrough and Preston. With the latter club he took up coaching, joining Northampton Town, as war broke out in 1939. Despite being over 40 he was pressed into service as an emergency full back, but returned to his first love, coaching. He would later act as coach to the England Amateur team, the British Olympic team of 1960, and became a physiotherapist not only with Northants County cricket team but also the Indian touring team of the 1960's

Harold Shepherdson was a centre half with Middlesbrough, guested for Northampton during the war, he finished his days with Southend, before returning to Middlesbrough as trainer, the pinnacle of his career came in 1966, when he trained the England team that won the World cup

Jack Jennings, looked over the new intakes, and asked the question; 'Any footballers?'. Two of the servicemen raised their hands.

'And which club do you play for ?' There was an element of disbelief, as the coach looked at Tommy, one of the players with his arm aloft. Seeing this small, slight youngster for the first time, His head wound still visible, the answer which followed took some believing. 'Everton !'

Jack Jenning's face was a picture. The other player was a Scotsman named, Archie Garrett. He was to make history for Northampton Town, over the next few years. Archie had started his career at Preston North End but unable to break into their first team on a regular basis, took the opportunity to return to his homeland, and signed for Hearts. The centre forward was a prolific scorer, but the war interrupted his career and like Tommy he also fell victim to war wounds. Once again fate played a hand.

Kempston was only 20 miles from Northampton, but it was very hard to travel between the two points. There was no direct train route, and the bus stopped at every village in between, making it a near two hour journey.

The two players were invited to train with the Cobblers and obviously gave a good account, as they were both picked for the next game, against West Bromwich Albion at the Hawthorns.

With travelling so hard, both players were given a weekend pass. They would catch a bus from Bedford on Saturday morning, play the game in the afternoon, stay overnight in Northampton, at the YMCA. before returning to Kempston on

Sunday morning, after a Saturday night at the Salon.

It was a lot of messing about for a game of football, but then Tommy had not played competitively for two years. Even worse, the players were only paid expenses. Tales that manager Tom Smith plied players with eggs and vegetables from his farm were nothing more than a Myth.

'We used to make a little bit on expenses, but it was not much', recalled Tommy. 'Tom Smith would pull a wad of notes out of his pocket after a game and approach each player: 'Expenses ?'

'Each player would give him a figure, but we weren't silly and each had a good idea how much he should be asking for'. In Tommy's case, it probably just about covered the cost of a few beers at the Salon on a Saturday night.

'The only thing I remember about the game at West Bromwich was someone coming out from the crowd and shaking my hand', Tommy remarked. 'It was someone I had served in France with. He told me he would meet me after the game, but it never happened, and I never saw him again'.'

In the Northampton team that day was goalkeeper Alf Wood, a Coventry City player, who was also training soldiers in unarmed combat. Tom Smalley, the ex-Wolves and England wing half was at right back, guesting from Norwich City, while his partner at left back was Andy Welch, previously with Darlington, Manchester City and Walsall. Gwyn Hughes, one of the half backs, was the only non-guest in the side. The young Welshman was from the Rugby area, recommended to the club by their ex-goalkeeper Len Hammond who lived in the area. Bill Coley a no-nonsense, hard tackling ex-Wolves player was Gwyn's wing half partner At the time he was on the books of Torquay. Between the two, at centre half was Bob Dennison, a physical, bustling centre half from Fulham, although he had previously played for Newcastle United and Nottingham Forest. as a forward.

Jim Brown the Irish international from Grimsby was on the right wing, Bill Fagan, of Liverpool and Scotland was his inside forward partner. Ironically, when Bill finished with football he became a prison officer at Wellingborough, and his son Gary had a spell on Northampton's books, although he did not play in the first team. His position was . . . outside left!

Travelling companion Archie Garret was at centre forward, and the inside left position was covered by Alf Morrall, who was based in the Midlands, having only played non-league football. Tommy took up the position he knew best, outside left.

The game was a disaster for the Cobblers, who lost 0-6. Andy Welch was injured and had to leave the field, which meant a forward moving to half back, as Bill Coley took Welch's position. Then Bob Dennison received a cut on the nose and left the field for a spell. Injuries disorganised the team and add to that the fact West Brom were on a run, of five games without defeat, and you had the recipe for a one sided affair. Ike Clarke hit his eighth war time hat trick and only a few weeks earlier they had beaten Smethwick 17-0 in a friendly.

All this happened in March 1945 The season was almost over, but even in the few games that Tommy played there were quite a few strange happenings. Like the match against Birmingham where the Cobblers had no centre forward. So they played reserve keeper Alex Lee, hoping his 6' 2" and 14 stone frame would upset the opposing defence. Very often Tom lined up with a player one week, only to find him in the opposing side the following week, while players missing trains or connections, were all common occurrences.

Tom managed four games during that season, winning the last one, against Derby, and scoring his first goal for the club. 'That was something I could not get over, my lack of goals at Northampton', The left winger mused. "At Everton I was averaging a goal every other game but here it was nearer one in five.'

Around the same time Tommy was moved again, this time to the 23rd Infantry Holding battalion, stationed in Herefordshire, just outside Ross-on-Wye. He went straight into their football side, and helped them to lift the Hereford-shire County Cup, that season. Among his team mates was Harry Ware of Norwich, who had played with Tom at Folkestone, and Arthur Cumberlidge, the ex-Stoke and Port Vale wing half.

There were also a few games for Hereford for the young winger as he strove to bring himself back to peak fitness. 'The war was over by now, and my mind on football, but at the present I was still in the Army, had time to serve, and that took priority, although they were very good when I was asked to be released for football,' Tommy said.

First posting was at Foxley, and then a centre just outside Ross on Wye. It was at the latter camp that Tommy found himself an enjoyable little job, He would cycle in to Ross and collect the post for the barracks as well as taking the camp mail to be posted. It was while in Ross that something happened which would change his life . . . for the better!

Lance Corporal Thomas Fowler 14550764, of the 2/6 Battalion
of the South Staffs. regiment.

The Chateau before the German Army took it over as their headquarters.

The same building after the hostilities. The Germans rebuilt it to its former glory, after the war.

Tommy and Joyce with the Lady who owned the Chateau. On one of their visits to Canbes-en-Plaine.

Visiting the grave of one of Tommy's army comrades who fell at Epron

Being decorated by the Mayor, on one of his visits to the cemetery.

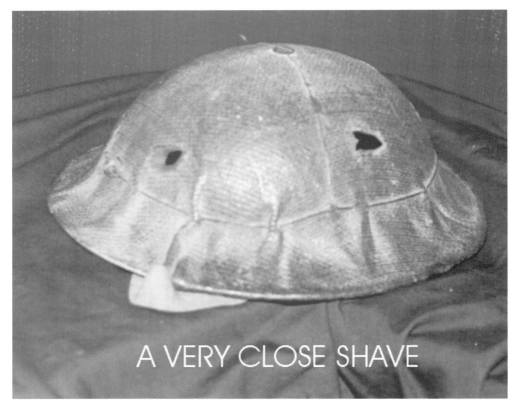

That famous helmet ! Complete with bullet holes.

TOMMY BECOMES A COBBLER

Joyce Wall was the daughter of a farm labourer in Ross. She had spent her life in tied cottages, sometimes moving from one home to another, at the drop of a hat, after her father and his employer had a disagreement.

Not only were these cottages isolated, but electricity and running water were a luxury rather than a standard auxiliary service. When she reached the age of 15, her Mother passed away, leaving her with her father and sister and six brothers, of which Joyce was the youngest. She was at an age where she wanted to get out and see something a little more than the four walls of her home, Ross-on-Wye may not be the pulsating, thriving centre of the universe, but it offered a bit more life.

On one of her jaunts into the market town, she attended a political meeting, on behalf of the Liberals with a friend. Their attention was drawn, not by the speaker, but by the two soldiers heckling him. 'I fancied the bigger one of the two, but it was the other one I ended up with', Joyce recalled. She little realised that the relationship would take them all over the country, and they would settle in a Town many miles away.

Despite being stationed near Hereford, Tommy was still turning out for Northampton Town, whenever he could get a weekend pass. He was keen for Joyce to join him on trips to Northampton but as he was existing on expenses for one plus his army pay, he took drastic action.

'I could have been shot for what I did', Tommy recalled, 'Someone gave me an A.T.S. pass for Joyce. This meant we could travel anywhere in the country for half the fare, which was very helpful for our trips to Northampton'.

They would leave Ross on the service bus to Hereford, very early in the morning, then travel by train at Northampton, grab a meal at a cafe in Sheep Street, then on to the game, before returning to Hereford or Gloucester.

Joyce remembered the time they arrived back too late for a bus, they could not afford a Taxi, so they walked the 15 miles to her home. 'It was dark, there was nothing on the roads, and when we reached the "Yew Tree pub", which was half way, we both let out a loud cheer'.

Another time they arrived at Gloucester station too late for a bus but there was an RAF driver outside, who offered them a lift on a shooting brake.

'Now that was a ride to remember, talk about white knuckle rides. We were hanging on for dear life and stuck it until we were about four miles from my home. Then we told the driver to drop us, at the first house we saw. He was told this was where we lived', Joyce recalled with a smile, reliving those early days.

'I often wonder how many RAF servicemen were left waiting at the station because he was taking us home', Tommy mused.

While he was stationed in the area, Tommy also turned out for Hereford United, then a non-league side, on a few occasions. The war was over by August 1945, but the Football League, in their wisdom, decided to have another season of 'Wartime' football, allowing teams to sign players on full contracts. This also allowed them another season to bring in much needed revenue, by cutting down on travel.

Fuel, like most things, was still rationed. The divisions were set out as they would have been in 1939. Then they were all split geographically into North and South. The Cobblers played in the Division Three South, Northern Section, this took the fixture list up to the new year.

At this stage the Midland clubs competed in a cup competition. Each team played each other on a home and away basis, comprising a league, with the top four teams playing off in a knock out finale.

Finally, the F.A. Cup made a return. For the one and only time it was played on a two legged basis, from the first round.

Added to this there were the County cup matches and a sprinkling of friendlies, enough to get the football-loving public back on the terraces.

The season almost started with a strike. The clubs wanted to continue paying war time wages, but the P.F.A. insisted that they revert to the pre-war system. Luckily, the F.A. stepped in and an agreement was reached before the first kick off date.

Slowly, Northampton Town Football club started to sign players on full contracts. Bob Dennison, took a job at a local timber yard, and moved into the area, Right winger Gordon Roberts, moved from Wolves once he located a job locally, as a draughtsman. Full back Tom Smalley moved from Norwich for an 'undisclosed fee', later disclosed to be £900, not bad for a man in his early 30s, while free scoring forward Alf Morrall also joined the professional ranks. The Northampton manager at the time was Tom Smith. As a player he was on the books of Leeds City, but failed to make their first team. He later moved to the village of Ravensthorpe in Northamptonshire in the 1930s, taking over a farm, and setting up a bakery. When war broke out the club invited him to become their manager, not an easy task considering the problems with fixtures and players. But he did the job, and quite successfully, and must have been looking forward to peacetime football, which would remove the pressure of getting players released or wondering if they would turn up for a game.

Tom's trademarks were the trilby hat he always wore, more often than not he could be seen drawing on a fat cigar.

'He was a good manager, never stood on the side of the pitch ranting or raving, never had a go at players in the dressing room and never, ever, singled out individuals for criticism,' Tommy, quoted. 'He was more "hands on" than Theo Kelly at Everton, getting more involved in the dressing room, but he had a good second man in Jack Jennings.'

A full contract was offered to Tommy, once he could get his release from Everton. A letter was sent to Enoch back in Prescot asking him to contact the club, and brother-in-law Walter rang them up, but was met with the curt reply, 'If Northampton Town want to sign one of our players, they must contact us'. Considering Tommy was only on amateur forms, and they ran out in 1943, it was felt the Merseyside club were being heavy handed. The two Toms decided to ignore the remarks, and the contract was signed.

At the age of 20, Tommy Fowler became a professional footballer. There were no further problems with Everton. Teams including the Cobblers, were still using the 'guest' system, some more than others.

In a friendly v Watford, Stanley Mortenson and Maurice Edleston lined up for the Hertfordshire club, and against Ipswich, the Suffolk club paraded all five forwards as guests.

In the meantime, Tommy was settling into the professional ranks. The post match report of a game v Port Vale, read; 'He can beat his man by a single expedient of tapping the ball past him, then shooting past him himself, like he was jet-propelled'. Northampton Town were having too much of an indifferent spell to make any serious progress up the league. Three consecutive victories were followed by four consecutive defeats, which in turn was followed by 23 goals scored in four games.

But the F.A.Cup was a different matter. The first round brought non-league Chelmsford to the County Ground, who had been defeated just once all season. The Cobblers doubled that figure with a thumping 5-1 victory, Tommy making two of Morrall's goals in a three minute spell. The scoreline was also amazing considering Northampton had lost centre-forward Sam Heaselgrave for most of the match. The Essex club, who later changed their colours to claret and white, as their chairman was a Cobblers fan, never recovered. The second leg recorded the Cobblers going nap again, this time without reply. Among the goalscorers this time was one, T. Fowler, and he laid on another of the five for Gordon Roberts, on the other wing.

The 10-1 aggregate victory saw Tommy's side through to the second round, and a tie against Notts County, who had earlier in the season won 2-1 at the County Ground, in a league fixture. There was no repeat of the league defeat. It took just 15 seconds for Alf Morrall to break away and put the Cobblers into an early lead. Then Tommy had a 'red letter day', laying on goals for Eddie Blunt and Alf Morrall. The 3-1 victory, was felt to be enough to take to the second leg at Meadow Lane. Again the newspaper reports were complimentary to the Cobblers left winger, stating; 'He outpaced Southwell and Harris, almost every time'. County won their home leg 1-0, and again the local press claimed that ' 'The Cobblers outside left was the most dangerous player in their forward line'. Northampton won through on a 3-2 aggregate, and for the one and only time lost an F.A.Cup tie, but progressed to the next round.

The third round saw Northampton's name come out of the bag with that of Millwall, then a second division club. It was hoped that luck would favour the Cobblers and they would be drawn out with a first division side, but on reflection, Millwall were struggling, and maybe there was a chance of progressing into the fourth round. It was not to be. Although the teams drew 2-2 at the County Ground, Millwall ran out 3-0 winners at the Den, and Northampton Town's interest in the F.A.Cup ended there.

However, the story did not, and what happened next, was to make the headlines in several national newspapers. Millwall made an offer, believed to be in the region of £10,000, for FIVE of the Cobblers team. No names were mentioned but if anyone sat down and worked it out, it was obvious the the bid was for the five forwards, as their own were reaching the veteran stage. John Richardson was 34, Dave Ripley and Russell Phillips a youthful 29, Eddie Smith 31 and Jimmy Jinks 30. In contrast the Cobblers forward line consisted of Gordon Roberts 20, Eddie Blunt 27, Alf Morrall, the 'old man' at 28, Gwyn Hughes at 23 and Tommy himself, just turned 21. The players knew nothing about this until they read it along with the supporters. None of them were ever approached by the manager or directors, but Tom Smith replied, through the press, that he had slowly built up a good young side and did not want to break it up now, regardless of how much money was involved. Millwall came back with a firm offer for Alf Morrall, that was rejected, giving the supporters hope that once league football started in earnest, the following season, Northampton Town really were going to be in the 'promotion pack'. With only one club being promoted, it was very hard to get out of this division.

Tommy won his first honour as a Northampton player, when the club lifted the Maunsell Cup that season. After beating Rushden Town 9-0 in the semi- final they went on to beat Kettering Town 4-2 in the final, it was to be the last ever game played on the Rockingham Road sloping pitch. During the close season Several tons of earth were used to level the playing surface. There were several memorable events that season, the last of war-time football, for Tommy. The game at Southend, kicked off at 6.15 p.m. and even with no half-time break, the game finished in darkness.

Then there were the 'Birmingham Three' – Jack Sankey, Harry Lowery and Sam Heaselgrave, all signed in a £4,500 deal from West Bromwich Albion, yet all missed their intended debut v Orient. They travelled to Northampton by car, but were held up. The bus taking the Northampton players to Orient could not wait any longer, hence they left without the three prospective debutants. On arriving at Northampton they realised the rest of the team had gone on, so decided to follow by car. On their way down they broke down. Mean-while the bus, trying to catch up on time, was involved in a slight accident, but still managed to make it to the venue in time. Not so the three 'ex-Baggies'. They turned up at half time, to see three reserves in their places, and to rub further salt into the wound, Orient won 1-0.

A Scottish newspaper circulated a story that a Northampton director was in Scotland with £40,000 to spend on new players which was strongly denied by Northampton director Phil Hutton, 'It's absurd to think that a Third Division club has £40,000, to spend on players.' Tommy missed a game at Norwich when he failed to catch his connection at one of the stations, and also missed a few games when he picked up an injury playing for the Western Command. Team mates included Gil Merrick of Birmingham and Bert Sposton of Spurs and Manchester City.

When it was realised that the club were in the running for nothing the supporters started to barrack some of the players. This led to Tom Smith publicly defending his staff. He explained that many of them had been serving their country all over the world, where some never had the chance to kick a ball. There were others on reserve occupations, like mining or farming, where football was of secondary importance and there were some like Tommy, who were recovering from war wounds.

The first season of league football, since 1939, kicked off on the 31st of August 1946. The league, decided to use the fixture list that was abandoned after three matches of the ill-fated 1939-1940 season. There were no new players in the Cobblers side, Goalkeeper Jack Jones returned to the club after a seven years absence, replacing Alf Wood, who had returned to Coventry City. The opening

Training on the County Ground.

game was at home to Swindon Town. It was to be the last time the club opened with a home fixture for 27 years, because of the cricket club's games at the County Ground. Gordon Roberts, Dave Smith, Alf Morrall, Sam Heaselgrave and Tommy were the forward line that day,. They were regular members of last season's side, yet this was the first time they had played together! The goals came fast and furious, as Northampton eased into a comfortable 4-2 victory, with a brace of goals from Morrall and Heaselgrave, Tommy supplying one of them. Supporters left the ground that Saturday, talking of promotion and national newspapers were tipping the Cobblers as a team to watch, unfortunately, it was to be a false dawn. Swindon had not played football all through the war. Their ground had been used as a prison camp, although their players may have served other sides as guests. They had not played together yet, no one could have thought, as they left the County Ground after the match, that by the end of the season, that Swindon would finish nine places above the Cobblers.

Another of those ironies that happen in football came in the shape of the Swindon Town manager, Louis Page. Twenty five years earlier he was the darling of the Northampton supporters, thrilling them with his dashes down the left wing. In the 1920s the supporters talked about the wingers Pease and Page, like they would talk about English and Fowler in the 1950s.

After the euphoria of the Swindon game, the club came down to earth with a bang. They picked up just one point from their next five games, one of them at

Port Vale, which Tommy missed when he could not get leave for the evening fixture. The matches were covered by the *Chronicle and Echo*, their reporter was always known as 'Flagkick', giving the reporter a certain amount of anonymity, although most people knew who it was. These games were being covered by Fred Speakman, a knowledgeable man when it came to local sport, being something of an expert on events on both sides of the County Ground. He could also be quite scathing. At some time or another most players felt the sharp end of his pen, and Tommy was no exception. An example was the game against Exeter, when Alf Morrall was injured and Tommy switched over to the right wing, Speakman wrote: 'Fowler plays better at outside right, than he does at outside left'. Then in a game against Bristol Rovers at Eastville the scribe penned the following: 'Why does Fowler always play his better games away from home?' In a match against Torquay, Tommy had the chance to equalise from 6 yards out, but missed. This brought the quote: 'The worse miss I have ever seen by a Cobblers player'. It was after a 0-1 defeat at Exeter, early in the season that 'Flagkick' wrote: 'Why does the management insist on playing Fowler?'. Tommy replied, in the only way he knew possible. He scored twice in the next game, a 3-2 victory at Norwich. For Tommy it was a double celebration, it also was the day after his release from the Army.

'Bad match reports, and barracking from the crowd, never worried me', Tommy admitted. 'I always tried my best, sometimes it came off, sometimes it did not. But I never let it get to me. The supporters paid their money, and were entitled to have a go, but if I did have a bad game, it was never through lack of effort.' Maybe it did not worry Tommy, but Joyce was different. On more than one occasion she has been known to defend Tommy, and she was not afraid to take on anyone, including local scribe Speakman.

They came face-to-face with each other at a game against Notts County, and she made her feelings known to the reporter. 'Going to write some more of your rubbish?' she inquired. The situation got to a stage where he would nervously look out for Joyce at a game, and say to his colleagues, 'Keep that – – – – woman away from me'. There was never any animosity between Tommy and the reporter and when Fred Speakman passed away in August 1985, Tommy attended the funeral together with Nev Ronson, the chairman of the club at the time, Jack English, Graham Carr, Frank Jenner and Harry Warden.

Joyce would go on defending Tommy throughout his playing days, it was some years later, that she was travelling back to the town centre on a bus, after watching a game, and heard two men behind her berating Tommy's performance, all the way from Abington Avenue to Abington Street. As she got off the bus, she turned to the two men. 'Did you know he's been in bed with flu all week?' she asked. 'What do you know about it?' one of the men sarcastically enquired. 'Well I ought to, I'm the one who's been getting in and out of bed with him for the past six years.' With that she upped and left. A few days later a piece appeared in the 'Old Hamtune' column of the *Chronicle and Echo* titled 'My most embarrassing moment', and one of the men in question, related the story.

Back to September 1946. Manager Tom Smith was disappointed with his fire power, so he paid out £3,000 to bring Archie Garrett back to the County Ground, together with his colleague Jim Briscoe from Hearts. The Scottish club had over 40 players on their books, and the two ex-Preston North End players made it

Tommy Becomes a Cobbler

CARTOONS: How Adams of the Chronicle and Echo, *saw the Cobblers side of the late 1940s. Top Row, left to right: Tommy Fowler, Archie Garrett, Harry Lowery; Middle Row, left to right: Jack Jones, Bobby King, Gwyn Hughes Sam Heaselgrave; Bottom Row, left to right: Tom Smalley, A. J. Darnell (president).*

known they would like to return to English football after their exploits guesting for a host of league sides during the war.

Garrett continued where he had left off in war-time football at the County Ground, scoring goals, He netted a brace in his first league match, helping the Cobblers to a 2-1 victory over Notts County. Throughout the season the outside left position was Tommy's but after a bad run in February and March, in which the club picked up just one point from five games, manager Tom Smith made changes. He moved Gordon Roberts to the left wing, while Jim Briscoe, Alf Morrall and Stan Frost shared the outside right duties. Tommy was restricted to reserve team football. Stan Frost had played for Northampton before the war. He was transferred to Leicester City but before his career could take off he was called up for national service.

On his return, Leicester had a change of manager and the new man made it clear Stan was not part of his plans. He suggested he returned to Northampton, maybe they would have a place for him. Tom Smith did take him on, but he found several players vying for his right wing position. At this time Frost recalled a job he was given by Jack Jennings. He was given a sack full of footballs and told him to aim them at Tommy's head. The left winger just did not like heading the ball, some made the excuse that it was because of his war wounds, but Tommy admitted that he hated heading the ball, even as a schoolboy. 'I sent ball after ball over to Tom, but you could see he had no enthusiasm to head them. He would either stick his head out at the ball, so it bounced off it, or let it hit him. It must have been obvious he was never going to be an exponent of heading,' Stan recalled.

The ex-Leicester man had a short career at Northampton. He took up the offer of a job with Cleavers the building merchants and played part-time for Rushden Town. Being demoted to the reserves, Tommy asked for a free Saturday, which was granted, and on the 8th of April 1947, Tommy and Joyce were married in Liverpool. After the ceremony they were in a pub having a drink when someone walked in with a sports paper. The newly wed groom asked to borrow it to see how his team had fared, you can imagine his shock when he saw deep among results for Division Three South:

NORTHAMPTON TOWN 0 WALSALL 8!

IN, AND OUT, AND IN, AND OUT

The Fowlers moved to Northampton in August 1947.

Although Tommy never won his first team place back for the rest of the season, he received the letter he was waiting for. Just a short note offering him terms for the following season with his proposed wages. Terms were only for 12 months, with a winter wage and a lower one in the summer, plus the added incentive of £2 for a win and £1 for a draw. There were no agents in those days, and no room for negotiation when it came to contracts. You accepted what you were offered. If you did not, you were released or your registration was held by your club and you would remain their player, unpaid, until you either changed your mind, or another club came in.

In those days, clubs had the controlling hand. 'It was something I worried about, all my footballing life', Tommy admitted. 'I had no trade or skills to fall back on. I was doing what I always wanted to do, play football'. Some of the players, in the Cobblers squad around that era had made plans for such an eventuality.

It was mentioned earlier that Bob Dennison had taken a management job in the timber trade and Gordon Roberts was a draughtsman. Sam Heaselgrave took law exams and became a solicitor in Birmingham when he retired. Reserve goalkeeper Dave Scott was a schoolteacher, whilst Dave Smith learned the workings of the administrator, as he was soon to take over as the Club Secretary. Others felt the need to hold down a secure job as well as playing football. Stan Frost took a job with a builders merchant, Jack English managed a clothing manufacturers, while Latvian, Eddie Freimanis continued in his job as an interpreter.

'I thought Northampton was a lot like Prescot', Tommy recalled. 'A lot bigger, but it reminded me a lot of home'. For Joyce it was something of a culture shock. 'I did not like it, at all', she remarked. 'After all those years in isolation I was suddenly surrounded by noise, people and traffic. It took some time to come to terms with it all'.

Home was one room in a house in Abington Avenue, handy for Tommy when it came to getting to 'work', but today, they both wonder how they managed to live in their confined quarters. Houses were at a premium just after the war, hence the erection of 'prefabs' that were quickly assembled as a temporary measure, though some were not demolished until the late 1970s.

'House sharing' and living with the in-laws was quite a common thing in those days. It was a case of living wherever you could find a home. The club was not obliged to find their players homes, although it is fair to say they played their part. They had to, if they wanted quality players turning out for them every week. 'The Birmingham Three' – Sam Heaselgrave, Jack Sankey and Harry Lowery – were allowed to remain in their Midlands homes and travel to Northampton, rather than find rented accommodation.

Tommy and Joyce recalled those early days. 'We did everything in one room

We cooked, ate, slept and lived between those four walls, with its sparse furniture. It was all new to us, we were young and starting out on married life. It was almost an adventure'.

Their next home was shared with an old lady in King Edward Road, in the Abington area of the town. 'We had one room upstairs and another down. The "Birmingham Three" often came to visit us, and always left with their pockets full of apples "scrumped" from the old lady's orchard', they both recalled.

One day Tommy came home from training and made the announcement: 'I've got us a house, and a brand new one at that'.

Con Wilson was building a new estate in Parkfield Avenue, and number 72 was to be rented to the Fowlers. The cost was £800, and Tommy was to pay £2 to £3 a week rent, which at the time was rather high.

Joyce insisted they would have nothing they could not pay for. The bedroom suite came from Liverpool. There was a table and chairs for downstairs, and that was the extent of furnishing in those early days. When Tommy's team mates asked if they could come and look around, they were told they would have to 'take us as you find us'.

Again Joyce remembered, 'We did not have a stair carpet for six years, and the first living room suite came from Wades of Liverpool, and cost £42' The 'no credit' decision was relaxed when Joyce took a job at Arnolds, the box manufacturer in Barrack Road. 'We bought a radio and paid Ten shillings a week for it'. Over the years, the couple were to have many of Tommy's team mates as neighbours as other houses on the estate became 'club houses'.

The 1947/48 season started with Tommy still in the reserves, but he was getting some good reviews. 'Coming back into form' was one, while another stated 'returning the promise he has shown in the past'.

In October, he won back his first team place, for a match at Exeter City. Six different players had been tried at outside right, with only limited success. It was declared that Gordon Roberts was the best man for the job, and he switched wings, allowing Tommy back into the side. November 15th 1947 was a date that would stand out in the history of Northampton Town Football Club. It was to be of national interest to the football loving public of England, which the Cobblers played a small part in. England international centre forward, Tommy Lawton had joined Notts County, and was to continue his career in Division Three South. The Tommys had been team mates at Everton, but their careers took different turns.

While Fowler was on the battlefields of France, Lawton remained in this country as a P.T. instructor. He took some flak over it because like a lot of top pro footballers at the time he did not see active service, and while on a post war tour of Europe playing against service sides, he and his team mates were often met with the cries of: 'workers against the shirkers'.

Tommy Lawton defended himself venomously. He pointed out that he did not decide where the army sent him. Like all soldiers he had to do as he was told. Also as he quite rightly pointed out, many footballers were killed in battle during the war. Although Lawton played quite a bit of football during the war, like Tommy, and a great many other players of the day, a large chunk of his career was lost through the hostilities. He left Everton for Chelsea in 1945, because he was concerned over his wife's health, and felt the southern air would be better for her. His first attempt to ask for a move from the Merseyside club saw him ejected from

Theo Kelly's office, in no uncertain manner. But in the end he got his way, joining the London club in time to play for them in the famous Moscow Dynamo game. Two seasons later he joined Notts County, and made headline news, It was hard to believe a current England International would join a Third Division club. The facts were that Notts County had made the best offer of £20,000, added to the fact that wherever he moved to he would get the same wage, as there was a 'ceiling' on professional footballers wages at the time.

Everyone was in Northampton that day. Crowds began to form four hours before kick off. The police marshalled crowds using mobile radio equipment. As the kick off drew nearer, so the crowds got bigger, snaking 100 yards long, and in places ten people deep. The Press sought out the man who was first through the gate, discovering he had left his Olney home at 8.00 am to get to the ground.

Toffee apple vendors were doing a roaring trade and programme sellers were running back for more copies. Tommy Fowler met up with his old team mate and they talked about their time at Everton, discussing the whereabouts of old playing colleagues, and of their own careers since they played together some four years earlier.

Meanwhile, the tension mounted as over 18,000 supporters poured into the County Ground, wearing either claret or black and white rosettes. In the Cobblers dressing room, someone tried to relax by playing the penny whistle. Tommy could not remember who, but confirmed, it was not him! The crowd were still pouring into the ground, When Tommy Lawton opened the scoring, one of the quickest debut goals in the football league, it had its repercussions. From that moment on, Cobblers centre half Bob Dennison had the England player in his pocket, to such an extent he moved out on the wing for a spell in the second half, trying to escape his shadow. The ground erupted when Northampton's own scoring supremo Archie Garrett equalised. It seemed on the cards that the Cobblers could win the game, Tommy playing his part sending in cross after cross But the County defence were equal to the task, soaking up all the Cobblers could throw at them. They stole the match at the death, Jack Marsh netting the goal from a break, after another spate of Northampton pressure. Supporters were still talking about the Notts County game, when Northampton Town hit the national sports papers again. The time was December 1947, the event was the transfer of Archie Garrett to Birmingham for a club record fee of £10,000. There were other players involved in the deal. A reserve keeper called Lloyd went to St. Andrews along with Archie and two Birmingham reserve team players, Sid Stanton and Ron James joined the Cobblers. With the money, the Northampton board bought the 'Trueform' sports ground, on the Kettering road. It was their intention to run the 'Colts' side from this ground, while at the same time slowly converting it into a stadium suitable for league football, before leaving the County Ground. This idea died a death when residents of the Spinney Hill area made their displeasure of such a move known in no uncertain manner.

The complaints came thick and fast. So much so, that the council offered the club alternative land, near to Thornton Park in the Queens Park/Kingsthorpe area of the town. On the field, manager Tom Smith brought Bobby King back from Wolves, He had joined them from Northampton in 1939, the first war time transfer, but Bobby was a winger, not a goalscorer, and Archie's goals were being missed. Around this time, Tommy was having an indifferent spell, and found himself playing a few games in the reserves. However it worked in his favour, for as he was finding form again, scoring twice against Coventry reserves, the first team were going through a very barren spell, with one victory in the last 11 games.

A new forward line was tried for an away match at Watford. Jim Briscoe returned at outside right, Gwyn Hughes at centre forward and Tommy on the left wing. Bobby King and Randy Jenkins took the inside forward positions. The result was 1-1, but that made less significant news than the fact Watford paraded SEVEN debutants including five who had signed the day before, from Leicester City. Northampton manager Tom Smith must have been pleased for he kept the forward line together for the following match, and they repaid him with a 4-0 victory over Brighton.

Because of the poor mid-season results Northampton had little to play for, by this time, except pride. Tommy maintained his place and well remembered the away match against Notts County at Meadow Lane. The Magpies were holding on to a 2-1 lead, roared on by a 30,000 plus crowd, when Tommy broke free and netted an equaliser. in the dying minutes of the game. Everyone expected a two all draw, and some of the supporters were streaming out of the ground, when that man Tommy Lawton hit that all important goal, giving County both points again. When he fired in the winner, the referee was only seconds from ending the game.

During the close season, Tommy and Joyce returned to the Ross area, where they would supplement their summer wages with jobs like pea picking or strawberry picking, while staying with Joyce's relatives.

Tommy started the 1948/1949 season with a bang. He scored his first goal of the season in the opening game, against Exeter City, at St. James Park. Unfortunately, the Cobblers conceded five! They could have used the excuse that there were four new men in the side. Goalkeeper Edgar Williams, full back Norman Aldridge, wing half Ron James and the Latvian forward Eddie Fremanis.

Tommy scored again in the 3-0 victory over Leyton Orient, at Brisbane Road, the club's second away win on the trot, but the game was marred when the London club's full back, Len Ritson suffered a broken leg. He later had to have it amputated. Things were not going well on the field. By the end of October, Northampton Town boasted just five wins, in 15 games, and Bill Coley, Harry Lowery and Tom Smalley had all missed penalties.

There were rumours of discord, fuelled by national press reports, in the camp. This came about when new centre forward Eddie Fremanis was injured and lay motionless on the ground. His team mates seemed to ignore him, and kept their distance, from the injured player, 'It's because I told them to', Jack Jennings informed the inquisitive press men. 'You can do more damage trying to move, or lift an injured player, than if you leave him alone. It only takes me a few seconds to reach any part of the pitch so there is no need for anyone else to go near the player. The players are acting on my instructions. If you think there is no team spirit come into the dressing room before or after a game, you'll see if there is discord. Now let's hear no more about it', Jack instructed, and he didn't!

A few weeks later Eddie was in the news again when he played as a stand in goalkeeper. Jack Ansell was carried off injured in a match at Swansea, and the Latvian international put up such a fine display between the sticks, the Swansea crowd gave him a standing ovation, as he left the field. He had joined the Cobblers from Peterborough, where he was a scoring sensation, but found life a little harder in the Football League. After netting three goals in his first five games they dried up, and he w.as later dropped, The fact that he remained a 'part time player', probably did not help his cause.

An effort was made to sign Fred Durrant, the Queens Park Rangers centre forward, but personal terms could not be agreed. Instead Tom Smith took a trip up to Birmingham and signed Archie Garrett, again. He joined an elite band of Cobblers who had three different spells with the club. Herbert Chapman, William Nobles, Albert Dunkley, and later Frank Large and Billy Best. Archie had suffered a bad injury at Birmingham and in his 12 months at St. Andrews he had made just 18 appearances, although he had also netted six goals. Also joining the club was Wilf McCoy, a centre half from Portsmouth. He was known as 'Tim' and signed to fill the void left by the retirement of Bob Dennison. Harry Lowery had been tried in the position with little success and the young Ben Collins was still learning his trade.

There may have been harmony in the dressing room but that was not the case in the boardroom. In January 1949, manager Tom Smith resigned. He cited his reasons as 'disagreements with the directors', stating that it started almost 12 months earlier. He was promised the £10,000 received on the Archie Garrett deal, to buy new players, but the money went on the ground at Spinney Hill. It all came to a head at the match v Leyton Orient, the manager was criticised for his team selection, despite the Cobblers winning 4- 1. No one could question the manager's commitment. During the war he brought such players as Bill Shankley, Andy Beattie, Gilbert Alsop, Don Dearson, Ron Starling, George Cummings, Bob Dennison and many many more to the County Ground.

He also later admitted that he had turned down the chance to manage two first division teams. The players were sad to see Tom go, they all respected him and felt he had the right attitude towards the job, and towards them. They all received a letter from their ex-manager. Tommy still has his copy today. They were all hand written, relaying the following; Dear Tommy, Just a line to wish you the very best of luck in the future and to thank you for the loyalty to me, since you have been at Northampton. You know my address and if I am able to help I shall be only too happy to do so. Remember me to your good wife and I shall be hoping to see you in the near future. Sincerely yours Tom Smith.

There were 31 applications for the post of manager at Northampton Town, and the press put forward four names. There was Jack Jennings, the coach, he knew the set up at the County ground; ex-defender Bob Dennison, who was now the youth team coach; ex-football league referee, Jack Barrick was also a contender, he had been in the middle at the 1948 F.A. Cup Final. There was also George Hardwick, the Middlesbrough and England full back.

'We were all pleased that Bob Dennison got the job', Tommy said. 'He was a real gentleman, was also very straight talking, you knew where you stood with him. He was a lot like Tom Smith in many ways, never ranted or raved, and always watched a game from the bench without jumping up and shouting. If we did have a bad game on a Saturday we would have a meeting the following Monday, and discuss it'. Tommy smiled as he recalled. 'Sometimes he and Jack Jennings would shut theirselves in the treatment room, and talk in low voices. If things were not going well at half time, but they never pointed the finger at any particular player'.

Tommy made an impressive start for his new boss, he netted his first Cobblers hat-trick, in a 4-0 victory over Millwall . It was never on the cards, Northampton were coasting to a 2-0 victory, with just Five minutes to go, Tommy had netted one and Bill Smith the other. Then as supporters were thinking of leaving early, Tommy struck twice, in the 85th and 87th minute.

The season ended early for Northampton Town's number 11. It was during a Tuesday night game at the County ground, in April that he picked up an injury and spent most of the game limping on the left wing. The game, against Brighton, ended 0-0. It was hoped he would make his come back the following week but after a try out in the morning, he broke down and it was decided to rest the injury. This brought about a catalogue of disruptions and changes. For reserve winger Alf Horne went sick, this meant a car trip for the new manager, to Symingtons of Market Harborough, where the Colts were playing. He took colts player Nickells with him, and brought back Gwyn Hughes to replace the injured Tommy.

Although he would not know it at the time, it would be almost a year before Tommy played in the first team, again. With the club avoiding re-election on goal average, Bob Dennison decided on revamping the side. He brought in Maurice Candlin, a hard tackling, no nonsense wing half, or centre half. Jack Southam, a much travelled full back came via Newport County, Eddie Murphy, a skilful, ball playing inside forward, came from Scotland, Adam McCulloch, a free scoring centre forward arrived with him, and a fifth signing was an outside left! Bert Mitchell, had played for Stoke and Blackburn, with little success, he then moved into Southern league football with Kettering Town, although technically he was still a Blackburn player. He went straight into the new look first team, and it would not matter how well Tommy played for the reserves there was no way that he was going to shift Mitchell from his spot. The team were doing well and Bert Mitchell was scoring goals.

'I cannot remember a lot about it, I suppose I played for the reserves. I was never bitter or angry about losing my place, you had to play for it and if the manager thought there was someone playing better, in your position, then you had to accept the fact, and get on with the game', Tommy stated. 'The Mitchells were not only our neighbours, but our best friends', Joyce continued. 'They were a lovely couple, and had two lovely, although uncontrollable girls. One day they emptied the neighbour's fish pond of all its fish'.

Tommy spent most of the 1949/50 season in the reserves that season, although he was in good company – Bill Barron, Ben Collins, Jack English, Eddie Freimanis, Archie Garrett, and Gwyn Hughes were his team mates for most of the Football Combination games. The standard of football was obviously lower than at league level, but still high, after all, there were no squads in those days, if you played the second Eleven of Tottenham or Arsenal, then it was the Second best Eleven players on their books, not a mixture of youth and trialists like a lot of reserve teams are today. Away travel had not taken off at this stage, except for some cup matches, so attendances of five figures were not unknown especially at places like Highbury or Upton Park.

Mitchell was injured in a 0-0 draw at Aldershot, allowing Tommy a five match run in the first team during October, but once the ex-Blackburn man was fit, it was back to the reserves. For the last six games of the season, Mitchell was switched to the right wing and Tommy came back into the side, the same time as

Left to Right; Ben Collins, Tommy Fowler Jack English.

The Four 'Wingers' on the Cobblers books in the Early 1950's. Left to Right; Bert Mitchell, Tommy Fowler Jack English, Dave Bowen.

Ben Collins took over the centre half spot. There was still an outside chance of promotion to the Second Division at the time.

With Six games left Notts County had 53 points, the Cobblers 42. Even if they won all the remaining games they would have to rely on County picking up less than two points for the remainder of the season. Prior to Tommy's inclusion in the side, Northampton had not had the best of runs. Four wins and six draws in the previous 14 games had knocked them off the top spot and they never seemed able to catch up with Notts County. A 3-1 home win against Norwich, the day after County lost to Port Vale saw the Cobblers edge closer, then Bristol Rovers were beaten 2-0, one of the goals coming from the reinstated winger, while County faltered again, this time losing 0-2 at Aldershot.

Over 13,000 supporters watched Northampton at Southend, who were just one place behind, them, and they saw the Cobblers emerge victorious, winning the game 2-1. One of the goals coming from Archie Garrett, who had also been recalled from the reserves. However news filtered through from Meadow Lane that County had beaten local rivals, Nottingham Forest 2-0.

With just three games left, there was no way that Northampton could make up the seven point deficit, Notts County were the Division Three South Champions!

In a way it took a little gloss off of the remaining three games, because Northampton and Notts County were to meet twice within the following week. Despite the title being signed and sealed well over 31,000 attended the game at Meadow Lane, not bad considering in was a Thursday afternoon kick off. The result was academic, County won the game 2-0 and 'that man', Tommy Lawton scored his 30th and 31st league goals of the season.

Tommy could not recall any special instructions for the run in, just the usual pep talk, and there was most certainly no offer of a cash incentive to lift the championship. Two days later, the two clubs met again at the County ground, this time a certain amount of revenge was extracted, the Cobblers coasted to a 5-1 victory, but it was somewhat hollow, there was nothing at stake and under 10,000 supporters paid to watch the game. Second place was a vast improvement on the last season, but it counted for nothing in a division that only the champions were promoted. For Northampton Town it was back to the drawing board. Bob Dennison had built a side capable of better things, he also had strength in reserve. The side had balance, skilful players, like Eddie Murphy and Bert Mitchell, 'grafters' like Adam McCulloch, experienced players like Tom Smalley and Bill Barron, and youth like Ben Collins, Gwyn Hughes and Tommy.

There were also the players who could look after theirselves, and others, like Smalley, Maurice Candlin, and Bill Coley. Tommy recalls one match in which he was well and truly 'clattered' to the ground by a defender. The referee gave a free kick. Tommy was lifting himself from the ground, still feeling the effects of the tackle, Bill Coley came along side him, as he placed the ball for the free kick. 'Don't worry about him', he whispered 'Leave him to me'. Tommy did, and Bill was as true as his word!

BENEFITS, TRANSFER REQUESTS AND A NEW MANAGER

The problem with playing in a specialist position, like goalkeeper or outside left, was that there were no alternative positions. A wing half could interchange with an inside forward, a centre half could go full back or centre forward, but the winger was one on its own.

More so in Tommy's case, because he was a left footed player, he was only really comfortable on the left side of the field. The 1950-51 season started the same way as the previous season, Bert Mitchell still maintained the first team shirt, with Tommy playing for the second string. Manager Bob Dennison strengthened the side with players like Arthur Dixon, a goal grabbing inside forward from Hearts, Jim Davie, a solid wing half from Preston and Ted Duckhouse, a raw boned, no nonsense centre half from Birmingham. Despite these class signings, the club struggled, winning just three of their first 12 games, a bitter disappointment after the runners-up spot they achieved the season before.

Injuries to key players played a large part in the club's poor performance, goalkeeper Jack Ansell suffered a broken leg at Southend, while wing half Maurice Candlin and full back Tom Smalley both missed part of the season. It was through injury to both wingers, Jack English and Bert Mitchell, that Tommy won back his place, he took over the number 11 shirt, while Dave Smith played his first game, in the first team, for over a year. Tommy's return was an away match, at Brighton. Unfortunately the new pair of wide men could not reverse the club's dismal run, and the 'Seagulls' came away 5-1 winners. However, Bob Dennison must have been pleased, with Tommy's performance, as when Bert Mitchell regained full fitness, he was switched to the right wing.

With no reflection on Tommy, the 13 games he played that season, realised five draws and eight defeats. He played his part by scoring in three of them, and laying on one or two more, for his team mates. 'The results may not have been going for us, but there was still a lot of camaraderie, in the side, and always a few jokers in the pack.' Tommy recalled, relating to two particular incidents. 'We were staying at a hotel, I think it was in Torquay, we all left our shoes outside the rooms to be cleaned by the staff, but in the morning, when we stepped outside our rooms to collect them, they had all been switched around! Not only had the players had their footwear swapped, but the other guests had their shoes switched. It was all played down and an apology was made to the hotel management, but the culprits never owned up. Most of us knew it was set up by the hard tackling wing half and the ball playing inside forward, butter would not melt in their mouths.

At another hotel, the reception was on the first floor. Someone pointed out that Jack Jennings was pacing the path outside the hotel. We all stood at the window watching, then we realised that two of our party were missing, the same two that switched the shoes. It then became apparent that the two, who were known for their love of a drink, were out on the town, sampling the local brew'.

Bob Dennison made big changes for the start of the 1951-52 season. Eddie Murphy had been sold to Barnsley for a near record fee. Barnsley using the money they received from Aston Villa for a certain Danny Blanchflower. Veteran full backs Tom Smalley and Bill Barron had been released, and Bert Mitchell moved on to Luton Town. It was to be a 'bitter-sweet' life for the winger, at Luton. He was to be selected for an England 'B' trial match, during his stay there, but was to also tragically lose his wife to cancer, while still in her 30s, leaving him with two young girls. In to the side came a free scoring centre forward, Willie O'Donnell from Scotland, a skillful inside forward, Freddie Ramscar, and another Winger! Felix Starocsik was from Poland, he had been signed from St. Mirren, and like Bert Mitchell was equally at home on either wing. Often his name was to be found among the goal scorers, he was a talented, yet temperamental player. It was the Pole who kicked off the season in the number 11 shirt, but Tommy took over when he was injured, and never looked back, he reformed the relationship with Jack English that they had started in the reserve side. It was also one of his best seasons for goals. Ten were netted throughout the season, including a brace against Port Vale, and five during a seven match spell. Most of March was lost through injury, but as soon as he was fit, he retained his place again, helping the side to a respectable eighth position, a far better effort than the previous season.

This was also to be Tommy's benefit year. A match was arranged at the end of the season between the club and a 'Select Eleven', with the proceeds to be shared with Gwyn Hughes, who had also completed his five years. Tommy was to lead the Northampton side, while Gwyn's side would be the select, the line up was; COBBLERS: Alf Wood; Ben Collins, Jim Southam; Jim Davie, Maurice Candlin, Ron Burgess (Tottenham); Felix Starocsik, Jack English, Willie O'Donnell, Freddie Ramscar and Tommy Fowler. The 'SELECT' team; Sonny Feehan (Cobblers) Charles Withers (Tottenham) Les Jones (Luton), Bill Nicholson (Spurs), Syd Owen (Luton), Gwyn Hughes; Bert Mitchell (Luton), Tommy Harmer (Tottenham), George Lowerie (Coventry), Eddie Bailey (Tottenham), Norman Lockhart (Coventry) The match referee was Norman Hillier, who was to play a part in Tommy's career, but for all the wrong reasons. Although the result was academic, Tommy's side won 5-0, and the two recipients received £120 apiece. 'I remember Jack Jennings saying to me, "Tommy, let me run you down to the building society with that cheque, you want to get that straight into savings" ', Tommy recalled, as he read the receipt that he still possesses today.

Joyce had suffered two miscarriages during the early part of their marriage, and the first child born to the couple, was stillborn. A boy of 9lbs 7oz. 'I received a lovely letter from Bob Dennison's wife, offering me her condolences. It was very moving', Joyce recalled. 'There was also my friend Vera, we became friends very early in my stay at Northampton, and she has been my friend ever since. She was a rock, and helped me through those days'. When it was discovered Joyce was pregnant again, the Baby doctor at the Northampton General Hospital made her a promise'. I'll make sure this time you will have a bouncing baby, even if I have to keep you in hospital for the whole of your pregnancy!' After five months in hospital Joyce gave birth to Tommy junior in 1953. Things went from one extreme to another, for until the age of two the youngster would wake up every night, around one or two o'clock and keep his parents awake.

'I did not have a good night's sleep for two years', Joyce said. 'Tommy junior would get me up, and I would have to sit and play with him, or watch him'. 'But, she made sure I did get some shut-eye', Tommy added. 'Every Friday night, before a game, I was sent to the box room to sleep, and sometimes in mid-week, if we had an evening game.' It all became too much in the end and they spoke to the Doctor who told them as long as he was not in a position to harm himself, just leave him, he'll get over it – ignore his cries and screams. 'Joe Payne was our neighbour then, we had to go round and tell them to ignore any screaming they might hear', Joyce continued. 'It was hell to go through, but it worked, he settled down well after that.

When Susan was born in 1960, everything went so smooth with her, we did not know we had her'. By now Enoch, Tommy's father had retired. He would come down to Northampton during the close season and stay with his younger son, giving Tommy's sister, Ada, a break. He was just as keen on cricket as he was on football and in the early days would discuss the virtues of the Lancashire County Cricket Club's players. There was nothing he loved better than watching Northamptonshire play, especially Freddie Brown. Joyce would pack him up some sandwiches and he would spend most of the day watching the County, breaking off for a pint in the County Tavern, while he ate his lunch. He made many friends there, not only with the supporters but also the players, and became quite a popular figure.

On the books of Northampton Town Football club, at the time, was a young reserve winger, called Arnold Woollard. He was from Bermuda, and had been recommended to Northampton by the high commissioner of Bermuda. He recalled a conversation he had with manager Bob Dennison. 'You are never going to shift Tommy from his left wing spot, I'm going to convert you to a full back'. It was a career move that paid off, for although Arnold was released by the club, and dropped into non-league football with Peterborough United, it kick-started his career again, and he turned out for Newcastle United, Bournemouth and back to Northampton.

The supporters loved to see Tommy running at defenders, he was so good at that, and his relationship with Jack English, on the field, was second to none, I cannot understand why a bigger club never snapped them up. When I returned to Northampton in the early 1960s Tommy had gone, he was replaced by Barry Lines, who I thought was in the same mould as Tommy'. Tommy was back in the first team to stay. It was Ben Collins who quoted 'The Northampton manager always put Tommy's name down on the team sheet first, then gave careful consideration to the other ten players'. That may not quite have been the situation, but he was an integral part of the Northampton Town side, and was growing in stature every season. A few more pieces were added to the jigsaw for the 1952-53 season, and it almost worked, promotion was missed by just two points. 'That was the best Cobblers side I ever played in,' Tommy admitted. 'It had everything – skill, commitment, balance, and a great bunch of lads'.

By this time Alf Wood, who had guested for the club during the war, returned to keep goal. Full backs Ron Patterson and Jim Southam, were ever present, while Maurice Candlin and Ben Collins shared the centre-half spots. It was a case of pick two from three at wing half, Tommy McLain, Gwyn Hughes and Norman

Dodgin, all sharing first team duties. Jack English covered the right wing, and his inside forward partner was Maurice Edelston, who was capped for England at Amateur level. Willie O'Donnell was the number Nine, with the talented Freddie Ramscar playing as Tommy's inside forward partner. The compliments were not all one way, many of the side were grateful to have a player like Tommy in the side.

Ron Patterson was a talented no nonsense full back, who had left his Gateshead home to take up a career with Crystal Palace, but it did not take off. He returned to the North East, where he signed for Middlesbrough, but found first team opportunities at a premium. When Bob Dennison offered to sign him he jumped at the chance, and soon fitted into the side, 'I always "fired" a pass to Tommy', recalled Ron. 'If you rolled a ball to a winger, an opposing defender could intercept it, or tackle the player before he turned, but that was never the case with Tom. He had the ability to either pass to a team mate, and then get into a position where he could receive the ball back, or turn, put the ball one side of the defender, and he would run the other side, leaving the opposing full back in two minds as to which way he should go'. Ron was enthusiastic in his praise for his ex-team mate. 'He had this ability to kill a ball dead, regardless of how hard you passed it to him, add to that his speed and his accuracy at pin point centres, he was a hell of a player to have in your side.' 'Ron also recalled the dressing room banter before a match. 'There were a lot of big lads in the side, and they were always having a dig at each other, about the pending game, but Tommy never got involved, he would quietly change into his kit, and let it all pass over his head, that was something else that won him a lot of admirers'.

At the time there were also a couple of youngsters who were looking for first team places, both full of praise for the first team winger. Ken Leek was a Welsh lad, who would become something of a footballing nomad, as well as collect a few Welsh caps on the way. He was to have two spells at the County Ground, but at this stage he was yet to break into the first team. 'I used to look at that forward line, English, Edelston, O'Donnell, Ramscar and Fowler, and had nothing but admiration for the players, they were as good as any in that division', Ken recalled, 'and I had to try to break into that side! I never played as many times as I would have liked to with Tommy. As soon as I made the first team, I was called up for National Service. On my return I had to fight for my first team place again. No sooner had I won it over, than I was transferred'. Another player who was impressed with the winger's ability was Frank Upton. A blacksmith's apprentice, he was spotted playing for Nuneaton, and so keen were the Cobblers to sign him, they not only paid a fee, but lent Nuneaton two players until the end of the season. 'I was always thankful to Bob Dennison for giving me the chance to play league football', Frank said. I would get on the Northampton train at Nuneaton and travel down with Jim Southam who came via Birmingham. Tommy was fast and quick, I admired his professionalism, often outpacing the defenders. The players all accepted me as one of them, which made me feel at home. However, one thing I never got involved with was their post training 'flutter'. I was never a gambler then, or now'.

May 1953 saw the Club net 109 goals, each of the five forwards reaching double figures, on only four occasions did the club fail to score, and five goals were hit on five occasions, with six being netted against Reading The supporters were talking eagerly of next season. realising it was defence that needed strengthening, Bob Dennison took a plane to the North East and signed full back Maurice Marston, and centre half Bill Walsh from Middlesbrough. Despite the fact that the nucleus of the side was that of last season, it just was not clicking, it took five games before they recorded their first win, a 2- 1 victory over Bournemouth. A 4-1 victory over Watford could have been higher, had Freddie Ramscar not missed two penalties, it cost him his position as the club's penalty taker, and the job was given to Tommy. It was said he had a hard shot, although he himself denied it was any harder than many of his colleagues, but despite his wiry frame he could pack a lot of power from that left foot. Testimony to this came from Harry Brown, the Queens Park Rangers goalkeeper. He made two finger tip saves from Tommy in a 1-1 draw in London, and later admitted that; It was two days before I dare take my gloves off, to see if my fingers were still there'. Freddie Ramscar always believed in "placing" his penalties, and to do this he would always side foot them in, It is fair to say that in most cases it came off but in the game against Watford it failed, Twice! 'I would always blast my penalties' Tommy remarked. 'Even if the goalkeeper got his hand to a shot, the chances were that he would not be able to hold it, or if he got his body behind it, there was the chance it would rebound to you'.

Jack Jennings, preferred a left footed penalty taker, he believed they would put the ball to the goalkeeper's left hand side, which was their weakest side, a theory not shared by everyone. Tommy converted his first penalty via Reading. 'I cannot remember how many I converted, but I missed one, then I lost the job!'

October 1953 saw Jack Cross, a centre forward join the club from Bournemouth. Dennison had been after the forward for some time, but after a long and lengthy struggle, he finally got his man, a prolific scorer, and a man with a B.A, after his name. Willie O'Donnell had lost form, he had scored just three goals in 17 league games, but as soon as the new centre forward arrived, the Scotsman slapped in a transfer request. It was fair to say that the new man revitalised the side, he netted nine goals in 12 games, and only appeared in a losing side twice, but as quickly as he came – he left!

In January, Sheffield United made an offer for the player, that was believed to be double what the Cobblers paid for him, the board accepted it, and the player moved on. 'We were all shocked and surprised', said Tommy. 'He was a good quality player, he was easy to work with, was fast, keen, and got himself into positions that were easy for me to find him with crosses'. The board of directors claimed that he had to be sold because the gate receipts were not bringing in enough money, however the average attendance for home matches stood at around 11,000. Facts show that after the sale of Jack Cross, the goals dried up. Tommy managed just five, half last season's total, despite being the club penalty taker, and Freddie Ramscar scored ten. Only Jack English was finding goals easy to come by, scoring 31, including three hat tricks in that total. The sale of Cross was to have far reaching consequences.

At the end of the season, the Club's popular manager, Bob Dennison, announced that he was leaving to join Middlesbrough, in a similar position. He stated he was frustrated at not being able to keep his better players because of the low gates. Both supporters and players were sorry to see him leave. Although he had three years of his contract left, the directors allowed him to go, realising his frustration. He also admitted that two seasons earlier he had turned down the chance of managing Southampton.

Fifth was the best position the club could attain at the close of the 1953-54 season, and never really made a serious attempt for the promotion spot. This was mainly due to the lack of goals. Any interest in the F.A. Cup ended at Hartlepool in a second round replay. The 'Pools' scored the only goal of the game. However there was an interesting match report of the first round tie, at home to Llanelly. Ken Maxwell, the Llanelly right back, was one of Tommy's ex-team mates and a neighbour on his housing estate, a few seasons earlier. The local Welsh press made a story of how the two ex-team mates would meet up again, and who would come out on top.

The Cobblers won 3-0, Tommy scored one and made one, playing to his usual high standards, regardless of who the opposition were. The local press had a field day and related part of the match report thus: 'Tommy Fowler and Ken Maxwell shook hands at the start of the game, and it was the last time the two players met again, until they shook hands at the end. The Scotsman, never got near the Northampton winger, often getting left for dead as he moved in for a tackle only to find Tommy had moved the other side of him'. It was no reflection on Ken Maxwell's ability, even players in the third division cursed their luck when they knew Tommy was playing against them. Dave Smith stepped up from Secretary to team manager. It seemed a logical move, he knew the set up at Northampton, and who was who at the County Ground. It was an appointment that did not need a lot of alteration to things as they stood, it also meant the playing and coaching staff, remained the same. One of Dave's first signings was Don Hazeldine, a centre forward from Derby County. 'I remember living in lodgings in King Edward road, I was a single man in those days and Maurice Marston and his wife often used to invite me to their home for Sunday lunch', Don recalled. 'Tommy could easily have played at a higher level of football, he was most certainly capable of it, He was fast and tricky, I was surprised no clubs ever came in for him'.

Don was not offered new terms after his stay in 1954-55, and left to join his brother at Boston, they were to play together in the side that beat Derby County 6-0 in the F.A.Cup a few years later. Meanwhile, the Cobblers new manager was having to deal with a spate of transfer requests. There was no real reason for players wanting to leave but they came in thick and fast. First was Freddie Ramscar, then Ron Patterson, followed by Tommy Mulgrew and Larry Baxter. The latter two were unable to hold down places in the first team and their requests were granted, Baxter joining Norwich and Mulgrew, Newcastle. Freddie Ramscar was also granted a move, he put pen to paper with Millwall, remembering the happy days he spent in London with Queens Park Rangers. Despite this he continued to live in Northampton, which threw up a strange anomaly. When the Cobblers travelled to Millwall for a league game, Freddie got permission to travel with them on the coach, he played in the game for the Lions, laid on the winning goal, and then travelled back with the Cobblers players. 'I cannot remember too much about the game', Tommy tried to recall. 'But there must have been something said, some remark, but probably not in Fred's earshot'.

In late October there was a bombshell dropped, Tommy asked for a transfer!.

Joyce and Tommy Junior, pictured after Tommy had withdrawn his transfer request.

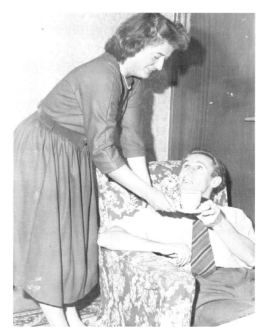

Relaxing at home

'It's nothing against the Club, they have treated us and the other players well, it is a private and personal matter', Tommy quoted.

'I felt we needed to get away, I was not worried if we moved nearer to my family in Herefordshire or Tommy's family in Lancashire, but I felt we needed a break, and Tommy agreed,' Joyce recalled. Even Chairman Edwin Hawtin made a public statement. 'Of course we do not want to let this man go, the matter has to be gone in to very seriously indeed' Whatever happened over the next few days were kept between the people closely involved, but on the 10th of November, Northampton Town supporters heard the news they wanted to hear, 'Tommy was staying'.

After a lengthy discussion between Tommy and Joyce, they decided that their future did lie in this small market Town and the request was withdrawn. It was almost a case of 'bringing out the flags and buntings' to celebrate, firstly a *Chronicle and Echo* reporter and cameraman travelled to Parkfield Avenue to take Joyce's photograph, while manager Dave Smith made a press announcement. 'The matter has now been settled to the satisfaction of all, we are all happy about it'.

The side was too inconsistent to mount any serious challenge for promotion, Southend were beaten 6-2, Colchester 6-1 and Bournemouth 5-0, but then defeats were suffered at Reading (2-6), Bristol City (1-5) and there was a 1-6 defeat at

Walsall. The Club also lost their life vice-president, A. J. Darnell, at the age of 90. 'He always travelled away with the reserve team, always had his stick with him, and sometimes he had a job to walk, but he would never miss a reserve game, he never came to away games with the first team, just the reserves, almost right up to his death', said Tommy. 'He was a lovely man, everyone at the club respected him. I was proud to have been one of the Club's representatives at the funeral.' Darnell had founded the football club in 1897, and had been a honorary club member since 1945. He had also sat on the NFA, the Southern League, and the Football League as the Division Three Representative. And that was not to mention his involvement with the County Cricket Club, the Conservative Party, and boys football in the Town.

The 1954-55 season closed, reflecting on a nine month period where more happened off the field than on it, but no one could realise what was to come.

Tommy and Tommy Junior, in the back garden at Parkfield Avenue.

ENGLISH SCORES FROM A FOWLER CROSS

Over the years Northampton Town have boasted many great wingers. In the very first side of 1897, Albert Dunkley was the first player they signed on professional terms. He would later play for a host of League and Southern League clubs. Soon after him Billy Brawn emerged, who at six feet tall and 13 stone in weight, lived up to his name. Billy would later wear an England shirt, as would John Coleman, a right winger who played just after the turn of the 20th century.

No one could forget the 'mighty midget', Fanny Walden, who was capped for England both sides of the first world war, after he left Northampton for Tottenham Hotspur. The 1920s saw the famous pair, Billy Pease and Louis Page, flank the Cobblers forward line, again both players moved to first division clubs, and both won England caps. Jack Rawlings and 'Shadow' Wells were the wingmen of the 1930s. Rawlings, a right winger, and the son of an ex-Cobblers player had a short but successful stay at the County ground, whilst Wells, like Tommy, made the left-wing berth his own, for many years. Then came the 1950s and two more exciting wingers emerged, Tommy Fowler and Jack English!

It was the perfect scenario, Tommy on the left wing had the ability to beat his marker and put pin-point passes into the opposing goal mouth where Jack would ghost in, and score. The fact that Tommy made the most appearances for the club, and Jack scored the most goals must prove the point that they were such an important part of the Northampton Town set up of their day.

Without being disrespectful to Jack English, he was never as fast as Tommy, he never had Tommy's ability to beat his man, and lacked the left winger's ball control. What he did have, was an amazing burst of speed over a small distance, and an uncanny ability to be in the right place at the right time. Regardless of how many defenders were in the penalty box, Jack always seemed to be exactly where the ball fell. He was also ice cool in the box Never panicked or flapped, neither did he have to dive or stretch out a leg, he had an unusual sixth sense. Sometimes it worked against him, he scored 135 league goals for the Cobblers, but it must be wondered how many more legitimate goals were ruled out for offside, because he was so quick, officials must have felt he was in an offside position.

One national newspaper made a tongue-in-cheek remark, suggesting the local press must have a permanent piece of type set, which read. 'English scores from a Fowler cross'. However, like Tommy, Jack also served in the armed forces during the hostilities, and like Tommy came close to losing his life.

Jack was the son of a professional footballer, also called Jack. He had appeared for Preston North End, Watford, and Sheffield United, winning an F.A. Cup-winners medal with them in 1915. Jack senior, had won representative honours with the football league and it was thought he was on the fringe of an international cap, before the first world war broke out. Sheffield United wanted him to continue his performances as a polished full back with them, but he chose to go into management, taking the post of player/manager at Darlington. After leading the 'Quakers' to the North Eastern League championship, followed by the Third Division North championship, he moved on to Nelson followed by Northampton Town in 1931.

His son Jack junior went to a private school, and during his term holidays, would go with his father to the County Ground, and loved nothing more than to get involved with the training sessions, playing alongside the professionals. Many complained that 'young English was a nuisance', never realising some 20 years later, opposing defences at the County ground would be agreeing with that sentiment.

Jack senior was not long at the County ground, and returned to Darlington, after a spell at Exeter City, in between. Jack Junior completed his education and then, like Tommy, found himself on National Service, serving with the R.A.F. in India. Here he played football, and emulated his father, by winning the cup final. But this was the all-India Cup Final, no medal, but a neatly printed certificate, with his achievement in black and white. Jack was playing for Delhi and they beat Bengal in the final. He was not only one of the few white men playing, but also one of the few that wore boots! That was not necessarily an advantage, for he advised people later to avoid a kick from those bare feet. They were like cast iron, and if they did catch you, you knew about it, double shin pads or not!

He returned to England and was stationed at Bristol. Despite travelling halfway around the world, it was here that he came closest to losing his life.

He was in a building at the Filton aviation plant when for some reason he was called away. It was at the same time that the German airforce decided to make a day-time raid on the plant, leaving the building that Jack had just vacated, a pile of rubble. Many of its occupants died, something Jack was to remember for the rest of his life. While at Bristol he made two war time appearances for Bristol City. Both at inside left. Neither were memorable, a 1-5 defeat at Aldershot, and a 1-7 defeat at Bournemouth, although just like Tommy made his war time appearances alongside Tommy Lawton, Jack could boast he played alongside Roy Bentley.

In October 1946 he was offered terms by Northampton Town, and appeared several times for the 'Colts', who were in effect the reserves. Ironically, finding lodgings in Abington Avenue, it took some time for the Durham lad to make an impression. It was not until January 1948 that he made his debut, against the club he once played for, Bristol City. Almost twelve months later he netted his first goal for the club in a 4-0 victory over Exeter City, the club once managed by his father. By the end of the 1949/1950 season he had appeared 47 times for the club and scored seven goals, but that was over a three year period. Jack was made, 'open to offer' on the transfer market, the Cobblers did not have a regular place for him, but felt they did not want to lose his services without some compensation.

Bristol City, who were well aware of the Winger's talents, made enquiries, but it never went any further. It was also said that two Midlands clubs, believed to be Walsall and Coventry, were interested, but it seemed that Jack would be starting the next season still a Northampton player. However he took things into his own hands, and made the best decision of his career. Jack English became a part-time player. He took a job with the Brook Clothes' Manufacturers factory, and just trained a couple of days a week at the County ground. He was by now in his late 20s and had one eye on the future. He found it hard to keep up with the rigour of first-team training, lacking the stamina needed to compete. This led to Jack Jennings arranging a special training package that suited his style. It worked, the goals kept coming; 21 in 1952, 24 in 1953, and a record 31 in 1954. No opponents seemed to have the answer to Jack's phenomenal scoring record. It was legend that he had scored on every ground of Clubs in the Third Division South.

It would be impossible to gauge how many of Jack's goals came from Tommy's crosses or how many he missed or were saved, but it must have been in the hundreds, as Northampton were well among the goals during that period.

'People asked us if we worked these moves out in training, they used to seem surprised that we did not. We never practised any tactical moves it was just fitness training, followed by practise matches', recalled Tommy.

'They asked how I always managed to find Jack with my passes, but I put that down to him, he moved so fast in the box, he used to catch defenders out of position'. Peter Pickering knew a bit about the English/Fowler relationship. He was a goalkeeper with York City and then joined Chelsea for a record fee for a player in that position. After three seasons at Chelsea he dropped into non-league football with Kettering. He was given the opportunity to return to league football when Northampton found themselves without a keeper on their books in 1955.

'I played with, and against, the pair of wing men, and I know which I preferred!' the ex-Cobblers custodian stated.

'When I played for Kettering against Northampton in County cup games, I really had to be on my toes. Tommy would beat his marker, then bring the ball down the bye-line. As goalkeeper, I would automatically cover my near post, knowing full well, Jack would be lurking at the far post, just waiting for half a chance. Playing in the same side was a different matter, I knew exactly where Tommy would be when I had possession. He was a thinking player, not robust but he avoided physical contact with his exceptional turn of speed. I was blessed with a long kick, and throw so Tommy would leave his full back and come into our half of the field, allowing me to throw the ball to his feet. He would then play a one-two with a team mate then run down the wing for the return.

At other times he would draw the full back to follow him, then I would kick the ball out towards the opposition corner flag, and then watch Tommy sprint towards the ball, with the full back trailing behind him, desperately chasing him like a startled stoat.

Jack would be waiting the other side of the pitch, for the pass, that more often than not, resulted in a goal. It was a pleasure to play with them.' With over 150 goals in League, cup and friendlies, there was always the chance that one or two of Jack's goals were going to be 'freaks'.

In one game he latched on to a back pass, but the goalkeeper seemed to have the ball covered. Jack opened his feet hoping the ball would run between them and he would flick it with his back foot, but it never happened. The ball was going

Jack English

faster than he thought, hit his foot, and diverted into the net, fooling the goalkeeper and him! During another match, against Gillingham, their goalkeeper Rigg, dropped the ball after he was challenged. Jack thought he would drop on to the ball as it bounced, so he caught it between his knees, and hopped over the goal line!

Although Jack was on the Cobblers books from 1946 to 1960, it was between 1951 and 1958 that the two players had their best seasons. Tommy missed just 18 matches during that period while Jack scored goals at will.

During the three months between September and December 1953, he scored FOUR hat tricks. Throughout his stay at Northampton he played in all the forward positions - except outside left!

It was a different life for the professional footballer in those days, than it is today. It would be fair to say that some people in industry were earning more money, there was no sponsorship, no sponsored cars, and many of the players did not have their own home. They could be moving on after a year. Summer wages were hardly enough to live on, while a player had to spend five seasons with a club to earn a benefit, and even that had a ceiling.

'We were happy. Money never really worried me, as long as we had enough money to live on, we got by', Tommy recalled.

'I would cycle to the ground every day, for training, although on match days, I always caught the bus. After training we would all go to the betting shop and have a flutter, then I would cycle home. When Jack Smith played for the club, he lived nearby and gave me a lift on his motor cycle, no crash helmets in those days. It was to be some years later before I bought my first car – a Ford Popular. On Fridays I would meet Joyce in town, and we would walk back to Parkfield Avenue, pushing Tommy in his pram,' Tommy recalled.

'Then I would spend the afternoons in the garden. I enjoyed gardening, it was always nice seeing the potatoes grow.' From an early age, Enoch told Tommy to always keep himself to himself, speak when spoken to, and never offer opinions, unless asked.

'That always stuck in my mind', said Tommy. This was confirmed by all the players who played with him over the years, they all made comments like 'He was quiet, never said a lot, did his talking on the field' or 'a real Gentleman, both on and off the park'.

One player who knew him well was Ben Collins. The Kislingbury defender joined the club in 1948, and stayed 11 seasons, playing centre-half, or right-back. He remembered Tommy with affection.

'I will always feel very privileged and proud to have played with him many, many times, and I will always remember dear Flash. Pulled muscles, strains, colds, flu never worried us much in those days, just that £2 win bonus.

One of Tom's features was that he would roll the tops of his shorts up several times, showing plenty of leg (something that Archie Garret used to do as well).

Trainer Jack Jennings used to say he had seen bigger legs on a rabbit, but Tommy knew how to use them, his speed was second to none. His spirit was a big feature of his game, his crosses on the run were a gem to see.'

Ben recalled the great relationship between Jack English and Tommy, stating that 'Jack scored more goals in a season than whole teams do these days'. 'Tommy's closest friend was Gwyn Hughes, who in my opinion was the club's best all-round player. He could, and did, appear in almost every position for the Cobblers. They would sit in the corner of the dressing room and between them became the dressing room lawyers.

They knew about most things, from team changes to general knowledge and politics, and even who would win the 2.30. Each morning they would find time to read the Daily Herald, Sporting Life and even the Daily Worker. They would jog around the County Ground together, doing their laps, and putting the world to rights. Two great servants to the club'

It is fair to say that Tommy and Gwyn remained friends well after their playing days were over, and both Tommy and Joyce were regular visitors to the Welshman, until he sadly passed away in February 1999.

By the 1955/1956 season, the side was picking itself; Peter Pickering, Maurice Marston, Ron Patterson, Ray Yeomans, Ben Collins, Jack Smith, Jack English, Roly Mills, Bill Draper, Eddie Smith and Tommy Fowler. A great start was made, the first seven games all ended in victory, and Peter Pickering repaid a large chunk of his transfer fee, by saving TWO penalties in a match against Aldershot.

Once again the club failed to maintain their great start, they lost their way during the second half of the season, winning just three of their last 15 games. The F.A. cup brought up an interesting fact. Northampton made the third round, and each game was at home. A 4-1 victory over Millwall was a good start, to the competition. The London club were struggling, and Jack English, helped himself to a hat trick, while the Lions centre half Charlie Hurley, put through his own net. The second round brought Southern League Hastings to the County Ground, who were managed by ex-Cobbler, Jack Tresadern. This resulted in another 4-1 win, Bill Draper hitting a brace, and Jack English netting his fourth goal of the competition.

Then came Blackburn Rovers. Unfortunately, the game was played in a thick fog, which could have had something to do with the small crowd of 14,087, over 1,500 less than watched the match v Hastings. Northampton put up a good fight, but they ran out of steam, with three part-timers in the side, it was not surprising Rovers won 2-1.

With Tommy junior, now almost at school age, Tommy senior could no longer go out working on the land at Hereford during the close season. Firstly he took a job on the building sites, along with other Cobblers players. He then got a job at the Manfield shoe factory, mainly due to the fact that Ken Dear, a Cobblers director, was also a director of the shoe company.

Despite this there were no favours when it came to wages. Tommy was to work from 7.00 am to 6.00 p.m. Five days a week, making up orders, for the weekly wage of £7-15s (£7.75).

The Club made an indifferent start to the 1956/57 season. Manager Dave Smith had started to inject youth into his side; Tony Claypole, Geoff Coleman, Gerry Bright, Ken Leek, Roger Miller and Bobby Tebbutt all stepped up at some stage of the season to play in the first team. In all 25 players were used that season. The pack was shuffled so many times the inevitable happened, Tommy was dropped! Even then it was not a quick decision by the manager. The local press announced that for the home match v Walsall, a last minute decision would be made as to who should take the left wing spot, Tommy Fowler or Hugh Morrow, a winger, usually on the right, who was signed from Lockheed Leamington. Morrow got the nod.

After 226 consecutive games for the club – a record – Tommy found himself out of the first team.

'I do not remember too much about it', he said. 'It was all part and parcel of the set up in those days, players were chopped and changed all the while, my turn had to come sooner or later. I was never aware I was creating any kind of record with my appearances for the club, it was not until the newspapers recorded that I had played all those games that the realisation came home'. The experiment was a failure, Walsall beat the Cobblers 3-2 at the County Ground, and Tommy returned for the next game.

The season ended on a low note. Out of the F.A. Cup at the first hurdle and a lowly 14th place in the league, 15 points from promotion, and nine from re-election. Partick Thistle came down from Scotland to play in the joint testimonial for Tommy and Ron Patterson.

'I can not remember why it was against Partick', Tommy tried to recall. 'All I remember was that I did not make much more than the previous game'.

The 1957/58 season brought about a lot of changes in personnel. Maurice Robinson, a winger, had been signed from Kettering Town, after helping them win the Southern League championship. He was at home on either wing, but he started the season at outside left. This all changed after the Club picked up just one point from their first two games. Tommy was reinstated, Robinson moved over to the other wing and Coventry were beaten 4-0!

Northampton Town were going through a "Jekyll and Hyde" period. They beat Plymouth 5-0, Colchester 4-1, but lost 1-7 at Brentford, and 1-5 at Swindon. There never seemed to be a settled side, after a 2-4 home defeat by Brighton, the manager made SIX changes for the next match v Queens Park Rangers, and lost that one 1-5. Needless to say, the team that lost to Brighton were re-instated,en bloc.

It was around this period that Tommy once again asked for a transfer. 'I can not remember why, or what the outcome was, I suppose that I must have withdrawn it at some stage', he said.

A good cup run that season caused a backlog of fixtures. For the first time there was an added incentive to all clubs in the division to do well. It was to be the last ever season of the Division Three North and South.

Clubs finishing in the top half of the two divisions would make up the new Division Three, while the clubs below 12th position would be in the newly formed Division Four. It was not until March, that the Cobblers started to hit form, at that stage there was an even chance they could finish in the bottom two! Gillingham were beaten 3-1 in an Easter Saturday game, and on the following Monday, Millwall were hammered 7-2, Alan Woan netting a hat-trick. Two days were then spent on the South coast, a 1-1 draw with Bournemouth was followed by a 4-1 victory at Brighton. Two home matches followed, Bournemouth were beaten this time 4-0, and then on the 12th of April Exeter City were beaten 9-0. Both Alan Woan and Bobby Tebbutt netting hat tricks.

Earlier in the season, after Northampton's 1-0 victory over Exeter at St. James Park, their Right back shook hands with Tommy after the game and stated: 'I hate playing against you'.

After the County ground game, his sentiments must have been echoed tenfold. The player was Theo Foley, later to skipper the Cobblers into Division One, and manage them for a spell in the 1990s.

Tommy remembered a later meeting with Theo in 1998, at the Club's Centenary reunion. 'He introduced me to his wife, and said to her, "this is the little so and so, who used to run rings around me". We had a chat about those days, with fond memories.'

Theo admitted to being an admirer of Tommy's. 'I was well aware of his skills and his great left foot, but I was a tough lad, quite quick, I could handle him, or so I thought. Every time I got near him, he would release the ball, then run to another position to receive it. Oh, he was a tough nut to crack. Back to the run-in of 1958, the club faltered at Torquay, losing 0-1, but took revenge at the County Ground ten days later, by the same score. Gillingham were also beaten on the way, but a double defeat by Southend in the last two games of the season confined the Cobblers to Fourth division football the following season, although it is fair to say, by the time the Southend games came around, their fate was sealed, what ever the result, their destiny was no longer in their hands.

Northampton Town finished 14th one place and three points off of a place in the Third Division.

Tommy and Jack during a charity game after their playing days were over.

OUTGUNNING THE GUNNERS

Although the 1957/58 season was not a success as far as the league was concerned, it was a different story in the F.A. Cup. When the first round draw was made there was little excitement shown by the Northampton public. The Cobblers had been drawn at home to Newport County, who two weeks before the cup tie, had beaten them 3-0 at the County Ground.

Dave Smith was having a problem at centre forward and put centre half Colin Gale in the number nine shirt, having used four other players in that position up to that point in the season. The giant Welshman repaid his manager's faith by scoring one of the goals as the Cobblers avenged their league defeat, by the same score.

Tommy missed that game, as it fell during the period he had lost his place to Maurice Robinson.

Bournemouth were the second round opponents. They too were fellow bed-mates in the third division, and they too were riding high. By this time Tommy had retained his left wing spot and played his part in helping Ken Leek and Alan Woan score for the Cobblers. Bournemouth players, Hughes and Norris also scored, but it was in the Cobblers favour, in their own net, Northampton Town won the match 4-1.

The third round draw made the Northampton public sit up and take interest, Northampton Town were drawn at home to . . . the Arsenal! From the day of the draw to the day of the match, both local and national newspapers carried some story about the pending game. Dave Bowen, had left Northampton for Arsenal in July 1950, yet still lived in the town, where he had business interests, he also trained with the Cobblers during the week. One of the first moves the club made was to ban the Welsh International from the ground until after the match.

By the Thursday before the game the Cobblers top scorer, Alan Woan found himself confined to his bed, suffering from food poisoning. Manager Dave Smith replaced him with the ex-Colts player, Bobby Tebbutt. There was a gradual build up to the game over the week, with announcements coming from both camps.

A Northampton director had promised the players a close season tour of Sweden, should they beat the Arsenal. While club officials were rubbing their hands at what should be a bumper crowd.

For Tommy, it was his first real experience of playing against a quality team in the F.A. Cup, since joining Northampton. He was not in the side that lost to Preston North End in 1947, or the side that went out in the Fifth Round, to Derby County in 1950. Bert Mitchell was the outside left when the Club met Arsenal the previous time in 1951, leaving the match against Blackburn, two seasons ago, as his only real F.A.Cup match against higher opposition, although they were a Second Division side, at the time.

January 4th, 1958, saw the crowds emerge on Abington Avenue, in droves. The police had insisted the match was all ticket, as they patrolled the ground inside and out, keeping in contact with Walkie Talkies. The civil defence provided a Land Rover to be used as the radio H.Q. Meanwhile 'Crowd Marshalls' using megaphones tried to make more room for the supporters still entering the ground thick and fast.

Ex-England cricketer and footballer, Dennis Compton, took his place in the press box, his first time in such a capacity at the County ground, also his first since becoming a C.B.E. Cliff Michelmore was also at the ground, as commentator for BBC television. It was the first time their cameras had recorded a football match at the County Ground.

Regretfully in those days once a reel of film was shown it was used again. No one had the foresight to keep it for future use and the game was lost forever to those who were unlucky enough not to have seen it.

The Cobblers side that day comprised of goalkeeper Reg Elvy, he had replaced Peter Pickering who had emigrated to South Africa. Reg had seen it all before having played in the first division with Blackburn. Ben Collins was at right back, having replaced the amateur player Terry Robinson, Ben's full back partner was club captain, Ron Patterson. The giant Welsh centre half Colin Gale had been restored to his rightful position, after his early season run at centre forward, he was flanked by Scotsman Ray Yeoman and the 'play anywhere', Roly Mills. Jack English had been in and out of the side, at outside right but had retained his place for his important match. His experience would be a great assistance to Bobby Tebbutt who was playing inside him.

The Irchester lad was playing only his ninth game in the Northampton first team. Barry Hawkings, had played at outside right, inside right this season, but was now wearing the number Nine shirt, Ken Leek, the Welshman who had worked his way through the ranks was at inside left, with Tommy taking up the left flank.

As the players changed, the crowd outside were getting noisier. The banter between the rival fans was friendly, no segregation in those days. An Arsenal supporter ran on the pitch, swinging a rattle and kicking a small Red and White ball, this brought a great cheer from their supporters in the crowd, as he ran towards the goal. An even bigger cheer went up as a Cobblers supporter ran on and 'robbed' him, with a clean crisp tackle. A large shield could be spotted in the crowd with the logo 'We the Arsenal supporters say, may the best team win', as it was proudly waved in the air, both sets of supporters gave out a loud cheer. Curious interest was shown at a horse box that drew up on the cricket side of the ground, this turned to amusement as a group of fans climbed out of the box and onto the roof, for their own 'grandstand view'.

In the 'Gunners' side there were changes, Wills was playing at right back, in place of the injured Stan Charlton, while Danny Clapton was preferred at outside right, over the South African Le Roux. The London side also announced that Dave Bowen would be the Club's permanent captain from now on, a baptism he would never forget.

Arsenal took the field in Gold shirts, their supporters giving them a hearty welcome. It was equalled by the Cobblers' supporters when their side emerged from the tunnel in blue. Mr. Cooper the referee followed carrying a brilliant white ball, it stood out well on a grey, misty, foggy day. Dave Bowen won the toss for his side, and elected to defend the hotel end, leaving the Cobblers to kick off.

Their first attack saw a long ball by Mills collected by the Arsenal keeper, Jack Kelsey. Then it was the turn of Ken Leek, he moved out to the left, but his shot was intercepted by Wills. Evans fouled Hawkings, but the free kick by Yeoman was far too powerful and sailed out of play. Tommy came into the game when he laid the ball at Hawkings feet but his centre was cleared, only for Ron Patterson to lob it back, aiming for English, but the Arsenal keeper cut it out. The Cobblers were having all of the play at this early stage, Arsenal's first attack came to nothing when Groves was caught offside, from the free kick. Tebbutt brought a gasp from the crowd, when he headed just wide from a Leek cross.

Cliff Holton was to score many goals for Northampton when he was to join them three years later, but the first one he made for them, was as an Arsenal player. He brought down Leek, and was spoken to by the referee, Yeoman took the free kick, it sailed deep into the Arsenal penalty area, and Tebbutt headed home. Dave Bowen made a desperate attempt to stop the ball entering the net, but all to no avail, the Northampton supporters showed their appreciation, and Bobby Tebbutt was mobbed by his team mates. This stung Arsenal into action, Bloomfield shot wide, and then Groves had a long range shot. Cobblers keeper, Reg Elvy was kept busy. The game was flowing backwards and forwards, Kelsey bravely dived at the feet of two onrushing forwards, then was in action again, saving a low cross from Tommy. David Herd had a stinging shot go wide of the Cobblers post, then Kelsey pushed a Leek cross over the bar, for the Cobblers first corner, which came to nothing.

It was after 25 minutes of the game that Arsenal secured their first corner. Elvy and Bloomfield collided as they both went for it, but it was cleared to Tommy who laid the ball in Tebbutt's path, Kelsey ran out to clear. Five minutes later, the game was all square, Elvy saved a shot from Groves, but could not hold on to it, Clapton followed up and scored. Seconds later the Gunners almost took the lead, Herd broke free, but Elvy ran out of his goal to smother the ball, before the big forward could reach it.

Yeoman sent over another free kick, from almost the identical place the first goal came from but Kelsey was wise to it this time. Both sides had the chance of taking the lead, first Clapton found himself on his own in the Cobblers penalty area, but hurried his shot, while at the other end Tommy again fed Tebbutt, but the Keeper was alert to the pass, and cut it out. Both sets of players were cheered off the field as they ran into the dressing rooms at half time, There was so much excitement few people noticed the fog was getting thicker as the day got darker and duller. 'We never got any pre-match instructions and the only thing I can remember was Dave Smith saying , "Watch their keeper on crosses, he's suspect".

When we got back into the dressing room, I turned to Dave and told him he was right about the keeper, Dave put a finger to his lips and pointed towards the opponents dressing room', Tommy reminisced, about the game that Cold January day.

A gasp was followed by a groan, at the start of the second half, Yeoman fed Hawkings, and the centre forward, stepped clear of the Arsenal defence, beat Kelsey, but agonisingly watched his shot narrowly miss the post. The Arsenal defence was now beginning to dominate, both Holton and Dodgin conceded corners, then Gale conceded one at the other end. Groves and Bloomfield both saw chances go wide, and English's shot was cleared by Wills.

Visibility was getting poorer, the darkness and mist were drawing in. Elvy was applauded as he dived at the feet of Groves, when he broke clear, followed by gasps when a shot from Herd cannoned off the post, it was sent back by Groves, but this time Elvy saved. On the hour, Northampton Town took the lead! English passed to Hawkings, who had his back to goal, he flicked the ball over his shoulder completely fooling Kelsey, and the rest of the Arsenal defence. That was how the papers reported it, but in fact the scorer tells a different story.

'Jack passed the ball to me at about 100 miles an hour. It was also heading for my nether regions, it was instinctive to lift my foot, to protect myself. It just fell into place, I deflected it, more in luck than judgement, over my shoulder and it took everyone by surprise, most of all me!'

This brought a tremendous outburst from the Cobblers supporters. Tommy recalled, 'From that moment on, I never felt that we would lose'. Arsenal renewed their efforts, Elvy was brought to his knees saving from Groves, then he collected a ball off of Herd's head and thankfully a thunderbolt shot from Holton was well wide of the mark. Northampton went back on the attack again, Tebbutt had the crowd cheering as he ran half the length of the field, but as he was about to shoot, the leg of an Arsenal player snaked out and put the ball in to touch, for a corner. Tommy sent the corner kick onto the head of Ken Leek, who's delicate flick beat Jack Kelsey, but Wills popped up on the line to head it away, bringing groans of disappointment from the Cobblers supporters in the crowd. Tommy was combining well with Bobby Tebbutt and between them they were leading some spirited attacks.

In one such attack they put Barry Hawkings away, but he was unfairly stopped by Bill Dodgin, who incurred a lecture from the referee for his troubles. Time was ticking by. Arsenal began to put on more and more pressure, at one stage Elvy bravely dived at the feet of two gold-shirted players, his clear-ance found Hawkings, who in turn found Leek. The Welshman sent a shot into the crowded penalty area, somehow the ball eluded everyone, and ended up in the Arsenal net. **NORTHAMPTON TOWN 3, ARSENAL 1.**

Now the London side really had their tails up, they mounted attack after attack on the Cobblers goal, willed on by their supporters. Bloomfield thought he had pulled one back as he sent his shot goalwards, only to see Yeoman appear from nowhere and hook the ball off the line. The Northampton players were getting tired, their fans realised this and got behind them even more, the County Ground was heaving, almost everyone of the 21,000 plus, were shouting at the top of their voices. Ben Collins made two excellent clearances, first he put the ball out for a corner, then from the resulting kick, he made a clearance that almost took a cameraman's head off ! Wills sent a free kick goalwards, Elvy punched clear, Herd sent it back, but it had no direction, the minutes were ticking away.

Supporters were asking each other 'how much longer?' They were looking at the referee, Mr. Cooper, waiting for him to put the whistle to his lips. One of the Arsenal players turned to the bench, pointing at his wrist, obviously asking the same question, his reply was a shrug of the shoulders. Barry Hawkings broke clear, but shot wide, it was to be the last move of the game, the final whistle followed, and this heralded a crescendo of cheering, clapping and shouts of 'Well done Cobblers'. 'We dragged ourselves back to the dressing room, tired but oh so happy', Tommy recalled.

The Arsenal players came off the pitch knowing they had been beaten by a better team on the day.

However, no one could realise that the half back line of Dave Bowen, Bill Dodgin and Cliff Holton, would all return to the County Ground, and become heros in the eyes of the Northampton public. The Northampton Town chairman, Phil Hutton, broadcast to the hospital networks, relaying the major points of the game. Skipper Ron Patterson was dragged from the dressing room, before he had the chance to shower, for an interview with the BBC television. He grabbed a spare keeper's shirt and a pair of track suit bottoms. In his short T.V. 'career' he paid tribute to the team, and to the supporters, 'They were worth a goal start', he quoted. The *green 'un*, the local sports paper, carried a match report that evening. In it 'Flagkick' wrote how the team played so well together, and for each other. The national papers gave more space to the Cobblers than they had all season, One even gave its whole back page to the match.

There was more than a tinge of excited anticipation at the training session, the following Monday. The players quickly showered and changed, after their stint, and collected in the club offices in Abington Avenue.

There, they sat around the radio, awaiting the fourth round draw of the F.A. Cup . . . 'Everton will play . . .', could it be a return to Goodison Park for Tommy. He must have wondered as he heard the name of his old club come out of the hat first. '. . . Blackburn Rovers!' 'Cardiff City will play . . .', this time it was centre half Colin Gale who began to show the most interest, would he be returning to play against his old club, now struggling at the foot of the First Division' '. . . Leyton Orient'. Northampton were the only Third Division South side left in the competition. Although Scunthorpe United and Darlington from the Division Three North were also still competing. The players knew there was a more than even chance that they would draw opposition from a higher sphere. 'Liverpool will play Northampton Town'.

The third tie out of the hat brought mixed reactions from the crowd of Cobblers players listening to the draw. Liverpool were in the Second division, but were challenging for promotion. They boasted such players as Jimmy Melia, Ronnie Moran, and the famous Billy Liddell, added to this Anfield was a stadium most players always wanted to play at. Tommy was overjoyed. He was born just Eight miles from the ground that he used to go to as a lad and watch his heros. Now after twenty odd years he would get the chance to play there in an F.A. Cup match.

The following week was hectic, the players were presented with footwear from different local factories, Tommy secured a pair of Boots from Manfield, that he never ever wore. Bobby Tebbutt was measured up for his suit, promised by a Wellingborough tailor if his side beat the Arsenal, while the National sporting press discovered there was a place called Northampton!

Tommy was busy trying to snap up as many spare tickets off of his team mates as possible. Nearly all of his family in Prescot wanted to come along to the match and watch him play, for some, it would be the first time since he became a Cobbler.

Four days before the game, the team were taken off to Southport, where they would train. It also kept them away from the blaze of publicity that came with a tie like this one. The weather was at it worse, deep snow surrounded their quarters, forcing a lot of training inside, although they did train outside as much as possible.

'It was cold, but bracing, all the players got on well together, and most training sessions ended with a snowball fight', recalled Tommy. On the big day, Northampton's Castle Station was heaving with Cobblers supporters. A train had been decked out in Claret and White for the occasion and the fans stood alongside it as Photographers ran up and down the platform taking snaps from different angles.

Meanwhile journalists were winkling out stories for their papers. Like the one where a husband and wife were going to Anfield, she was a Liverpool fan, he a Cobbler. Another woman was grateful to the Cobblers, she had wanted to visit her family in Liverpool for ages, but her husband always found an excuse, now he could not get there quick enough!

The Northampton team to meet the Reds was to be the same that beat the Arsenal three weeks earlier. Although Alan Woan was fit, he could not win back his place, which was disappointing for him as he too came from the Liverpool area and also had family there.

It was amazing that only six players, who played in that first round game against Newport County, were playing in the fourth round, just three months later. At one stage it was thought that the game would not take place, the snow had been cleared from the lines at Anfield but the pitch was cutting up badly and it was expected to become a quagmire. Over the other side of the City, the Everton

Jack Jennings (far left) watches Jack English, Alan Woan, Ken Leek, Tommy Fowler, Bobby Tebbutt and Barry Hawkings, training at Southport.

Woan, Tebbutt and English, about to 'Ambush' Hawkings, Fowler and Leek.

v Blackburn game was off, however the match referee at Anfield, Mr. Tirebuck deemed the match could be played, so it was.

The Scottish International, Billy Liddell, was the first to get the 57,000 fans cheering when he put the 'Reds' into the lead, just before the half hour. Liddell had been on Liverpool's books when Tommy was at Everton in 1942 but this was the first time they had played against each other. It was Tommy who got the Liverpool section of the 'Fowler' clan cheering when he ran down the left wing, as he had done so many times, and laid the ball off for Barry Hawkings to hammer home the equaliser. LIVERPOOL 1 NORTHAMPTON TOWN 1.

The pitch was cutting up badly, as expected, the snow had turned to slush, making parts of the pitch almost unplayable. The Cobblers stuck to their task, matching the mighty Liverpool side, just as they did against Arsenal. Several times they almost gave them a scare, but the Northampton defence was also kept busy.

With just eleven minutes to go, fate wielded it's heavy hand. Ben Collins went to clear an innocuous looking shot at goal when he slipped, the ball hit his head, and deflected past a startled Reg Elvy in the Cobblers goal. Barry Hawkings was back helping the defence in that game and he recalled: 'I saw Reg Elvy's face as the ball deflected over him, it was one of disbelief. Ben seemed to have it covered, the next thing we knew he was sprawled on the floor and poor Reg was helpless, he could do nothing as the ball sailed over him. 'The state of the pitch was to blame for the slip by Ben, but being the gentleman that he is he never looked for an excuse, and accepted full responsibility for the own goal. Louis Bimpson, virtually a reserve at Liverpool broke away and scored the third goal for his club, as the Cobblers strove hard for the leveller, in the 82nd minute. That in effect made the game safe for Liverpool.

Tribute to the Cobblers performance came at the end of the game, when the Liverpool fans applauded their opponents off the field, they were beaten, but by no way disgraced. Further evidence of this came from ex-England International goalkeeper Frank Swift, now a journalist. He covered the game and gave a glowing report of the Cobblers play, stating that had it been a better playing surface, he would not have been surprised if the result would have been different.

Sadly it was to be one of the last match reports the great player would ever write, as a few days later he perished in the Munich air disaster, while covering Manchester United's game in Belgrade. The cup run gave the poor league season some meaning, as well as making the season profitable for the club, but division four loomed, and Northampton Town needed to get out of this division, as quickly as possible.

Manager Dave Smith instructs the players. Standing; Left to Right; English, Tebbutt, Leek, Fowler Kneeling; Left to Right; Hawkings, Woan.

Tommy sets Barry Hawkings up for the Cobblers' goal at Anfield.

The opening of the Tommy "Flash" Fowler lounge at the White Hart Social Club.

YOU HAVE TO GO WHERE THE WORK IS

The tour never came off.

Tommy could not remember the reason why but talk of it died down and it was never mentioned again. It was not the first time this had happened, when Herbert Chapman's team won the Southern League in 1909, they were promised a tour of Bavaria, that too failed to materialise.

'I never did get the chance to go on a tour', Tommy remarked. 'I think all the lads would have enjoyed it'.

Northampton Town were among the favourites to win promotion out of the Fourth Division. For the first time in league history, four teams would be promoted and Alan Woan went into the record books, by scoring the first ever goal in Division Four, he netted against Port Vale, after two minutes, in the Cobblers 4-1 win. In fact the Club made a great start to the campaign by winning six of the first seven games, but things turned sour in mid-season and other teams started to catch up with them. December especially, was remembered by Tommy as a 'bitter-sweet' month. After putting Wycombe Wanderers out of the F.A. Cup on a foggy Saturday in November, (what was it about foggy F.A. Cup matches at the County Ground?), Northampton were drawn against amateur side, Tooting & Mitcham.

They had put Bournemouth out of the competition in the first round, but Dave Smith did not seem unduly concerned. Not even when centre half Colin Gale went down with chicken pox. However he did not realise what was to happen! During the game full back Jim Bannister was injured, he was taken off, Roly Mills dropped back from wing half to full back, and Kevin Baron vacated his place in the forward line to cover Roly's position. It completely threw the forward line and Tooting won 2-1. After beating the Arsenal less than twelve months previously, the team now had the shoe on the other foot.

Eleven days after his 34th birthday, Tommy scored the second hat-trick of his league career. It was against Gillingham and the Kent side had taken the lead until 'Flash' took control. Little did he realise that he had set yet another record, his previous hat-trick had been nine years and ten months previous.

Roly Mills was an all action utility player, the terrier type of 90 minute player the Cobblers supporters loved. He had appeared in almost every outfield position and had been selected at outside right for the Division Three South against the Division Three North, some years earlier. He was also Tommy's room mate when the team had 'stop overs'. 'Never a dull moment', mused Roly, recalling those early days. 'I was woken up one night to find my bedclothes being pulled off of me by Tommy. Thinking I had overslept I jumped out of bed, only to find it was still dark outside. Then I realised – Tommy was sleep walking.'

The Daventry-born Roly, who was to spend over 30 years with Northampton as player, assistant-trainer, youth-team coach and Promotions Manager, recalled another incident regarding his room mate.

'Not only did he sleep walk, but he also talked in his sleep. I was woken one night with his unintelligible ramblings. Suddenly, he shot up in bed and shouted; "for Christ sake Joyce, fetch the bloody coal in!". I never did ask what he was dreaming about.'

It was not just Tommy's nocturnal habits that stuck in Roly's memory. 'I was having a shave with an electric razor when Tommy asked if he could borrow it. I cleaned it out and handed it to him as I went off to do something else. When I returned the razor lay on my bed. "That's useless", Tommy complained, "It doesn't take anything off". I examined the rejected shaver and pointed out to Tommy, that to get a decent shave, you have to take the guard off!'. The two players were the best of friends, and had a mutual respect for each other.

'If Tommy had my right leg, or I had his left, we would have played for England,' Roly stated. 'He could do anything with his left foot, tie knots with it if he had to, together with his pace no one could live with him.

Northampton Town finished in a disappointing eighth place, seven points off promotion, twenty four players were used and the highlight of the season was Alan Woan's goals. He finished the season on 32 league goals, just two off the club record, held by Ted Bowen.

Dave Bowen returned to the club as player-manager, for the start of the 1959/1960 season. Dave Smith had wanted him to return as player coach but the directors had other ideas.

The ex Welsh International was given a free hand and he made it clear he wanted to bring his own men in, so slowly he replaced the team that a few years earlier had put the side he had given such good service to, out of the F.A. Cup. Goalkeeper Reg Elvy, full back Ron Patterson and centre half Ben Collins all retired. Ray Yeoman joined his old manager Bob Dennison at Middlesbrough, while Jack English decided to finish his days in non-league football with Rugby Town. Ken Leek had joined Leicester City some time previously and by now had some Welsh caps to his name, but Bobby Tebbutt suffered a broken leg and never recaptured his league form, but still gave sterling service to Kettering and Bedford Town. Barry Hawkings moved into non-league football with Gravesend while Alan Woan was sold on to Crystal Palace in exchange for Mike Deakin and a cash adjustment, leaving only Tommy and Roly of the originals.

In fairness, the new manager seemed to build the team around them, and the two players who could play in Tommy's place, Ken Tucker and Bela Olah, hardly got a look in.

Bela, who was a Hungarian, signed for the Cobblers as an amateur coming from Bedford town with his friend and colleague Zag Balough.

'At the time I joined Northampton, they were a noisy, boastful lot', Bela recalled. 'They would boast about anything, from how much they drank the night before or how active their love lives were, but not Tommy. He was always quiet, polite, but quiet. He kept himself to himself, and only spoke when asked.'

Bela went on to recall Tommy's skill. 'What a player, what a left leg', he recalled. 'He could do anything with it. I'm sure his right leg was just for standing on, so he did not fall over when he kicked the ball!' As more and more players were brought in by the new manager, so players like Tommy became the Senior professionals, yet all of the 'new boys' had nothing but respect for him, and so did the management.

Alf Wood was assistant trainer at Coventry, when their left winger was injured they decided to go into the transfer market. 'Get Fowler, from Northampton', The Cobbler's ex-keeper advised. The Midlands side made an approach but were told by Dave Bowen, 'Nothing doing'.

Frank Griffin was Dave Bowen's first signing when he took over as boss. He was an outside right from Shrewsbury Town, who scored the winning goal for West Bromwich Albion in the 1953 F.A. Cup Final. 'We lived next door to the Fowler's, our daughter and their son were the same age and used to play together. What I remember most was Tom's ability to cross a ball on the run, few players could do it, but he could; he had a terrific left foot. I only had a season at Northampton, but that stands out in my mind', said Frank.

Goalkeeper Norman Coe, recalled Tommy's attitude. 'He's a lovely fellow, a real gentleman. He was also a very good player, and very professional, always quiet and reserved. Some of the new manager's signings were extroverts, but Tommy always remained the same, a model professional and he won a lot of respect because of it.'

'He was a gentleman on and off the field', echoed Tony Claypole. 'I called him "Shuffler". He was always available if you were under pressure. He would appear from nowhere and take the ball. Tommy never got the credit he deserved, his "off the ball" running was excellent. He never had a go at players if they did anything wrong, not when they were playing football, but if you were his partner at cards and you let him down, he would let you know, he took his card games very seriously'. Tony was an ex County youth team player, he gave the Cobblers eight seasons until a broken leg ended his league career.

He spent almost as long in non-league football, playing for Cheltenham, Bedford, Kettering, Corby and Wellingborough at either right or left back.

On the 24th of September 1960, Tommy made his 500th appearance for .Northampton Town. It was at Holker Street, Barrow. Sadly the match ended 1-0 in favour of Barrow. Back in Northampton, outside left Barry Lines was putting pen to paper, the youngster from Bletchley was the man earmarked to take over the mantle held by Tommy for so many years.

Prior to the F.A. Cup match v Hastings, Frank Jenner, the secretary presented Tommy with a wrist watch to commemorate his feat, something he still wears today. Tommy's Cobblers career virtually came to an end at London Road, home of the new league members, and the club's nearest rivals, Peterborough United!

Derek Leck put the Cobblers one up in the first minute, in this first league encounter between the two sides, then both Mike Deakin and Tommy himself added further goals. It was to be the last goal Tommy ever scored for the club.

'I turned too quickly', said Tommy. 'It was the ligament in my leg, it forced my knee to lock up. At first Jack Jennings diagnosed a cartilage, but after closer examination the fault was discovered. I used to go to the hospital for radiotherapy, then the nurse would free the knee by forcing it back down into place. I remember being out for some time. Almost adding insult to injury, Peterborough pulled three goals back to make the game 3-3. One player making his debut in that game was Terry Branston, a wing half converted to centre half, who was part of Northampton's climb from the fourth to the first division . He too remembered his time playing alongside Tommy, with some affection.

'I had signed for the club on amateur terms, and was working for a firm in Rugby. The Cobblers had a full scale practise game every Thursday afternoon. I told my company I had an on going appointment at the Northampton General hospital, so I could play in the game. I would mark Tom, and as he came towards me with the ball I would decide he was going to try and pass me on the outside, so I would step out, only for him to move inside. Another time he would pass the ball just before I committed myself then fly past me to take the return, leaving me for dead. He was never big headed or boastful, and certainly never taunted anyone because he could beat them. I played for ten seasons at the County ground, and I rated Tommy as one of the best I ever played with, along with John Reid who I called the "Rolls Royce", Theo Foley, Joe Kiernan, Barry Lines, Roly Mills and Cliff Holton'.

Another player to express a similar sentiment was Alex Carson. Alex was playing for the Corby and Kettering schoolboys when Ron Patterson suggested he had a trial with the Cobblers. 'I was playing left half, Ron Patterson played behind me, threatening me with 'death' if I lost the ball. Everyone from Jack Jennings to the ball boys would be shouting at me screaming advice, I never knew fear like it. My mind was doing somersaults. It seemed everyone was telling me what to do, as the opponents were bearing down on me. My inexperienced brain was looking for help. It came in the shape of an older man, hunch backed and bow legged.

"Alex here", he said "give it to me". Tommy would be there, appearing from nowhere. He would take the ball and the game would change from defending to attacking, I would breathe a sigh of relief. He was a wing back 40 years before such an animal was created, his pace was electric, but mentally he was quite the opposite, calm and quiet.'

It was three months on the sidelines for the Cobblers player with the most appearances, as he tried to return to full fitness. While he was out he was asked to meet a young player off the train at Castle station. His name was Tommy Robson, and he was also an outside left and would spend five years at the County Ground before joining Chelsea. He later returned to his home in Newcastle before signing for Peterborough, where he emulated Tommy's record at Northampton, he made the most appearances for the Posh.

'He met me off the train', recalled Tommy. 'He then took me to his home and we had something to eat and drink, before we went to the County Ground'. This was the man I had been signed to replace, yet he could not be more helpful. 'Things were so different then, an apprentice could not enter the first team dressing room unless he knocked first. If a first team player thought his boots were not clean enough then they were thrown back at the apprentice. Respect was the name of the game then'.

Northampton Town won promotion for the first time in their history, finishing third in the division, behind Peterborough and Crystal Palace, Bradford Park Avenue clinching the other promotion place. In fairness the four teams were there or thereabouts for most of the season, It was just a case of which order they would finish in after Peterborough, who ran away with the championship.

Tommy was retained for the 1961/1962 season, although he was now one of three outside lefts on the books.

Barry Lines started off in the number 11 shirt but after two games Tommy was recalled. Things were not going well, After five games the club had scored just one goal and picked up just two points, then fortunes changed. When the team coach was travelling down towards Crystal Palace, Dave Bowen told the players they were stopping off at Watford, to pick up a player they had just signed. It was Cliff Holton, and he marked his debut with a hat trick as the club notched their first win of the season. Tommy also played in the 2-2 draw at home to Lincoln City, the following Saturday, little realising it was to be the last first team game he would ever play in for Northampton Town. Barry Lines returned and Tommy found himself in the stiffs, but he still gave his all. Garry Knibb, a goalkeeper, spent over 10 years as youth, 'A' team and reserve team goalkeeper at Northampton, he remembered one particular reserve game, and Tommy in particular.

'It was against Crystal Palace Reserves, we won 2-1, but I gave them their goal. I threw the ball at the feet of their forward, who scored. Centre half Jim Fotheringham went mad at me, shouting and screaming, at my mistake, but Tommy just walked past me saying, "forget it, you are doing all right just play your natural game". He was always a gent, never had a go at anyone, never complained never moaned, a true professional'. By the end of 1961 Tommy had lost his place in both the first and reserve sides, Barry Lines and Tommy Robson taking up the positions as numbers one and two.

Dave Bowen told Tommy that Kings Lynn, then a Southern league side were interested in signing him, so he took a trip with Joyce to the Norfolk Town, but they decided it was not for them, and the money was not up to much. It was to be a well trodden path from Northampton to Kings Lynn over the years, Tony Haskins, Tom Flynn, Colin Sharpe, Mickey Wright and Norman Coe all found their way there but Tommy was the one that got away.

Tommy's career change came on a day he was laying in bed, suffering from tonsillitis. A knock came on the door and Dave Smith, the ex-Northampton manager, then at Aldershot, stood on the door step.

'I want you to come and join us', he told Tommy, then related the terms. Tommy had just become interested in the bookmaking business, and was learning the trade. He did not want to give this up so the agreement was that he would still train at Northampton, and travel to London on a Saturday morning, where he would meet the rest of the team if they were playing away.

If it was a home match, he would catch another train to Aldershot. Everything hinged on the Cobblers allowing him to stay in the club house as housing in Aldershot was at a premium.

Northampton Town agreed, so on the 21st of December 1961, five days after Tommy's 37th birthday, he signed for Aldershot. 'I don't want to go', Tommy told the press. 'But it's like everything else, you have to go where the work is.

Aldershot have made an attractive offer to me. I've enjoyed my stay here, and I like Northampton, but I realise I am getting towards the end now, and the Cobblers had to find someone to replace me. Barry Lines and Tommy Robson, both have a lot to learn, but I reckon both will make good players' Chairman at the time, Wally Penn, summed it up, 'I do not know of a better servant to the club, than Tommy Fowler'.

At Aldershot, as well as teaming up again with Dave Smith, there was Alan Woan, Brian Kirkup and Mike Deakin. He would also team up with Bill Shipwright who was captain of the R.A.F. side while serving in Egypt and Bobby Howfield who had two spells with Aldershot and two with Watford. In between he became a grid iron player for the New Yorkers.

Howfield was playing on the left wing and manager Dave Smith wanted him back inside where he would have a better chance of scoring which was the reasoning behind signing Tommy.

It all started well, the first four games were won, but all the good work was undone when the next five were lost, along with it went the club's chance of promotion, they finished seventh, three points off a promotion place.

While training at the County Ground, Tommy was approached by the administration staff and told he would have to vacate his house, despite the promise that he could remain in it after his transfer. The club followed the threat up with a solicitor's letter. When he informed Aldershot of the Cobbler's action Tommy was told to ignore it, but by the time a second solicitor's letter arrived, he and Joyce decided to do something about it. They bought the cosy little terraced house that was to become their home for over 40 years.

Tommy played his last game of league football at Edgley Park, where the Shots went down 0-3 to Stockport County. This took place just eight days prior to Tommy's 38th birthday and he decided that it was time to take a job outside the game. 'I did not want to stay as a coach or trainer, it was too precarious, when a manager was sacked, the new manager often brought in his own staff, I had 16 years of living on a yearly contract. I wanted something more stable'.

He took to the bookmaking trade and after a period with McGleish learning the ropes he took over as manager of their Overstone road branch. There was a job offer from Tiffield reformatory, as a sports master. He would have to have taken an exam and it would mean living in. Joyce would have been responsible for cooking 16 breakfasts every morning. They thought long and hard about it, but having just purchased their own house and with Tommy junior settled at school, they decided against it.

Joyce had always gone along to the County Ground to watch her husband play, she had acquired an interest in the game from those early days when they used to travel from Ross on Wye to Northampton. She could always be seen sitting in 'D' stand regardless of the weather or conditions; now Tommy Junior started to get involved.

When England won the World Cup in 1966, the Fowlers were on holiday in France. Once the news reached them of England's victory over the Germans, Tommy Junior hung up his team photograph of the England squad in the back window of the car. A brave move since France were one of the teams England eliminated on the way. Tommy was a left winger, in more ways than one! He never forgot his roots and because of it he was a strong socialist so much so that come election times he could be seen canvassing for Reggie Paget, the Labour M.P. for South Northants.

Paget was a Queen's Counsellor and was a strong advocate of the anti-hanging campaign. One amusing incident during Tommy's days with the local labour party happened at the retirement party of George Attwell, member for South Northants in March 1970. 'How are you getting on since leaving football ?'

the retiring labour member asked. 'Fine', replied Tommy, 'Except, young boys used to run after me for my autograph, but now, ten years on, they do not recognise me'.to which Attwell replied, 'You're lucky, no one ever asks me for my autograph !' On one of Tommy and Joyce's visit to France, to visit the graves of his fallen comrades, Tommy signed the visitors book as normal, not realising what lay ahead. Some time later he received a letter from a French schoolteacher who had taken Tommy's details from the the visitors book. He was writing a book about the Normandy invasion, and asked the ex-Staffs regiment man for his story. On their next visit, the Fowlers visited the ex-Schoolteacher, an Albert Grandais, and not only related his war time recollections but also had his photograph taken with 'that' famous helmet!

It was almost 10 years later when a copy of the book turned up in the post, with Tommy's photograph, wearing the helmet. proudly among the prints. Of course being written in French someone kindly took the pages relating to Tommy and translated them into English! By this time he had left the bookies and joined British Timken, working with many people who had watched him play. As the Cobblers rose to the first division and fell back to the fourth, Tommy also kept an eye on results and events, but distanced himself from any involvement with the game except for the odd piece in the local sports paper, should they wish to do a 'nostalgic' article on Northampton Town.

However in the late 1990s, several events brought Tommy's name back into the limelight. A reunion of ex-players on the evening of 22nd May 1997, saw Tommy and over 60 ex-players turn up to celebrate Northampton Town's centenary. Here he met up with Bill Barron, Barry Lines, Tommy Robson, Freddie Ramscar and Barry Hawkings, someone he had not seen for nearly thirty years. Northampton suffered some severe flooding some months later, one of the places to suffer was the 'Old White Hart Social club' a favourite drinking hole of Tommy's.

When the floods subsided and the place was being rebuilt, the committee decided to turn a store room/office into the 'Tommy "Flash" Fowler Lounge'. The walls were adorned with photographs and memorabilia relating to Tommy's career, and a special opening ceremony took place involving several of the ex winger's playing colleagues. A fitting tribute, and record of his achievements. In 1998, the local newspaper the *Chronicle and Echo* asked supporters to vote for their 'Cobblers legend'.

It took nearly a month to collate the figures but the winner, and by a large margin was Tommy! He also found himself in the 'Cobblers team of the Century' again voted for by the supporters of Northampton Town. Eleven players and five substitutes, in all. Of the sixteen players, nine came to the ceremony at Sixfields, plus the family of the late Jack English to receive their awards. In over 700 games in the league, F.A. Cup, friendlies, and reserve games, Tommy only had his name taken once!

'It was in a Maunsell Cup match', recalled Tommy. 'I can not remember the opponents that day, but I remember the referee, it was Norman Hillier!'

'To make matters worse, it was not him at fault, it was Archie Garrett', Joyce remarked. Norman Hillier, later to become secretary of the Northamptonshire F.A. was a known stickler for discipline, there was no grey areas it was black or white. When the linesman called him over and pointed out he was being verbally

Tommy and Joyce at the opening of the 'Flash' Fowler Lounge at the White Hart Social club

abused he pointed the finger at Tommy, instead of the real culprit. One can only assume that the linesman went about his business, blissfully unaware that every time he ran past the 'D' stand, his life was in mortal danger!

Tommy reflected on all the players he played with at Northampton, and when asked to name the best ten team mates to make a 'dream team' he had to think long and hard. 'We had some good goalkeepers. it would be hard to choose. Jack Jones was small, but totally committed, Alf Wood was good reliable and solid, and of course Peter Pickering was very strong, another safe, solid and reliable player.

Maurice Marston would be my choice at right back, a good tackler and good in the air. For his partner I would select Ron Patterson, he could easily have played in a higher division, if he was half a yard faster, his distribution was first class. Bill Coley and Maurice Candlin would be my choices at half back. Bill had class, but he played hard. Maurice was another full blooded player, he never stopped until the final whistle. At centre half I would play Ben Collins he was always 100% reliable and there could be no other contender than Jack English for the number seven shirt, his finishing was out of this world, and he was so cool.

For his partner I would choose Maurice Edelston, he was a great ball player, despite the fact he was in the twilight of his career when he came to Northampton. We have had many great centre forwards at Northampton, Jack Cross, Willie O'Donnell, Adam McCulloch, Cliff Holton and many more. However , I have to say that the greatest centre forward I ever played with, was not a Cobblers player, but Tommy Lawton, when we were together at Everton. I felt very proud to have played in the same team as him. For my inside forward partner I would select Freddie Ramscar, skillful, clever and with an eye for goals. There can be no more fitting tribute to a man than those that come from his ex-team mates, these are just some of the comments they made.

'What a lucky man I was to have shared such times as I did with the never to be forgotten, Tom Fowler' – (Ben Collins); 'I had the greatest respect for Tommy, he was a thorough professional and a very good footballer' – (Derek Leck); 'They say that when he dipped his shoulder, half the Hotel end crowd, ended up in Abington Avenue' – (Jim Hall); 'Anyone who spends sixteen years at any club, deserves a medal' – (Larry Canning); 'He had a droll sense of humour and wit, and in my mind will always be remembered as the man who never whinged, on or off the field' – (Ron Spelman); 'Like most legends, Tommy had a natural sense of goodness' – (Alex Carson); 'On the park he was a more than useful player, who created a number of chances above and beyond those that were converted into goals. Off the park he was a gentleman, I can never remember him losing his temper' – (Arthur Dixon); 'regarding Tommy, words that come to mind are "quiet, unassuming, introvert and unobtrusive", but above all "dependable" – (Peter Pickering); 'A brilliant player with a wonderful left foot' – (Theo Foley); 'A gentleman on and off the field' – (Ron Patterson); 'One of the fastest, quickest players I have ever played with' – (Frank Upton); 'One of football's nice guys, could have played a lot higher than Division Three South' – (Don Hazeldine); 'Despite all his appearances and goals, his prize possession, was that "tin helmet" ' – (Alan Woan); 'One of the fastest players I had ever seen" – (Derek Danks); 'If I had his left leg, or he had my right, one of us would have played for England' – (Roly Mills); 'He was fast, pacey and quick' – (Ken Leek); 'If ever you were in trouble on the field, Tommy was always a "get out" ' – (Tony Claypole); 'A class footballer and a gentleman, what a combination' – (Barry Hawkings); 'His right foot was just for standing on, but what a left foot' – (Bela Olha); 'A great crosser of a ball, while on a run' – (Frank Griffin); 'Always a gentleman, one of the old school' – (Norman Coe); 'He often beat you in training sessions, but never mocked or gloated over it, a real gent' – (Terry Branston); 'I will always look up to Tommy, he made me feel at home' – (Tommy Robson); 'Never blamed anyone if they made a mistake, a true gentleman' – (Garry Knibb); 'If ever he scored a goal with his head, the County Ground erupted' – (supporter, R. L. Draper).

The cabinet may not be full of trophies, the wages were a pittance compared to today, but Tommy can lay claim to have something that thousands of others can not. He has a host of admirers. Those that watched him, those that played with him, and those that played against him. All have the greatest respect and admiration for him, for his ability and for his talent. No player deserves the mantle more than; ' Tommy Fowler, Cobblers legend'.

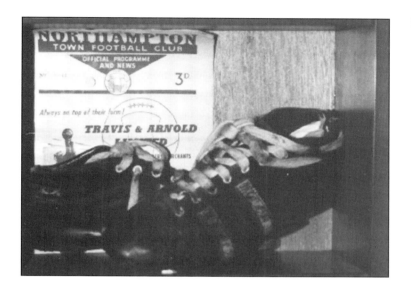

The boots presented to Tommy, by Manfield, in 1958, but never worn !

The trophy cabinet Boots and Trophy Cabinet

TOMMY FOWLER JUNIOR

At one stage it seemed that Tommy Junior would emulate his father.

In the late 1960s he was selected for both the Northampton Town and Northamptonshire County schoolboys.

'I remember lining up against 'knocker' Gregory in the County team', Tommy recalled. Gregory later starred for the Cobblers, Aston Villa, Brighton and Queens Park Rangers, before turning his hand to management, with Wycombe and Villa.

Tommy scored both goals when Northampton Schoolboys beat Peterborough schoolboys 2-1, from the position his father appeared in so many times, outside left. The match report headlines read 'Fowler outshines Hornsby'. This was a proud moment for Tommy as Brian Hornsby was being hailed as the new 'whizz kid' at Peterborough. He was quickly snapped up by Arsenal where he went on to make his name.

England trials followed at the same level, and the Far Cotton lad was selected for 'the South' to play against the North. Regretfully it all came to nothing at International level, he never received that England cap. If the International selection committee were not interested, then the league clubs most certainly were, but things were not always plain sailing.

'I was invited by Watford, to play in a trial match, unfortunately, it clashed with my club, Delapre Old Boys, playing in the final of the Grant Cup. I informed Watford that I would be playing in the final, hoping they would give me another date, but they did not, and never contacted me again.'

Peterborough United were another club to offer Tommy a trial, they suggested he came in the school holidays. Just before the break arrived they sacked their manager Jim Iley, and that too fell by the wayside.

Tommy recalled a lasting memory of those schoolboy days. 'I was playing for the Northampton schoolboys against the Isle of Ely, in an English schools shield match, at the old County Ground. It was a night match, played under floodlights, anyone who witnessed the game stated that it was one of the best games ever seen at the home of the Cobblers. It was end-to-end play, with everyone giving their all.

We won the game 6-5, and what was memorable for me was that I scored the winner in the dying seconds of the game'. While playing for Delapre youth, the Liverpool Scout Geoff Twentyman approached Tommy regarding a trial with the 'Reds'.

Twentyman was later responsible for the transfer of Phil Neal to Liverpool from Northampton for a then record fee.

'I was only there for a short while', Tommy recalled. 'It was an experience I would never forget. At most clubs the first team train separate from the reserves, who train separate from the youth team, at Liverpool we all trained together. I would be rubbing shoulders with Steve Heighway, and Ian St. John, training with them and playing with or against them in those famous Liverpool five a side practice games, even Bill Shankley took part'.

Coventry City accepted three Northampton lads for trials, Nicky Hudson, Glen Burdett and Tommy.

'Dad would drive me up there every week end, we were all on associate schoolboy forms, and this went on for almost a year, but when it came to the decision of taking us on as apprentices, only Glen Burdett was signed' Nicky Hudson was taken on by the Cobblers, and Tommy was also offered terms by them, but he declined them.

'Dad was not too keen on me signing for them, I don't think it was because of what happened to him regarding the house, I think it was more a fact that I would always be living in his shadow. He was a very hard act to follow'. Joyce would always go to watch her son whenever she could, just as she would never miss an opportunity of watching Tommy senior play.

'I think he was a better player than his father', she stated. 'He was as fast, and he had more skill, he would dribble around an opponent, where his father would tend to outpace them.'

Joyce felt there was something missing from his play, and he confirmed her suspicions when he announced, 'I only want to play football for pleasure'. No one was too upset that he did not want to become a professional footballer, for both Tommy senior and Joyce had spent sixteen years living on the precarious tight-rope that the professional footballer had to endure.

They knew only a few make it, Tommy had seen so many of his old team mates quit league football after a few years to take a job in industry, Tommy Junior played for Queen Eleanor in the Town League for many years, when his playing days were over, he turned to management and became a member of the management committee at the club. He was also a good cricketer and turned out for Delapre in the summer, following the tradition of the love of the summer game that his grandfather had.

It was back to Liverpool, but in a far different capacity to trialist. While cricket and football filled Tommy's leisure hours, his work time was spent at the Carlsberg brewery company, situated in the Southerly part of the Northampton Town centre. The Brewery company were also the sponsors of the 'Reds', and Tommy travelled to Liverpool for a League cup match v Fulham in October 1993, as a representative of the Sponsors.

'It was another highlight of my footballing life', Tommy related. 'I went to get Robbie Fowler's autograph for my son, as he was signing it someone pointed out we had the same surname, and a photographer seized the opportunity to capture the signing, with a 'Fowler meets Fowler' caption.' Tommy proudly has the photograph in his possession. 'It was a time I will always remember'. The same could also be said of Robbie, not so much because of the signing, but because Liverpool had beaten Fulham 5-0, and he had scored ALL five goals.

Tommy never had any regrets about not turning professional, he made a contribution to grass roots football, as both a player and a manager, ironically just as John English, son of Jack, also did. There is no doubt that Tommy is fiercely proud of his father's achievements at the County Ground, and even prouder to be his son, but whatever he would have achieved as a professional, he would always be; 'Tommy Fowler, son of Tommy Fowler'

Tommy Fowler Junior

Fowler Junior meets Robbie Fowler

Tommy and Tommy junior on holiday in France when England won the World Cup in '66

EVERTON
1942-1943

---

24. October. 1942   League North (first section)   Goodison Park   7,000

EVERTON 9   BURY 2

Everton: Burnett; Cook, Greenhaulgh;Bentham, Jones H, Watson; Dellow, Mutch, Curran, Stevenson, Fowler.   **Scorers:** Curran 3, Bentham 2, Dellow2, Fowler, Mutch.
Bury: Smith; Griffiths G, Gemmell; Griffiths W, Mathewson, Hart,: Potts, Davies G, Urmson,Burdett, Carver.   **Scorers:** Davies, Potts
Tommy opened his career with a goal. Smith the Bury keeper was taken off injured.

---

31. October 1942   League North (first section)   Gigg Lane   2,748

BURY 4   EVERTON 1

Bury: Whitehead, Hart, Gemmell;Griffiths W. Mathewson, Halton; Potts, Jones, Davies G, Dougal, Carter.   **Scorers:** Davies 2 (1 pen) Carter, Halton .
Everton: Burnett; Cook, Grenhaulgh; Bentham, McDonnell, Watson; Dellow, Mutch, Curran, Stevenson, Fowler.   **Scorer:** Fowler
Tommy scores his second goal, in as many games.

---

7. November 1942   League North (first section)   Prenton Park   5,994

TRANMERE ROVERS 1   EVERTON 3

Tranmere: line up not available.   **Scorer:** Bridges
Everton: Burnett; Cook, Greenhaulgh; Mercer, Jones, Watson; Bentham, Mutch, Curran, Stevenson, Fowler.   **Scorers:** Curran 2, Stevenson
Tranmere's best attendance since 1939.

---

14 November 1942   League North (first section)   Goodison Park   5,000

EVERTON 2   TRANMERE ROVERS 5

Everton: Burnett, Cook, Greenhaulgh; Bentham, Jones H. Watson; Boyes, Murch, Curran, Stevenson, Fowler.   **Scorers:** Curran 2, Fowler
Tranmere: line up not available.   **Scorers:** Saunders 2, Jackson, 2 Bell.
Tranmere's first win in seven games, Everton's first home defeat in six.

---

21 November 1942   League North (first section)   Goodison Park   5,000

EVERTON 4   CREWE ALEXANDRA 0

Everton: Burnett, Jackson, Greenhaulgh; Bentham, Jones T, Watson; Dellow, Mutch, Jones H, Stevenson, Fowler.   **Scorers:** Fowler, Jones H, Mutch, Stevenson.
Crewe Alexandra: line up not available.
Now recorded four goals in five games

---

28 November 1942   League North (first section)   Gresty Road   5,000

CREWE ALEXANDRA 4   EVERTON 2

Crewe Alexandra: line up not available.   **Scorers:** Cray 2, Bateman, Hallam
Everton: Burnett; Jackson, Greenhaulgh; Fairfoull, Jones H, Watson; Dellow, Mutch, Curran, Stevenson, Fowler.   **Scorers:** Curran, Jackson
Tommy laid on one of the goals

---

12 December 1942   League North (first section)   Sealand Road   2,500

CHESTER 2   EVERTON 3

Chester: Shortt; Bates, McNeil; Diutton, Williams, Booth; Roberts, Astbury, Yates, McIntosh, Thow.   **Scorers:** McIntosh, Roberts
Everton: Burnett; Jackson, Greenhaulgh; Bentham, Jones H, Watson; Dellow, Mutch, Curran, Stevenson, Fowler.   **Scorers:** Mutch 2, Curran.
Chester's sixth defeat in their last seven games, their seventh was a draw!

25 December 1942   League North (first section)   Goodison Park   10,000

EVERTON 6 MANCHESTER CITY 3

Everton: Burnett; Cook, Greenhaulgh; Bentham, Humphreys, Watson; Wyles, Grant, Lawton, Stevenson, Fowler. **Scorers:** Lawton 3, Grant, Stevenson, Wyles

Manchester City: Scales; Clarke, Eastwood, Robinson, Cardell, Bray; King, Walsh, Currier, Doherty, Stuart. **Scorers:** Currier 2, King

Six days earlier, City had beaten Everton 7-1, without Tommy in the side.

26 December 1942   League North (second section)   Prenton Park   10,000

TRANMERE ROVERS 2 EVERTON 1

Tranmere: line ups not available; Scorers; Jackson w. Frost

Everton: Watson, Jackson, Greenhaulgh; Bentham, Jones H. Boyes; Wyles, Mutch, Lawton, Stevenson, Fowler. **Scorers:** Lawton

Wing half Tom Watson, plays in goal for Everton.

9 January 1943   League North (second section)   Goodison Park   18,206

EVERTON 1 LIVERPOOL 3

Everton: Burnett; Cook, Greenhaulgh; Bentham, Humphries, Mercer; Jackson, Mutch, Jones H., Stevenson, Fowler. **Scorer:** Mutch

Liverpool: Hobson; Guttridge, Lambert, Kaye, Wesby, Pilling. Shepherd, Fagan, Done, Haycock, Hulligan. **Scorers:** Hulligan 2, Shepherd

Liverpool have been undefeated since the 5th of December.

13 February 1943   League North (second section)   Sealand Road   6,000

CHESTER 0 EVERTON 1

Chester: Shortt; Hughes, McNeil; Clarke, Williams, Booth; Roberts, Astbury, Kelly, Sharp, McIntosh

Everton: Birkett; Cook, Greenhaulgh; Mercer, Jones H, Curwen; Dellow, Mutch, Bentham, Stevenson, Fowler. **Scorer:** Fowler

Tommy scores a first half winner.

20 February 1943   League North (second section)   Haig Avenue   4,000

SOUTHPORT 3 EVERTON 8

Southport: line up not available. **Scorers:** Rawlings, Ball, Butler

Everton: Birkett; Cook, Greenhaulgh; Bentham, Carey, Humphreys; Delow, Mutch, Wyles, Stevenson, Fowler. **Scorers:** Wyles 3, Mutch 2, Stevenson, 2 Fowler

Ireland International John Carey makes his Everton debut, as a guest.

27 February 1943   League North (second section)   Goodison Park   20,000

EVERTON 10 SOUTHPORT 2

Everton: Birkett; Cook, Greenhaulgh; Bentham, Carey, Humphreys; Dellow, Mutch, Lawton, Stevenson, Fowler. **Scorers:** Lawton 4, Mutch 2, Cook, Fowler, Stevenson og

Southport: line up not available. **Scorers:** Frost, Deverall

Everton's biggest win of the season.

13 March 1943   League war k.o. cup   Goodison Park   35,000

EVERTON 4 BLACKPOOL 3

Everton: Birkett; Jackson, Greenhaulgh; Fairfoull, Jones T, Curwen; Ashcroft, Rosenthall, Lawton, Stevenson, Fowler. **Scorers:** Lawton 2, Curwen, Stevenson

Blackpool: Roxborough; Pope, Jones; Farrow, Atkinson, Johnston; Matthews, Dix, Dodds, Jones C. Burbanks. **Scorers:** Dodds 2, Burbanks

Tommy comes up against Stanley Matthews for the first time.

20 March 1943	League North/Lancs Cup	Haig Avenue	3,000

SOUTHPORT 4   EVERTON 1
Southport: Line up not available.   **Scorers:** Frost 2, Ball, Deverall
Everton: Birkett; Jackson, Greenhaulgh; Humphreys, Jones T. Boyes; Dellow, Mutch, Lawton, Stevenson, Fowler   **Scorer:** Fowler
Lose to Southport after scoring 18 goals in two previous matches against the side.

27 March 1943	League North/Lancs Cup	Goodison Park	4,000

EVERTON 2   SOUTHPORT 1
Everton: Burnett; Jackson, Greenhaulgh; Bentham, McDonnell, Curwen; Dunkley, Mutch, Lawton, Stevenson, Fowler.   **Scorers:** Lawton, Mutch
Southport: line up not available.   **Scorer:** Flack
Despite the victory, Everton exit from the Lancashire Cup

3 April 1943	League North (second section)	The Racecourse	4,045

WREXHAM 4   EVERTON 1
Wrexham: Burnett;Jones C. Meade; Blunt, Stuttard, Hill F.:Collins, Smith Bremner, Baines, Rogers.   **Scorers:** Rogers 3, Bremner
Everton: Williams; Jackson, Greenhaulgh; Wyles, Jones J. Watson; Dellow, Bentham, Lawton, Stevenson, Fowler.   **Scorer:** Stevenson
Tommy comes up against Eddie Blunt, later to be a team mate at Northampton

NORTHAMPTON TOWN.
1944 - 1945

17 March 1945	War Cup Qualifier	The Hawthorns	6,000

WEST BROMWICH ALBION 6   NORTHAMPTON TOWN 0
W.B.A.: Lewis; Shelton. Male; Lowery, Gripton, McNab; Hodgetts, Heaselgrave, Clarke, Parkes, Johnson.   **Scorers:** Clarke 3, Johnson, Hodgetts o.g.
Northampton: Wood; Smalley, Welsh; Hughes, Dennison, Coley; Brown, Fagan, Garrett, Morrall, Fowler.
Welsh and Dennison injured during match, Tommy switched to outside right.

24 March 1945	War cup qualifier	St. Andrews	18,000

BIRMINGHAM CITY 2   NORTHAMPTON TOWN 2
Birmingham: Merrick; Jennings, Metcalfe, Booth, Turner; Dearson, Mulraney, Small, Massart, Shaw, White.   **Scorers:** Mulraney, Massart
Northampton: Wood; Smalley, Jones; Harris, Shepherdson, Coley; Syme, Hughes, Lee, Morrall, Fowler.   **Scorers:** Syme, Morrall
Cobblers play reserve goalkeeper Alex Lee, at centre forward.

2 April 1945	Friendly	County Ground	'small'

NORTHAMPTON TOWN 3   WATFORD 3
Northampton: Wood; Smalley, Jones: Gardner, Stephens, Coley; Brown, Dixon, Lee, Morrall, Fowler.   **Scorers:** Brown, Dixon, unknown.
Watford: Sanders; Stone, Brown W: Browne R, Groves, Williams; Tivendale, Jones, Lewis, Franklin, Browne J.   **Scorers:** Lewis, Browne J (2)
Cobblers score a last minute goal

21 April 1945   Midland Cup   County Ground   5,000
NORTHAMPTON TOWN 2   DERBY COUNTY 1
Northampton: Wood; Smalley, Dennison, Harris, Shepherdson, Coley; Brown, Dixon,
Sparshot, Morrall, Fowler.   **Scorers:** Dixon, Fowler
DERBY: Savage; Parr, Butler; Bullions, Levty, Musson; Jones, Carter, Lyman, Doherty,
Duncan.   **Scorer:** Carter
Tommy nets his first goal for the Cobblers. Raich Carter, and Peter Doherty in the Derby
side

1945 - 1946

29 August 1945   Div. 3South(North)   Vicarage Road   2,768
WATFORD 4   NORTHAMPTON TOWN 2
Watford: Saunders; Brown, Poole, Gillespie, Shaw, Gray, Jones, Mortensen, Lewis,
Edelston, Jezzards.   **Scorers:** Jezzards (2), Edelston, Lewis
Northampton: Lee; Smalley, Jones; Harris, Shepherdson, Barron; Maskell, Dixon,
Phillips. Morall, Fowler.   **Scorers:** Dixon 2
Stanley Mortensen and Maurice Edelston are guest players for Watford.

1 September 1945   Div. 3 South (North)   County Ground   6,000
NORTHAMPTON TOWN 1   WALSALL 0
Northampton: Lee; Smalley, Barron; Neal, Dennison, Welsh; Roberts, Ellwood, Dixon,
Morrall, Fowler.   **Scorer:** Roberts
Walsall: Lewis; Stone, Smith; Crutchley, Sankey, Payne; Hancock, Brown, Alsop, Harvey,
Booth.
Game kicked off 7 minutes late ,

 5 September 1945   Div. 3 South (North)   Southend Stadium 5,000
SOUTHEND UNITED 0   NORTHAMPTON TOWN 1
Southend Joslin; Calder, Harris, Jones L, Jones C, Jackson R: Smith, Robinson,
Jackson, H, Smith, Walton.
Northampton: Lee ; Smalley, Dennison; Neal, Shepherdson, Baron; Roberts, Ellwood,
Dixon, Morall, Fowler.   **Scorer:** Morrall
Players stayed on the field at half time, but still the game finished in darkness

8 September 1945   Div. 3 South (North)   County Ground   7,000
NORTHAMPTON TOWN 1   PORT VALE 0
Northampton: Lee, Smalley, Welsh; Neal, Dennison, Barron; Roberts, Ellwood, Dixon,
Morrall, Fowler.   **Scorer:** Roberts
Port Vale: Prince; Purcell, Potts; Jervis, Griffiths, Felton, Dickie, McDowell, Gregory,
Wootton, Bellis.
Both Northampton's wingers get excellent reviews. Go 2nd in the division.

15 September 1945   Div. 3 South (North)   Vale Park   7,000
PORT VALE 0   NORTHAMPTON TOWN 0
Port Vale: Prince H: Purnell, Felton; Jervis, Griffiths, Cooper;Crunn, McDowall, Prince
E. Cumner, Bellis
Northampton: Lee; Smalley, Welsh; Neal, Dennison, Barron; Roberts, Wilson, Dixon,
Morrall, Fowler.
Cobblers lucky to take a point, goalkeeper Lee was the star player.

22 September 1945   Div. 3 South (North)   Portman Road   12,000

IPSWICH TOWN 2   NORTHAMPTON TOWN 1

Ipswich: Saphin; Harris, Parry; Bell, O'Mahoney, McLuckey; Sommerfield, Antonio, Day, Gillespie Hornby   **Scorers:** Day, Hornby

Northampton: Lee; Smalley, Welsh; Neal, Dennison, Barron; Roberts, Wilson, Dixon, Morrall, Fowler.   **Scorer:** Roberts

Ipswich paraded the maximum 6 'guest' players, including all 5 forwards.

---

6 October 1945   Div. 3 South (North)   County Ground   7,151

NORTHAMPTON TOWN 1   NOTTS COUNTY 2

Northampton: Lee;Smalley, Allen; McNab, Neal, Coley;Roberts, Hughes, Heaselgrave, Haycock, Fowler.   **Scorer:** Roberts

Notts County: Wiseman; Southwell, Allen; Harris, Corkhill, Peacock, Berrisford, McPherson, Hubbard, Kye, Strain.   **Scorers:** McPherson, Berrisford.

Allen of Notts County injured after 65 minutes, they continued with 10 men.

---

20 October 1945   Div. 3 South (North)   County Ground   9,000

NORTHAMPTON TOWN 0   QUEENS PARK RANGERS 2

Northampton: Wood; Smalley,Welsh; Neal, Dennison, Barron; Roberts, Blunt, Dixon, Morrall, Fowler.

Q.P.R. Allen; Rose, Jefferson; Daniel, Alexander, Farrow; Adonnell, Mallett, Heathcote, Neary, Whitehead. **Scorers:** Heathcote, Neary

The Cobblers have not won at home since the 18th September.

---

3 November1945   Div. 3 South (North   Brisbane Road   5,000

CLAPTON ORIENT 1   NORTHAMPTON TOWN 0

Clapton: Hall;Ringrose, Rumbold; Walters, Bartlett, Moss; Gore, Parr, Stock, Merritt, Owers. **Scorer:** Gore

Northampton: Scott; Smalley, Welsh; Neal, Dennison, Allen; Roberts, Blunt, Dixon, Barron, Fowler.

Heaselgrave, Sankey and Lowery, the Cobblers new men, failed to arrive until half time.

---

10 November 1945   Div. 3 South (North)   County Ground   5,000

NORTHAMPTON TOWN 6   CLAPTON ORIENT 1

Northampton: Scott; Smalley, Barron; Lowery. Sankey, Yarker; Roberts, Heaselgrave, Morrall, Wilson, Fowler.   **Scorers:** Roberts 3, Heaselgrave 2, Morrall

Clapton: Hall; Ringrose, Rumbold; Walters, Bartlett, Barnes; Gore, Parr, Stock, Merritt, Owen.   **Scorer:** Parr

Bill Barron was taken off injured during the game, but returned later.

---

17 November 1945   F.A.Cup Round. 1   County Ground   6,000

NORTHAMPTON TOWN 5   CHELMSFORD 1

Northampton: Scott; Smalley, Barron; Lowery, Sankey, Yarker; Roberts, Heaselgrave, Morrall, Hughes, Fowler. **Scorers:** Morrall 2, Hughes 2, Roberts

Chelmsford: Willsher; Thomas, Parry, Williams; Farley, Tunncliffe, Clarke, Eaton, Foreman Burley, Marden.   **Scorer:** Foreman

Tommy laid on both Morrall's goals, in a 3 minute spell. Heaselgrave taken to hospital.

---

24 November 1945   F.A. Cup Round 1   Whaddon Road   6,700

CHELMSFORD 0   NORTHAMPTON TOWN 5

Chelmsford: Willsher; Clapham, Potter; Eaton, Farley, Parry; Marden R. Burley, Foreman, Tunncliffe, Marsden B.

Northampton: Scott; Smalley, Barron; Lowery, Dennison, Yarker, Roberts, Smith, Morrall, Hughes, Fowler.   **Scorers:** Morrall 2, Roberts, Smith, Fowler

Tommy scored one, and made one for Roberts, Chelmsford netted but goal was disallowed

1 December 1945   Friendly   Recreation Ground   2,000
ALDERSHOT 2   NORTHAMPTON TOWN 7
Aldershot: Reynolds, Rogers, White A; Morris, White J , Summerbee; Bell, Sommerfield, Brooks, Fitzgerald, Hobbs.   **Scorers:** Bell Hobbs
Northampton: Scott, Smalley, Welsh, Sankey, Dennison, Yarker, Roberts, Smith, Morrall, Hughes, Fowler.   **Scorers:** Morrall 2, Roberts, Smith, Hughes, Fowler, o.g.
Aldershot play their 'league' side, without any guests from the local barracks.

 8 December 1945   F.A.Cup Round 2   County Ground   10,000
NORTHAMPTON TOWN 3   NOTTS COUNTY 1
Northampton: Scott; Smalley, Barron; Lowery, Dennison, Sankey; Roberts, Blunt, Morrall, Hughes, Fowler.   **Scorers:** Morrall 2, Blunt
Notts County: Kirkby; Southwell, Ratcliffe; Harris, Corkhill, Peacock, Berrisford, McPherson, Hubbard, Pye, Meredith.   **Scorer:** McPherson
Tommy laid on the 2 goals. Pye of Notts County misses a penalty.

15 December 1945   F.A.Cup Round 2   Meadow Lane   17,000
NOTTS COUNTY 1   NORTHAMPTON TOWN 0
Notts County: Kirkby; Southwell, Ratcliffe, Harris, Corkhill, Peacock, Berrisford, Pye, Martin, Hubbard, Meredith.   **Scorer:** Martin
Northampton:: Scott; Smalley, Welsh; Lowery, Dennison, Sankey; Roberts, Blunt, Morrall, Hughes, Fowler.
Despite losing the match, the Cobblers go through to the third round on a 3-2 aggregate.

25 December 1945   Div. 3 South (North)   Field Mill   unknown
MANSFIELD TOWN 2   NORTHAMPTON TOWN 0
Mansfield: Urien; Chessells, Marsh; Smith L.,Barke; Harkin, Thorpe, Womwell, Carter, Smith W. Allen.   **Scorer:** Carter 2
Northampton: Lee, Neal, Welsh, Harris, Skelton, Yarker, Roberts, Blunt, Ellwood, Wilson, Fowler.
Only 5 regular first teamers could make this Christmas Day game.

27 December 1945   Div. 3 South (North)   County Ground   7,000
NORTHAMPTON TOWN 4   MANSFIELD TOWN 0
Northampton: Scott; Smalley, Barron; Sankey, Dennison, Lowery; Roberts, Blunt, Morrall, Hughes, Fowler.   **Scorers:** Sankey, Lowery, Roberts, Blunt
Mansfield: Urien, Chesell, Marsh; Smith L, Barke, Harkin; Womwell, Thorpe, Carter, Allen, Smith B.
Two of the Cobblers goals came from long distance. Sankey's from 30 yards, Lowery's from 50

29 December1945   Div. 3 South (North)   County Ground   7,000
NORTHAMPTON TOWN 6   SOUTHEND UNITED 2
Northampton: Scott: Smalley, Barron; Sankey, Skelton, Welsh; Roberts, Blunt, Morrall, Hughes, Fowler.   **Scorers:** Morrall 3, Roberts, Blunt, Hughes.
Southend: Conway; Savage, Bell; Bennett, Jackson, Linton; Macklin, Thompson, Dudley, Gibson, Ormandy.   **Scorer:** Dudley 2
Reports state that although Tommy was the only forward not to score, he was the danger.

1 January 1946   Div. 3 South (North)   County Ground   2,000
NORTHAMPTON TOWN 4   NORWICH CITY 1
Northampton: Lee; Collins, Allen; Neal, Skelton, Yarker; Roberts, Wilson, Dixon, Hughes, Fowler.   **Scorers:** Dixon 2, Hughes, Roberts
Norwich: Davis;Frost, Reid; Ware, Young, Armes; Duffield, Russell,Maskell, Aquaroff, Rackman.   **Scorer:** Duffield
Cobblers make seven changes from the previous game.

5 January 1946   F.A.Cup Round 3   County Ground   13,000
NORTHAMPTON TOWN 2   MILLWALL 2
Northampton: Scott; Smalley, Barron; Lowery, Sankey, Yarker; Roberts, Blunt, Morrall, Hughes, Fowler.   **Scorers:** Blunt, Hughes
Millwall: Dunkley; Dudley, Fisher; Ross, Brolly, Tyler; Richardson, Gordon, Ridley, Brown, Smith.   **Scorers:** Richardson, Ridley
Morrall scored a winner for the Cobblers but it was ruled offside.

7 January 1946   F.A.Cup Round 3   The Den   15,384
MILLWALL 3   NORTHAMPTON TOWN 0
Millwall: Dunkley; Dudley, Fisher; Ross, Brolly, Tyler; Richardson, Gordon, Phillips, Brown, Smith.   **Scorers:** Phillips, Smith, og
Northampton: Scott; Smaley, Barron; Lowery, Sankey, Yarker, Roberts, Blunt, Morrall, Hughes, Fowler
Morrall again has a goal ruled out,after he scored and referee awarded a free kick instead.

12 January 1946   Div. 3 South (K.O. Cup)   Southend Stadium   4,000
SOUTHEND UNITED 4   NORTHAMPTON TOWN 3
Southend: Conway; Milne, Bell; Bennett, Jackson, Walton; Peters, Gilbey, Dudley, Gibson, Whitchurch.   **Scorers:** Peters, Gilby, Dudley, Whitchurch
Northampton: Scott; Smaley, Barron; Blunt, Skelton, Lowery; Roberts, Hughes, Morrall, Wilson, Fowler.   **Scorers:** Morrall 2, Smalley (p)
Tom Smalley makes up for his own goal last week, by converting a penalty.

19 January 1946   Div. 3 South (K.O. Cup)   County Ground   4,000
NORTHAMPTON TOWN 0   SOUTHEND UNITED 1
Northampton: Scott; Smalley, Barron; Bosse, Dennison, Lowery, Roberts, Hughes, Morrall, Wilson, Fowler.
Southend: Conway, Humphries, Bell; Montgomery, Jackson, Walton, Smith, Gilberg, Dudley, Richards, Pierson.   **Scorer:** Richards
Gilberg put a penalty for Southend, wide of the post.

26 January 1946   Div. 3 South (K.O. Cup)   Carrow Road   7,748
NORWICH CITY 2   NORTHAMPTON TOWN 1
Norwich: Davis; Reid, Taylor; Flack, Ware, Proctor; Duffield, Plunkett, Johnson, Furness, Jones.   **Scorers:** Furness, Jones
Northampton: Gillespie; Smalley, Barron; Neal, Dennison, Yarker; Roberts, Blunt, Morrall, Hughes, Fowler.   **Scorer:** o.g.
Norwich gifted the Cobblers an own goal within 3 minutes, but the Canaries emerged the victors

2 February 1946   Div. 3 South (K.O. Cup)   County Ground   4,000
NORTHAMPTON TOWN 1   NORWICH CITY 1
Northampton: Gillespie; Smalley, Barron; Neal, Dennison, Lowery, Roberts, Blunt, Morrall, Hughes, Fowler.   **Scorer:** Smalley (p)
Norwich: Hall; Reid, Taylor; Flack, Ware, Proctor; Church, Furness, Johnson, Plunkett, Jones.   **Scorer:** Furness
Tom Smalley converts a penalty against his old club

9 February 1946   Div. 3 South (K.O.Cup)   Vicarage Road   4,500
WATFORD 1   NORTHAMPTON TOWN 0
Watford: Mee; Harris, Gallimore; Gillespie, Shaw, Gray; Davies, Beckett, Lewis, Weir, Drinkwater.   **Scorer:** Davies
Northampton: Gillespie; Smalley, Barron; Lowery, Dennison, Yarker. Hughes, Blunt, McGregor, Morrall, Fowler.
The experiment of trying Gwyn Hughes as a winger, was a great success.

16 February, 1946   Div, 3 South (K.O.Cup)   County Ground   5,500
NORTHAMPTON TOWN 4   WATFORD 1
Northampton: Gillespie;Smalley, Barron; Sankey, Dennison, Lowery; Hughes, Haselgrave, Morrall, Bates, Fowler. **Scorers:** Morrall 2, Bates, Fowler
Watford: Mee; O'Brien, Gallimore; Gillespie, Shaw, Gray; Davies, Curran, Lewis, Weir, Drinkwater. **Scorer:** Davies
Edric Bates, later Southampton's manager, makes his only appearance for Northampton.

23 February 1946   Div. 3 South (K.O.Cup)   County Ground(Swindon)   8,815
SWINDON TOWN 1   NORTHAMPTON TOWN 4
Swindon: Wildman; Woodman, McDonald; Cousins, Tudor, Lloyd; Jones, Francis, Derrick, Lucas, Williams. **Scorer:** Lucas
Northampton: Gillespie, Smaley, Barron; Hughes, Dennison, Blunt; Roberts, Heaselgrave, Jones, Morrall, Fowler. **Scorers:** Morall 3, Jones
In only his 2nd come back game, Sam Heaselgrave is injured and spent the last hour limping

2 March 1946   Div. 3 South (K.O.Cup)   County Ground   4,000
NORTHAMPTON TOWN 5   SWINDON TOWN 1
Northampton: Gillespie; Smalley, Barron; Lowery, Dennison, Blunt; Hughes, Smith, Jones, Morrall, Fowler. **Scorers:** Lowery, Hughes, Jones, Morrall, og.
Swindon: Sturgess; Cousins, Kelso, Lloyd, Tudor, Loveday; Jones (E), Derrick, Saunders, Lucas, Williams. **Scorer:** o.g.
Both Smalley (Northampton) and Cousins (Swindon) put through their own goals.

9 March 1946   Div. 3 South (K.O.Cup)   County Ground   7,755
NORTHAMPTON TOWN 2   NOTTS COUNTY 1
Northampton: Saunders; Smalley, Baron; Sankey, Dennison, Blunt; Hughes, Smith, Jones, Morrall, Fowler. **Scorers:** Morrall, Fowler
Notts County: Brown, Southwell, Allen; Corkhill, Bagnell, Haines; Berrisford, McPherson, Lovering, Pye, Morrad. **Scorer:** Lovering.
Guest goalkeeper Gillespie was picked for a service game, guest goalkeeper Saunders plays.

16 March 1946   Div. 3 South (K.O.Cup)   Meadow Lane   9,925
NOTTS COUNTY 1   NORTHAMPTON TOWN 2
Notts County: Kirby; Ratcliffe, Allen; Haines, Southwell, Sheen; Berresford, Pye, Lovering, Hatton, Morrad. **Scorer:** Pye
Northampton: Gillespie, Smalley, Barron, Sankey, Dennison, Lowery; Hughes, Smith, Jones, Morrall, Fowler. **Scorers:** Hughes, Morrall.
Morrall injured after 15 minutes, Dennison also off for a spell.

23 March 1946   Div. 3 South (K.O Cup)   County Ground   10,000
NORTHAMPTON TOWN 1   MANSFIELD TOWN 1
Northampton: Gillespie; Smalley, Barron; Lowery, Sankey, Blunt; Hughes, Smith, Jones, Heaselgrave, Fowler. **Scorer:** Hughes
Mansfield: Cromack; Bramley, Chassells; Smith, Barke, Everitt; Hewitt, Harkin, Copestake, Hogg, Betts. **Scorer:** Betts
Cobblers first home defeat since the 19th of January.

30 March 1946   Div. 3 South (K.O. Cup)   Field Mill   4,000
MANSFIELD TOWN 3   NORTHAMPTON TOWN 1
Mansfield: Cromack; Bramley, Chessells; Smith, Barke, Everitt; Hewitt, Harkin, Copestake, Hogg, Betts. **Scorers:** Copestake, Hogg, Betts
Northampton: Gillespie, Smalley, Barron; Sankey, Dennison, Lowery, Hughes, Smith, Jones, Morrall, Fowler. **Scorer:** Morrall.
Dennison and Morrall returned to the Cobblers side, after injury.

| 6 April 1946 | Div. 3 South (K.O.Cup) | County Ground | 5,000 |

NORTHAMPTON TOWN 0   CLAPTON ORIENT 2
Northampton: Gillespie, Smalley, Barron; Lowery, Sankey, Blunt; Hughes, Smith, Jones, Morrall, Fowler.
Clapton Orient: Lewis, Clark, Ritson; Merritt, Bartlett, Ballard; Carter, Henley, Hunt, Pullen, Baynham.   **Scorers:** Pullen, Baynham
Cobblers wore black arm bands, due to death of director T.C. Gillett.

| 20 April 1946 | Div. 3 South (K.O.Cup) | County Ground | 8,000 |

NORTHAMPTON TOWN 1   WALSALL 4
Northampton: Gilespie, Smith, Barron; Hughes, Sankey, Blunt; Pritchard, Heaselgrave, Jennings, Morrall, Fowler.   **Scorer:** Fowler
Walsall: Lewis; Methley, Shelton; Crutchley, Foulkes, Newman; Hancock, Talbot, Mullard, Wilshaw, Alsop.   **Scorers:** Mullard 2, Talbot, Wilshaw
Mullard's first goal came 10 seconds after the kick off.

| 25. April. 1946 | Maunsell Cup Semi-Final | County Ground |

NORTHAMPTON TOWN 9   RUSHDEN TOWN 0
Northampton: Scott; Smalley, Barron, Sankey, Dennison, Yarker;Hughes, Smith, Jennings, Morrall, Fowler.   **Scorers:** Jennings 4, Hughes 3, Smith, Morrall
Rushden Town: Andrews; Mantle, Childs; Bland, Meacock, Peacock; Gell, Moore, Pipes, Starmer, Inwood.
Northampton's biggest ever win in the competition.

| 2. May 1946 | Maunsell Cup-Final | Rockingham Road |

KETTERING TOWN 2   NORTHAMPTON TOWN 4
Kettering: Olney; Smith, Campbell; Tear, Linnell, Wragg; Dean, White C, Henley, White A, Burgess.   **Scorers:** unknown
Northampton: Scott; Smalley, Barron; Sankey, Dennison, Allen; Hughes, Smith, Jennings, Morrall, Fowler.   **Scorers:** Sankey 2, Allen, Jennings.
Last game at Rockingham Road's sloping pitch, levelled in the close season.

1946- 1947

| 31. August 1946 | Division 3 South | County Ground | 12,013 |

NORTHAMPTON TOWN 4   SWINDON TOWN1
Northampton: Jones; Smalley, Barron; Sankey, Dennison, Blunt; Roberts, Smith, Morrall, Heaselgrave, Fowler.   **Scorers:** Heaselgrave 2. Morrall 2
Swindon Town: Boulton; Young, Trim; Lloyd, Itchell, Bingham; Jones, Lucas, Stephens J., Stephens A, Williams.   **Scorer:** Williams
Swindon's manager, is ex-Cobbler Louis Page.

| 2. September 1946 | Division 3 South | County Ground | 9,730 |

NORTHAMPTON TOWN 1   EXETER CITY 2
Northampton: Jones; Smalley, Barron; Sankey, Dennison, Blunt; Roberts, Smith, Morrall, Heaselgrave, Fowler.   **Scorer:** Morrall
Exeter: Hoyle; Thompson, Blood; Cutting, Hanford, Walker; Wardles, Hyde, Ebdon, Wright, Regan.   **Scorers:** Wright, Regan
Cobblers drop from first to tenth in the league table

7. September 1946   Division 3 South   Dean Court   13,461
BOURNEMOUTH AND BOSCOMBE 2   NORTHAMPTON TOWN 1
Bournemouth: Bird; Marsden, Sanaghan; Burke, Wilson, Gallagher; Longdon, Paton,
Kirkham, Hutchinson, Tunnicliffe.   **Scorers:** Kirkham, Paton
Northampton: Jones; Smalley, Strathie; Sankey, Dennison, Blunt; Roberts, Smith,
Heaselgrave, Morrall, Fowler.   **Scorer:** Morrall
Tom Smalley misses a penalty, Bournemouth's first win of the season.

14 September 1946   Division 3 South   County Ground   8,853
NORTHAMPTON TOWN 0   CARDIFF CITY 2
Northampton: Scott; Strathie, Barron; Smalley, Sankey, Blunt; Roberts, Smith. Morrall,
Heaselgrave ,Fowler
Cardiff: Cannin; Lever, Sherwood; Baker, Stansfield, Hill; Gibson, Rees, Jones, Allen,
Clarke.   **Scorer:** Allen 2
Rained all game, pitch cut up, became very heavy.

18. September 1946   Division 3 South   St. James Park   7.933
EXETER CITY 1   NORTHAMPTON TOWN 0
Exeter: Singleton, Thompson, Coles; Cuttings, Hanford, Walker; Mustard, Wardle,
Ebdon, Wright, Regan.   **Scorer:** Ebdon
Northampton: Jones; Smalley. Allen; Neal, Sankey, Barron; Roberts, Smith, Morall,
Blunt, Fowler
Tommy plays most of game at outide right, Roberts at Centre forward, Morrall injured

21. September 1946   Division 3 South   Carrow Road   16,215
NORWICH CITY 2   NORTHAMPTON TOWN 3
Norwich: Duke; Flack, Taylor; Robinson, Proctor, Williams; Johnson, Russell, Church,
Furness, Jones.   **Scorers:** Jones, Russell
Northampton: Jones; Smalley, Barron; Neal, Sankey, Blunt; Roberts, Smith, Jennings,
Heaselgrave, Fowler.   **Scorers:** Fowler 2, Smith.
Tommy's first goals for the club in league football, now joint second top scorer.

28. September 1946   Division 3 South   County Ground   11,906
NORTHAMPTON TOWN 2   NOTTS COUNTY 1
Northampton: Jones, Smalley, Barron, Sankey, Dennison, Blunt; Briscoe, Smith,
Garrett, Heaselgrave, Fowler.   **Scorer:** Garrett 2
Notts County: Brown; Bagnall, Robinson; Gannon, Lockie, Corkhill; Cumner, Brown,
Beresford, Sewell, Parks.   **Scorer:** Beresford.
Archie Garrett marks his debut with a brace of goals.

5. October. 1946   Division 3 South   Fellows Park   12,521
WALSALL 2   NORTHAMPTON TOWN 0
Walsall: Lewes; Netherley, Skidmore; Crutchley, Foulkes, Newman; Brown, Talbot,
Mullard, Wilshaw, Davies.   **Scorers:** Wilshaw. Talbot
Northampton: Jones; Smalley, Barron; Sankey, Dennison, Lowery; Briscoe, Smith,
Garrett, Blunt, Fowler.
Sankey a passenger for most of the game.

12. October 1946   Division 3 South   Recreation Ground   5,498
ALDERSHOT 1   NORTHAMPTON TOWN 1
Aldershot: Gage; Rogers, Shepherd; Fitzgerald, Rowland, Brown; Hobbs, Griffiths,
Hold, Gray, Hassall.   **Scorer:** Hassall
Northampton: Jones; Smalley, Barron; Lowery, Dennison, Blunt; Briscoe, Smith,
Garrett, Morrall, Fowler.   **Scorer:** Fowler
Tommy only one goal behind top scorer Morrall, who has 4.

| 19. October 1946 | Division 3 South | County Ground | 9,776 |

NORTHAMPTON TOWN 4   WATFORD 1
Northampton: Jones; Smalley, Barron; Lowery, Dennison, Blunt; Roberts, Smith, Garrett, Morrall, Fowler.   **Scorers:** Garrett 2, Smith, Morrall
Watford: Rigg, Morgan, Harris; Ross, Farnen, Harper; Davies, Young, Usher, Evans Wipfler.   **Scorer:** Ross (p)
Northampton two up in the first ten minutes.

| 26. October 1946 | Division 3 South | Portman Road | 13,280 |

IPSWICH TOWN 1   NORTHAMPTON TOWN 2
Ipswich: Burns; Rumbold, Parry; Bell, Mahoney, Fox; Little, Baird, Conner, Parker, Ray
Scorer: Baird
Northampton: Jones; Smalley, Barron; Lowery, Dennison, Blunt; Roberts, Smith, Garrett, Morrall, Fowler.   **Scorer:** Garrett 2
Rained all game, finished in semi-darkness.

| 2. November 1946 | Division 3 South | County Ground | 10,173 |

NORTHAMPTON TOWN 4   LEYTON ORIENT 1
Northampton: Jones; Smalley, Barron; Lowery, Dennison, Blunt; Roberts, Smith, Garrett, Morrall, Fowler.   **Scorer:** Garrett 2, Smith 2
Orient: King; Clark, Farley, Ballard, Ritson, Fullbrook, Baynham, Bacon, Hunt, Morrad, Pullen.   **Scorer:** Hunt.
King, the Orient goalkeeper makes his one and only league appearance.

| 9. November 1946 | Division 3 South | Loftus Road | 17,796 |

QUEENS PARK RANGERS 1   NORTHAMPTON TOWN 0
Q.P.R.: Allen; Rose, Jefferson; Smith, Barr, Powell; McEwan, Mallett, Heathcote, Hatton, Pattison.   **Scorer:** McEwan
Northampton: Jones, Smalley, Barron; Lowery, Dennison, Blunt; Jenkins, Smith, Garrett, Heaselgrave, Fowler.
Cobblers first defeat in five games.

| 16. November 1946 | Division 3 South | County Ground | 11,338 |

NORTHAMPTON TOWN 2   SOUTHEND UNITED 3
Northampton: Jones; Smalley, Barron; Lowery, Dennison, Blunt; Roberts, Smith, Garrett, Morrall, Fowler   **Scorer:** Garrett 2
Southend: Hankey, Linton, Walton; Harris, Jackson, Montgomery; Sibley, Smirke, Thompson, Bennett, Lane.   **Scorers:** Thompson, Bennett, Lane
Harris and Lane of Southend both appeared as guests for the Cobblers during the war.

| 23. November 1946 | Division 3 South | Eastville Stadium | 7,886 |

BRISTOL ROVERS 0   NORTHAMPTON TOWN 3
Rovers: Liley; Smith, Watkins; Warren, Winters, Pitt; Pethebridge, Bamford, Lambden, Morgan, Carr.
Northampton: Jones, Smalley, Barron; Lowery, Dennison, Blunt; Morrall, Smith, Garrett, Thompson, Fowler.   **Scorers:** Garrett, Smith, Morrall
Harry Thompson makes his Cobblers debut.

| 30. November 1946 | F.A. Cup Round 1 | County Ground | 15,600 |

NORTHAMPTON TOWN 2   MANSFIELD TOWN 0
Northampton: Jones; Smalley, Barron; Sankey, Dennison, Lowery; Morrall, Smith, Garrett, Blunt, Fowler.   **Scorers:** Garrett, Blunt.
Mansfield: Wright; Bradley, Fox; Hogg, Barke, Binnie; Harper, Brown, Copestake, Westland, Calvery.
Eddie Blunt's goal came from a 25 yard free kick.

7. December 1946   Division 3 South   Plainmoor   5,265

TORQUAY UNITED 2   NORTHAMPTON TOWN 1
Torquay: Matier; Keeton, Calland; Towers, Head, Coley; Phillips, Harrower, Connley, Cothliff, Mercer.   **Scorers:** Harrower, Connley.
Northampton: Jones; Smalley, Barron; Sankey, Dennison, Blunt; Morrall, Smith, Garrett, Thompson, Fowler.   **Scorer:** Garrett
Bill Coley ex-Cobblers war time guest. Tommy misses equaliser from 6 yards.

26. December 1946   Division 3 South   Ashton Gate   23,109

BRISTOL CITY 2   NORTHAMPTON TOWN 3
Bristol City: Eddalls; Bailey, Fox; Morgan, Roberts, Jones, Chilcott, Thomas, Clark, Williams, Hargreaves.   **Scorers:** Thomas, Clark
Northampton: Jones; Smalley, Barron; Thompson, Dennison, McKenna; Roberts, Smith, Garrett, Morrall, Fowler.   **Scorers:** Smith Garrett, Morrall.
City 2-0 up after 29 minutes. game stopped for a time due to thunderstorm.

28. December 1946   Division 3 South   County Ground(Swindon)   15,456

SWINDON TOWN 3   NORTHAMPTON TOWN 1
Swindon: Burton; Lloyd, Emery; Onslow, Bingham, Itchell; Jones, Lucas, Stephens, Paterson, Williams.   **Scorers:** Lucas 2, Stephens
Northampton: Jones; Smalley, Quinney; Thompson, Dennison, McKenna; Robers, Smith, Garrett, Morrall, Fowler.   **Scorer:** Garrett
Smith 'Scores' for the Cobblers, goals disallowed, Swindon attack and score.

23. January 1947   Division 3 South   County Ground   2,713

NORTHAMPTON TOWN 3   MANSFIELD TOWN 0
Northampton: Scott; Smalley, Barron; Smith, Dennison, McKenna; Morrall, Jenkins, Garrett, Thompson, Fowler.   **Scorers:** Fowler, Jenkins, Garrett
Mansfield: Wright, Fox. Bramley; Smith, Barke, Biney; Copestake, Hogg, Bryant, Westland, Calverley;
Began to snow at half time, lowest crowd of the season. Tommy nets his 4th goal .

25. January 1947   Division 3 South   County Ground   6,023

NORTHAMPTON TOWN 1   NORWICH CITY 0
Northampton: Jones; Smalley, Sankey, Lowery, Dennison, Blunt. Roberts, Smith, Garrett, Morrall, Fowler.   **Scorer:** Smith (p)
Norwich: Wiseman; Fleck, Tobin; Plunkett, Norman, Williams; Morgan, Dutton, Johnson, Eyre, Pembery.
Smith converts a penalty ten minutes after Garrett missed one.

1. February 1947   Division 3 South   Meadow Lane   13,096

NOTTS COUNTY 1   NORTHAMPTON TOWN 0
Notts County: Brown; Robinson, Southwell; Corkhill, Lockie, Dickson; Lunn, Cumner, Jayes, Sewell, Houghton.   **Scorer:** Sewell
Northampton: Scott; Smalley, Sankey; Lowery, Dennison, Blunt; Roberts, Smith, Garrett, Thompson, Fowler.
The Cobblers dispute the County goal, claiming it was offside.

8. March 1947   Division 3 South   Brisbane Road   8,567

LEYTON ORIENT 2   NORTHAMPTON TOWN 1
Leyton Orient: Tolliday; Fullbrook, Ritson, Bacon, Bartlett, Davidson,; Roberts, Hunt, Morrad, Pullen, Baynham.   **Scorers:** Pullen, Roberts
Northampton: Jones; Smalley, Barron; Lowery, Dennison, Sankey, Briscoe, Smith, Garrett, Thompson, Fowler.   **Scorer:** Garrett.
Northampton's first game for 5 weeks, due to weather.

| 15. March 1947 | Division 3 South | County Ground | 9,970 |

NORTHAMPTON TOWN 4   QUEENS PARK RANGERS 4
Northampton: Jones: Smalley, Barron; Sankey, Dennison, Lowery; Briscoe, Smith,
Garrett. Thompson, Fowler.   **Scorers:** Garrett 2, Smith 2.
Q.P.R.: Allen; Dudley, Jefferson; Blizzard, Powell, Chapman; McEwan, Parkinson,
Durrant, Mills, Pattison.   **Scorers:** Parkinson 2, Durrant, Mills.
Cobblers take a 6th minute lead, but are 2-4 down with 5 minutes to go!

| 22. March 1947 | Division 3 South | Southend Stadium 8,465 |

SOUTHEND UNITED 4   NORTHAMPTON TOWN 0
Southend: Hankey; Jackson, Walton; Harris, Sheard, Montgomery; Pritchard, Smirke,
Dudley, Thompson, Bennett.   **Scorers:** Dudley 3, Thompson 1.
Northampton: Jones; Smalley, Barron; Sankey, Dennison, Lowery; Briscoe, Smith,
Garrett, Thompson, Fowler.
Cobblers fifth consecutive away defeat.

| 29. March 1947 | Division 3 South | County Ground | 6,846 |

NORTHAMPTON TOWN 1   BRISTOL ROVERS 2
Northampton: McKee; Smalley, Barron; Lowery, Sankey, Thompson; Briscoe, Smith,
Garrett, Morrall, Fowler.   **Scorer:** Smalley
Bristol Rovers: Weare; Bamford, Watkins; Pitt, Warren, McArthur; Wookey, Hodges,
Leamon, Morgan, Carr.   **Scorers:** Morgan, Leamon.
Cobblers fifth game without a win. Tommy is one of four players dropped for next game.

1947- 1948

| 25. October 1947 | Division 3 South | St. James Park | 9,419 |

EXETER CITY 1   NORTHAMPTON TOWN 1
Exeter: Singleton; Thompson, Johnstone; Bartholomew, Gibson, Walker; Hutchings,
Mackay, Ebdon, Wright, Fallon.   **Scorer:** Fallon.
Northampton: Jones; Smalley, Barron; Lowery, Dennison, Coley; Roberts, Smith,
Garrett, Heaselgrave, Fowler.   **Scorer:** Garrett (p)
The Cobblers played in their new 'second' strip of Royal Blue jerseys, with White facings.

| 1. November 1947 | Division 3 South | County Ground | 9,289 |

NORTHAMPTON TOWN 1   NEWPORT COUNTY 1
Northampton: Jones, Smaley, Barron; Coley, Sankey, Thompson; Roberts, Smith,
Garrett, Heaselgrave, Fowler.   **Scorer:** Smith
Newport: Smith, Sutherland, Emmanuel; Hammill, Wilcox, McBlain; Williams, Lewis,
Mogford, Allen, Harper.   **Scorer:** Allen
The club were pleased with the crowd, considering the Towcester races, and the Saints.

| 8. November 1947 | Division 3 South | Southend Stadium 10,481 |

SOUTHEND UNITED 3   NORTHAMPTON TOWN 1
Southend: Robinson; Beach, Linton; Goodyear, Sheard, Montgomery; Pritchard,
Smirke, Dudley, Bennett, Whitchurch. **Scorers:** Dudley 2 (1 p), Smirke
Northampton: Jones, Smalley, Barron; Sankey, Dennison, Coley; Roberts, Smith,
Garrett, Heaselgrave, Fowler.   **Scorer:** Smith
Southend also had two goals disallowed.

15. November 1947   Division 3 South   County Ground   18,272
NORTHAMPTON TOWN 1   NOTTS COUNTY 2
Northampton: Jones; Smalley, Barron; Lowery, Dennison, Coley; Roberts, Smith,
Garrett, Thompson, Fowler.   **Scorer:** Garrett
Notts County: Brown; Southwell, Howe; Ganon, Baxter, Corkhill; Houghton, Sewell,
Lawton, Marsh, Cumner.   **Scorers:** Lawton, Marsh.
Tommy Lawton makes his Notts County debut, crowds queue 4 hours before kick off.

29. November 1947   F. A. Cup (Round 1)   St. James Park   13,143
EXETER CITY 1   NORTHAMPTON TOWN 1
Exeter: Singleton, Thompson, Johnstone; Barholemew, Gibson, Walker; Hutchings,
Mackay, Ebdon, Wright, Regan.   **Scorer:** Barholemew.
Northampton: Jones, Smaley, Barron, Lowery, Dennison, Coley, Roberts, Smith,
Briscoe, Thompson, Fowler.   **Scorer:** Roberts.
Thompson and Smith injured Cobblers play extra time with just 9 men.

6. December 1947   F.A. Cup (Round 1 replay)   County Ground   9,500
NORTHAMPTON TOWN 2   EXETER CITY 0
Northampton: Jones; Smalley, Barron; Lowery, Dennison, Coley; Roberts,
Heaselgrave, Briscoe, Jenkins, Fowler.   **Scorers:** Briscoe, Jenkins
Exeter: Singleton, Thompson, Johnstone; Bartholemew, Gibson, Walker; Hutchings,
Dymonmd, Smart, Wright, Regan.
Both Briscoe of the Cobblers and Thompson of Exeter miss penalties.

13 December. 1947   F.A.Cup (Round 2)   County Ground   12,000
NORTHAMPTON TOWN 1   TORQUAY UNITED 1
Northampton: Jones; Smalley, Barron; Lowery, Dennison, Coley; Roberts,
Heaselgrave, Briscoe, Jenkins, Fowler.   **Scorer:** Heaselgrave
Torquay: Joslin; Head, Calland; Towers, Evans, Stuttard; Lewis, Shaw, Conley, Hill,
Mercer.   **Scorer:** Hill
Extra time played. Poor attendance due to local bus strike.

20. December 1947   F. A. Cup (Round 2 replay)   Plainnmoor   7,000
TORQUAY UNITED 2   NORTHAMPTON TOWN 0
Torquay: Joslin; Head, Calland; Towers. Evans, Stutard; Lewis, Shaw, Conley, Hill,
Mercer.   **Scorers:** Hill, Mercer.
Northampton: Jones, Smalley, Barron; Lowery, Dennison, Coley; Roberts,
Heaselgrave, Briscoe, Jenkins, Fowler.
Dennison injured. Spent most of the second half limping.

25 December 1947   Division 3 South   Selhurst Park   15,095
CRYSTAL PALACE 1   NORTHAMPTON TOWN 0
Crystal Palace: Graham; Harding, Dawes; Buckley, Millbank, Reece; Mycock, Lewis,
Robson, Kurz, Clough.   **Scorer:** Mycock
Northampton: Jones, Smalley, Barron; Sankey, Lowery, Coley; Roberts, King, Briscoe,
Heaselgrave, Fowler.
Both Dick Graham and Fred Dawes were on the Cobblers books, before the war.

31. J anuary 1948   Division 3 South   Vicarage Road   13,834
WATFORD 1   NORTHAMPTON TOWN 1
Watford: Calvert; Harris, Jones; Eggleston, Hunt, Osborne; Davie, Paton, Thomas,
Hartley, Cheney.   **Scorer:** Cheney
Northampton: Jones, Smalley, Fisher; Lowery, Dennison, Coley; Briscoe, King,
Hughes, Jenkins, Fowler.   **Scorer:** Hughes
Peter Fisher makes his debut. Watford parade SEVEN debutants.

7. February 1948   Division 3 South   County Ground   6,661

NORTHAMPTON TOWN 4   BRIGHTON AND HOVE ALBION 0
Northampton: Jones; Smalley, Fisher; Lowery, Dennison, Coley; King, Hughes,
Briscoe, Jenkins, Fowler.   **Scorers:** Briscoe 2, Hughes, Lowery
Brighton: Baldwin; Marriott, Willemse. James, Dugnolle, Darling, Clelland, Hacking,
Thomas, Booth, Hanlon.
Booth of Brighton left the field with a broken collar bone.

14. February 1948   Division 3 South   Carrow Road   23,470

NORWICH CITY 2   NORTHAMPON TOWN 3
Norwich: Nethercott; Mansfield, Tobin; Robinson, Low, Dutton; Church, Kinsey, Driver,
Eyre, Morgan.   **Scorers:** Kinsey, Eyre
Northampton: Jones, Smalley, Barron; Stanton, Lowery, Coley; King, English,
Briscoe, Hughes, Fowler.   **Scorers:** Briscoe, Hughes, Fowler
Cobblers take a 2-0 lead, Norwich pull back to 2-2, Briscoe hits the winner.

21. February 1948   Division 3 South   County Ground   5,149

NORTHAMPTON TOWN 1   BRISTOL ROVERS 3
Northampton: Jones; Smalley, Barron; Coley, Lowery, Stanton; King, English. Briscoe,
Hughes, Fowler.   **Scorer:** Hughes
Bristol Rovers: Weare; Jones, Watkins; Pitt, Winter, McArthur; Pethbridge, Hodges,
Lambden, Morgan, Watling.   **Scorers:** Pitt (p), Lambden, Morgan.
So cold, only 6 people standing on the cricket side of the ground.

28. February 1948   Division 3 South   County Ground   8,353

NORTHAMPTON TOWN 2   WALSALL 1
Northampton: Jones; Smalley, Barron; Coley, Lowery, Blunt; King, Heaselgrave,
Briscoe, Hughes, Fowler.   **Scorers:** King, Hughes.
Walsall: Lewis; Walters, Male; Crutchley, Foulkes, Newman; Conde, Devlin, Massart,
Lishman, Wilshall.   **Scorer:** Devlin.
Blunt and Heaselgrave return to the Cobblers side.

6. March 1948   Division 3 South   Brisbane Road   14,714

LEYTON ORIENT 5   NORTHAMPTON TOWN 0
Leyton Orient: Tolliday, Banner, Ritson; Bacon, Sales, Stroud; Chapman, Richardson,
Neary, Naylor, Pullen.   **Scorers:** Naylor 2, Neary, Pullen, o.g.
Northampton: Jones; Smalley, Barron; Blunt, Lowery, Coley; King, Smith, Briscoe,
Hughes, Fowler.
Second time this season the club have conceded five goals

13. March 1948   Division 3 South   County Ground   6,163

NORTHAMPTON TOWN 3   EXETER CITY 1
Northampton: Ansell; Smalley, Barron; Lowery, Dennison, Coley; King, Heaselgrave,
Briscoe, Hughes, Fowler.   **Scorers:** Briscoe 2, Hughes
Exeter: O'Singleton; Johnstone, Rowe; Bartholomew, Gibson, Walker, Hutchings, Evans,
Dymond, Mackay, Regan.   **Scorer:** Regan
Jack Ansell makes his Northampton Town, debut.

18. March 1948   Division 3 South   County Ground   6,241

NORTHAMPTON TOWN 0   SWINDON TOWN 0
Northampton: Ansell; Smalley, Barron; Lowery, Dennison, Coley; King, Hughes,
Briscoe, Heaselgrave, Fowler.
Swindon: Boulton; Young, Lloyd; Kaye, Ithell, Nunn; Maguire, Dryden, Owen, Lucas,
Bain.
Gwyn Hughes injured after just 10 minutes.

20. March 1948   Division 3 South   Somerset Park   8,567
NEWPORT COUNTY 1   NORTHAMPTON TOWN 2
Newport: Loveman; Wilcox, Emmanuel; Joy, Smith, McBlain; Shergold, Rofi, Carr, Allen, Lewis.   **Scorer:** Allen
Northampton: Ansell; Smalley, Barron; Lowery, Dennison, Coley; King, Smith, Briscoe, Heaselgrave, Fowler.   **Scorers:** Coley (p), Briscoe.
Bus strike in Newport, affects the attendance.

26. March. 1948   Division 3 South   Elm Park   16,774
READING 1   NORTHAMPTON TOWN 1
Reading: McBride; Goldberg, Gulliver; Green, Ratcliffe, Deverall; Fisher, Edelston, Price, Dix, Amor.   **Scorer:** Fisher
Northampton: Ansell; Smalley, Barron, Sankey, Dennison, Coley; King, Smith, Briscoe, Heaselgrave, Fowler.   **Scorer:** King
Future Cobblers player Maurice Edelston is in the Reading team.

27. March 1948   Division 3 South   County Ground   9,104
NORTHAMPTON TOWN 2   SOUTHEND UNITED 0
Northampton: Ansell; Smalley, Barron; Sankey, Dennison, Coley; King, Smith, Briscoe, Heaselgrave, Fowler.   **Scorer:** Coley, 2 (2p)
Southend: Hankey; Beach, Linton; Montgomery, Sheard, Pryde; Tippett, Bennett, Grant, Thompson, Edwards.
Bill Coley converts two penalties, both in the first half.

29. March. 1948   Division 3 South   County Ground   8,855
NORTHAMPTON TOWN 1   READING 1
Northampton: Ansell, Smalley, Barron; Lowery, Dennison, Coley; King, Smith, Briscoe, Heaselgrave, Fowler.   **Scorer:** Briscoe
Reading: McBride; Goldberg, Gulliver; Green, Ratcliffe, Glidden; Smith, Barney, Price, Edelston, Deverall.   **Scorer:** Barney
Cobblers sixth game without defeat.

3. April 1948   Division 3 South   Meadow Lane   30,903
NOTTS COUNTY 3   NORTHAMPTON TOWN 2
Notts County: Brown; Southwell, Howe; Gannon, Corkhill, Pimbley; Freeman, Sewell, Lawton, Marsh, Cumner.   **Scorers:** Lawton 2, o.g.
Northampton: Ansell; Smalley, Fisher; Coley, Lowery, Bowen; King, Smith, Briscoe, Heaselgrave, Fowler.   **Scorers:** Smith, Fowler.
Dave Bowen's debut. Tommy scores equaliser in dying minutes, Lawton hits winner.

8. April 1948   Division 3 South   County Ground   11,260
NORTHAMPTON TOWN 1   QUEENS PARK RANGERS 1
Northampton: Ansell; Smalley, Baron; Coley, Dennison, Bowen; Smith, King, Heaselgrave, Lowery, Fowler.   **Scorer:** Coley
Q.P.R.: Saphin; Powell G, Jefferson; Powell I, Smith G, Smith A: Boxshall, Stewart, Heath, Mills, Hartburn.   **Scorer:** Hartburn.
Rangers stay top of the division

10. April 1948   Division 3 South   County Ground   8,506
NORTHAMPTON TOWN 0   SWANSEA TOWN 1
Northampton: Ansell; Smalley, Barron; Lowery, Dennison, Bowen; King, Smith, Jenkins, Heaselgrave, Fowler.
Swansea: Hooper; Feeney, Keane; Paul, Weston, Burns; Comley, McGory, Powell, Lucas, Morris.   **Scorer:** Powell
Cobblers fifth home defeat at home

12. April 1948   Maunsell cup (semi final)   London Road   7,600

PETERBOROUGH UNITED 5   NORTHAMPTON TOWN 1
Peterborough: Ferguson; Bryan, Parrott; Rickards, Warnes, Rawson; Burton, Brookbanks, Frieman, Osmond, Ranshaw.   **Scorers:** Freiman 2, Ranshaw, Brookbank, o.g.
Northampton: Ansell; Smalley, Fisher; Bowen, Dennison, Sankey; King, English, Roberts, Heaselgrave, Fowler.   **Scorer:** Roberts.
Bob Dennison off injured after just 10 minutes.

17. April 1948   Division 3 South   Dean Court   14,818

BOURNEMOUTH & BOSCOMBE ATHLETIC 2   NORTHAMPTON TOWN 0
Bournemouth: Bird, Marsden, Sanaghan; Blizzard, Wilson, Percival; Cross, Blair, Barclay, Lunn, McDonald.   **Scorer:** Cross, Blair
Northampton: Ansell; Smalley, Fisher, Blunt, Lowery, Bowen. English, King, Roberts, Heaselgrave, Fowler.
Now five games without a win.

21. April 1948   Division 3 South   Portman Road   9,285

IPSWICH TOWN 5   NORTHAMPTON TOWN 2
Ipswich: Brown; Rumbold, Parry; Perett, Bell, Bird; Day, Jennings, Pole, Parker, Little.   **Scorers:** Jennings 2, Day, Pole, o.g.
Northampton: Ansell; Smalley, Fisher;Gillespie, Thompson, Blunt; Roberts, King, Hughes, Heaselgrave, Fowler.   **Scorer:** King 2.
Gillespie makes his Cobblers debut, Jennings of Ipswich is an ex-Cobbler.

24. April 1948   Division 3 South   County Ground   4,410

NORTHAMPTON TOWN 4   IPSWICH TOWN 2
Northampton: Scott; Smalley, Fisher; Bowen, Lowery, Blunt; Roberts, King, Hughes, Heaselgrave, Fowler.   **Scorers:** King 3, Heaselgrave.
Ipswich: Brown, Rumbold, Parry; Perett, Bell, Baird; Day, Jennings, Pole, Parker, Little.   **Scorers:** Day, Parker.
Bobby King's first hat trick for Northampton.

29. April 1948   Division 3 South   County Ground   6,674

NORTHAMPTON TOWN 3   BOURNEMOUTH AND BOSCOMBE ATHLETIC 6
Northampton: Scott; Smalley, Fisher; Blunt, Lowery, Hughes; Roberts, Smith, King, Heaselgrave, Fowler.   **Scorer:** Hughes 3.
Bournemouth: Bird; Marsden, Sanaghan; Blizzard, Wilson, Percival, Cross, Blair, Milligan, Lunn, McDonald.   **Scorers:** Milligan 2, Cross, McDonald, Blair, Lunn.
The most goals Northampton had conceded in a league match at the County Ground.

1. May. 1948   Division 3 South   Ashton Gate   8, 392

BRISTOL CITY 1   NORTHAMPTON TOWN 1
Bristol City: Clack; Stone, Bailey; Thomas, Morgan, Kearney; Collins, Townsend, Clark, Williams C, Williams S.   **Scorer:** Townsend.
Northampton: Ansell; Smalley, Fisher; Bowen, Lowery, Blunt; English, King, Hughes, Heaselgrave, Fowler.   **Scorer:** King.
Cobblers finish five points away from re-election.

1948-1949
21. August 1948   Division 3 South   St. James Park   9.588

EXETER CITY 5   NORTHAMPTON TOWN 1
Exeter: Hoyle; Johnstone, Rowe; Bartholemew, Gibson, Walker; Hutchings, Smart, Johnston, Mackay, Regan.   **Scorers:** Regan 3, Johnston, Smart
Northampton: Williams; Smalley, Aldridge, Lowery, James, Coley; Roberts, Smith, Freiman, Hughes, Fowler.   **Scorer:** Fowler.
Tommy scores. Cobblers field 4 debutants, including Freiman, first Russian in the league

| 26. August 1948 | Division 3 South | Carrow Road | 22,517 |

NORWICH CITY 2   NORTHAMPTON TOWN 1
Norwich: Nethercott; Morgan, Tobin; Kinsey. Low, Arnes; Ryder, Driver, Hollis, Eyre, Church.   **Scorer:** Hollis 2
Northampton: Williams; Stanton, Aldridge; Bowen, James, Coley; King, Smith, Freiman, Hughes, Fowler.   **Scorer:** Freiman.
Three players out injured , Stanton makes his debut.

| 28. August 1948 | Division 3 South | Ashton Gate | 22,663 |

BRISTOL CITY 3   NORTHAMPTON TOWN 0
Bristol City: Marks; Guy, Bailey; Edwards, Roberts, Kearney; Boxshall, Townsend, Clark, Thomas, Williams.   **Scorer:** Townsend 2. Thomas.
Northampton: Williams; Smalley, Barron; Bowen, Lowery, Coley; King, Smith, Freiman, Hughes, Fowler.
Played in brilliant sunshine. Bill Barron returns from his season with Northants CCC

| 2. September 1948 | Division 3 South | County Ground | 7,127 |

NORTHAMPTON TOWN 1   NORWICH CITY 0
Northampton: Ansell; Smalley, Barron; Bowen, Collins, Coley; English, Smith, Freiman, Thompson, Fowler.   **Scorer:** Smith
Norwich: Nethercott; Robinson, Tobin; Pickwick, Low, Armes; Golding, Driver, Hollis, Eyre, Church.
Bill Smith scores on debut. Coley misses a penalty, played in a heavy rain storm.

| 4 September 1948 | Division 3 South | County Ground | 9,410 |

NORTHAMPTON TOWN 0   SWINDON TOWN 1
Northampton: Ansell; Smalley, Barron; Bowen, Collins, Coley; English, Smith, Freiman, Thompson, Fowler.
Swindon: Boulton; White, Young; Cowie, Ithell, Kaye; Lunn, Dawson, Owen, Jones, Williams.   **Scorer:** Owen.
The Cobblers have two goals disallowed, and Coley also misses another penalty.

| 7. September 1948 | Division 3 South | Southend Stadium 8,454 |

SOUTHEND UNITED 0   NORTHAMPTON TOWN 1
Southend: Nash; Beach, Walton; French, Thornhill, Pritchard;Tippett, Dudley, Montgomery, Brown, Bell.
Northampton: Ansell; Smalley, Barron; Blunt, Collins, Coley; King, Smith, Freiman, Hughes, Fowler.   **Scorer:** Freiman
The Cobblers first away win since March.

| 11. September 1948 | Division 3 South | Brisbane Road | 12,747 |

LEYTON ORIENT 0   NORTHAMPTON TOWN 3
Leyton Orient: Newton, Banner, Ritson; Bacon, Davidson, Deverall; Dryden, Taylor, Johnson, Connelly, McGeachy.
Northampton: Ansell; Smalley, Barron; Blunt, Lowery, Coley, King, Smith, Freiman, Hughes, Fowler.   **Scorers:** Freiman, Hughes, Fowler
Len Ritson the Orient full back breaks his leg, he later has it amputated

| 16. September 1948 | Division 3 South | County Ground | 8,850 |

NORTHAMPTON TOWN 2   SOUTHEND UNITED 2
Northampton: Ansell; Smalley, Barron; Blunt, Lowery, Coley; King, James, Freiman, Hughes, Fowler.   **Scorers:** James, Coley
Southend: Nash; Beach,Walton; Goodyear, Sheard, Montgomery; Tippett, Dudley, Grant, French, Lane.   **Scorer:** Dudley 2
Bill Coley scores the Cobblers equaliser with just 3 minutes left.

Career Results

18. September 1948   Division 3 South   County Ground   9,964
NORTHAMPTON TOWN 2   PORT VALE 2
Northampton: Ansell; Smalley, Barron; Blunt, Lowery, Coley; Briscoe, Smith D,
Freiman, Hughes, Fowler.   **Scorers:** Briscoe, o.g.
Port Vale: Heppell; Cheadle, Potts, McGarry, Hayward, Martin; Allen, Keeley, Aveyard,
Polk, Halligan.   **Scorer:** Aveyard 2
Smalley missed a penalty. All four goals scored in first 26 minutes of the game.

25. September 1948   Division 3 South   The Den   25,690
MILLWALL 3   NORTHAMPTON TOWN 2
Millwall: Hobins; Evans, Fisher; Reeves, Morton, Brolly; Johnson, Hurrell, Constantine,
Brown, Mansfield.   **Scorers:** Constantine 2 , Mansfield
Northampton: Ansell; Smalley, Barron; Blunt. Lowery, Coley; Briscoe, Smith D,,
Freiman, Hughes, Fowler.   **Scorers:** Smith, Hughes.
Brolly was a Cobblers guest during the war. Millwall's third win of the season.

2. October 1948   Division 3 South   County Ground   7,924
NORTHAMPTON TOWN 2   ALDERSHOT 0
Northampton: Ansell; Jackson, Barron, Lowery, Collins, Coley; Briscoe, Smith D,
Freiman, Smith W, Fowler.   **Scorers:** Briscoe, Smith D.
Aldershot: Reynolds; Rogers, Shepherd; Sherwood, Rowland, Cropley; Hobbs, Sears,
Rawcliffe, White, Sinclair.
The crowd was low because of a counter attraction at Silverstone. Jackson's debut.

 9. October 1948   Division 3 South   County Ground   9, 589
NORTHAMPTON TOWN 1   IPSWICH TOWN 1
Northampton: Ansell; Jackson, Barron; Lowery, Collins, Coley; Briscoe, Smith D,
Freiman, Smith W, Fowler.   **Scorer:** Smith D
Ipswich: Brown; Rumbold, Parry; Bell, O'Mahoney, Perrett; Brown, Dempsey, Jennings,
Parker, McGinn.   **Scorer:** Parker.
The Cobblers have a goal ruled offside and miss a penalty.

16. October 1948   Division 3 South   Dean Court   16,803
BOURNEMOUTH & BOSCOMBE ATHLETIC 5   NORTHAMPTON TOWN 2
Bournemouth: Bird, Cunningham, Sanaghan; Woodward, Stirling, Percival; Rampling,
Blair, McGibbon, Bennett, Cheney.   **Scorers:** McGibbon 2, Blair, Rampling, Bennett
Northampton: Ansell; Smalley, Barron; Lowery, Collins, Coley; Briscoe, Smith D,
Smith W, Hughes, Fowler.   **Scorer:** Smith D, 2
Cheney makes his debut for Cherries, last season made debut for Watford v Cobblers.

23. October 1948   Division 3 South   County Ground   8,178
NORTHAMPTON TOWN 2   NEWPORT COUNTY 1
Northampton: Ansell; Smalley, Barron; Lowery, Collins, Coley; Briscoe, Smith D,
Smith W, Hughes, Fowler.   **Scorer:** Smith W. 2
Newport: Loveman, Wilcox, Hayward; Morrall, Roffi, Newall; Williams, Comley, Parker,
Carr, Harper.   **Scorer:** Parker (p)
Ex Cobbler Alf Morrall is in the Newport team. Parker scores his 9th goal of the season.

30. October. 1948   Division 3 South   Eastville Stadium   15,363
BRISTOL ROVERS 1   NORTHAMPTON TOWN 0
Bristol Rovers: Weare; Bamford, Fox; Pitt, Warren, McArthur; Petherbridge, Hodges,
Lambden, Morgan, Watling,   **Scorer:** Morgan
Northampton: Ansell; Smalley, Barron; Thompson, Lowery, Coley; Briscoe, Smith D.
Smith W. Hughes, Fowler.
Rovers ninth win of the season, and the Cobblers seventh defeat

6. November 1948   Division 3 South   County Ground   8,365
NORTHAMPTON TOWN 1   READING 2
Northampton: Ansell; Smalley, Barron; Thompson, Collins, Coley; Smith W, Smith D, Freiman, Hughes, Fowler.   **Scorer:** Smith W
Reading: Marks: Gaunt, Gulliver; Henly, Brice, Reeve; Jordon, Edelston, MacPhee, Dix, Amor.   **Scorer:** MacPhee 2
Reading's fourth conseutive win, and Sixth game without defeat

13. November 1948   Division 3 South   Vetch Field   23,095
SWANSEA TOWN   1   NORTHAMPTON TOWN   0
Swansea: Parry, Newall, Keane; Paul, Weston, Burns; O'Driscoll, McGrory, Richards, Lucas, Scrine.   **Scorer:** Richards
Northampton: Ansell; Smalley, Barron; Thompson, Lowery, Coley; Smith W. Smith D, Freiman, Hughes, Fowler.
Ansell and W. Smith both go off injured, Freiman in goal for last 35 minutes.

20. November 1948   Division 3 South   County Ground   8.437
NORTHAMPTON TOWN 1   WATFORD 1
Northampton: Ansell; Smalley, Barron; James, Lowery, Coley; Smith W, Smith D, Freiman, Hughes, Fowler.   **Scorer:** Smith D.
Watford: Rigg; Harris, Oliver; Eggleston, Ratcliffe, Paton; High, Davies, Thomas, Woodruffe, Cumner.   **Scorer:** High
Inclement weather affected the attendance, it was a poor game.

27. November 1948   F. A. Cup (Round 1)   County Ground   10,300
NORTHAMPTON TOWN 2   DULWICH HAMLET 1
Northampton: Ansell; Smalley, Barron; Thompson, Lowery, Coley; English, Smith D, Briscoe, Smith W, Fowler.   **Scorers:** Smith D, Smith W.
Dulwich Hamlet: Freeman; Setters, Penney; Whitworth, Hall, Brown; Davies, Pheebey, Green,Connett, Beglan.   **Scorer:** Davies.
The game started in thick fog, but it lifted during the game.

4. December 1948   Division 3 South   County Ground   11,934
NORTHAMPTON TOWN 0   TORQUAY UNITED 0
Northampton: Ansell; Smalley, Barron; Stanton, McCoy, Lowery; English, Smith D, Garrett, Smith W, Fowler.
Torquay: Davis, Stuttard, Topping; Towers, Head, Hill; Lewis, Collins, Conley, Shaw, Cameron.
McCoy makes his debut for Northampton, Archie Garrett returns, Lowery injured in match.

11. December, 1948   F. A. Cup (Round 2)   Field Mill   13,501
MANSFIELD TOWN 2   NORTHAMPTON TOWN 1
Mansfield: Wright; Chessell, Jones; Devan, Grogan, Croft; Wheatley, Banks, Mercer, Oscroft, McArthur.   **Scorers:** Mercer, Oscroft.
Northampton: Ansell; Smalley, Barron; Blunt, McCoy, Coley; English, Smith D, Briscoe, Smith D, Fowler.   **Scorer:** Smith W.
Extra time played, 1-1 after 90 minutes, Cobblers disputed Manfield's winner.

18. December 1948   Division 3 South   County Ground   7,876
NORTHAMPTON TOWN 4   EXETER CITY 0
Northampton: Ansell; Smalley, Barron; Smith D, McCoy, Stanton; English, Smith W. Garrett, Freiman, Fowler.   **Scorers:** Garrett 2, English, Fowler.
Exeter City: Hoyle; Warren, Rowe; Bartholemew, Walker, Fallon; Dymond, Harrower, Smith A, Mackay, Regan.
First time the Cobblers scored 4 goals in a game since April.

25. December 1948   Division 3 South   County Ground   17,724

NORTHAMPTON TOWN 1   NOTTS COUNTY 2

Northampton: Ansell; Smalley, Barron; Lowery, McCoy, Stanton; English, Smith D, Garrett, Smith W, Fowler   **Scorer:** Garrett.

Notts County: Smith R.: Southwell, Purvis; Gannon, Baxter, Adamson. Houghton, Sewell, Lawton, Hold Johnston.   **Scorers:** Johnston, Sewell.

Receipts for the game £1,530, best home attendance since meeting County last season.

27. December 1948   Division 3 South   Meadow Lane   31,171

NOTTS COUNTY 2   NORTHAMPTON TOWN 0

Notts County: Smith R: Southwell, Purvis; Gannon, Baxter, Adamson; Houghton, Sewell, Lawton, Hold, Johnston.   **Scorers:** Hold, Sewell.

Northampton: Ansell, Smalley, Barron; Smith D. McCoy, Stanton; English, King, Garrett, Hughes, Fowler.

Biggest crowd at a Cobblers game since the war. Stanton goes off injured.

1. January 1949   Division 3 South   County Ground   6,901

NORTHAMPTON TOWN 3   BRISTOL CITY 1

Northampton: Ansell; Smalley, Barron; Smith D., McCoy, Blunt. English, King, Garrett, Hughes, Fowler.   **Scorers:** King, Garrett, Fowler.

Bristol City: Clack; Guy, Bailey; Edwards, Peacock, Davies; Boxshall , Townsend, Clark, Barney, Williams.   **Scorer:** Townsend

Game spoiled by wind, rain and a very heavy ground.

15. January 1949   Division 3 South   County Ground (Swindon)   14,306

SWINDON TOWN 2   NORTHAMPTON TOWN 2

Swindon Town: Burton; White, Young; Cowie, Ithell, Foxton; Lunn, Dawson, Owen, Jones, Bain.   **Scorers:** Owen, o.g.

Northampton: Ansell; Smalley, Barron; Smith, McCoy, Blunt; English, King, Garrett, Hughes, Fowler.   **Scorers:** King, o.g.

The Cobblers first away point since September 1948.

22. January 1949   Division 3 South   County Ground   8,661

NORTHAMPTON TOWN 4   LEYTON ORIENT 1

Northampton: Ansell; Smaley, Barron; Blunt, McCoy, Coley; English, Smith D, Garrett, King, Fowler.   **Scorers:** English, Smith, Garrett, King

Leyon Orient: Newton; Haslam, Davidson; Bacon, Rooney, Deverall; Dryden, Connelly, Neary, Naylor, McGeachy.   **Scorer:** Neary

Tom Smith resigns after the game, after a dispute with the directors.

29. January 1949   Division 3 South   Selhurst Park   13,972

CRYSTAL PALACE 2   NORTHAMPTON TOWN 2

Crystal Palace: Bumstead; Harding, Dawes ; Lewis, Bassett, Buckley; Broughton, Mullen, Thomas. Kurz, Clough.   **Scorers:** Lewis, Kurz.

Northampton: Ansell; Smalley, Barron; Blunt, McCoy, Coley; English, Smith D, Garrett, King, Fowler.   **Scorer:** Garrett 2.

Linesman failed to appear, Harry Thompson ran the line, Palace had 3 goals disallowed

5. February 1949   Division 3 South   Vale Park   9,369

PORT VALE 1   NORTHAMPTON TOWN 0

Port Vale: Heppell; Butler, Potts; McGarry, Hayward, Martin; Allen, Aveyard, Cheadle Polk, Hulligan.   **Scorer:** Allen.

Northampton: Ansell; Smalley, Barron; Blunt, McCoy, Coley; English, Smith D. Garrett, King, Fowler.

Bob Dennison's first match as manager.

12. February 1949   Division 3 South   County Ground   8,694

NORTHAMPTON TOWN 0   WALSALL 1

Northampton: Ansell; Smalley, Barron; Blunt, McCoy, Coley; Smith W.,Smith D., Garrett, King, Fowler.

Walsall: Lewis; Jones, Walters; Methley, Foulkes, Newman; Chapman, Mullard, Milligan, Clark, Condie.   **Scorer:** Clark.

English not yet recovered from injury, W. Smith comes into the side.

19. February 1949   Division 3 South   County Ground   10,775

NORTHAMPTON TOWN 4   MILLWALL 0

Northampton: Ansell; Smalley, Barron; Blunt, McCoy, Coley; Smith D, Smith W, Briscoe, King, Fowler.   **Scorers:** Fowler 3, Smith D.

Millwall: Finlayson; Fisher, Tyler, Reeves, McMillan, Brolly;Johnson , Simmonds, Constantine, Morgan, Mansfield.

Tommy nets his first league hat trick. The last two goals coming in the last 5 minutes.

26. February 1949   Division 3 South   Recreation Ground   5,635

ALDERSHOT 3   NORTHAMPTON TOWN 1

Aldershot: Reynolds; Rogers, Jales; White, Billington, Cropley; Hassell, Sears, Rawclife, Welsh, Sinclair.   **Scorer:** Rawcliffe 3.

Northampton: Ansell; Smalley, Barron; Blunt, McCoy, Coley; Smith W, Smith D, Briscoe, King, Fowler.   **Scorer:** Briscoe

Aldershot's first home win since October the 9th,

5. March 1949   Division 3 South   Portman Road   10,439

IPSWICH TOWN 4   NORTHAMPTON TOWN 2

Ipswich: Brown; Rumbold, Parry; Perett, Bell, Baird; Brown, Parker S, Jennings, Parker T, Little.   **Scorers:** Jennings 2, Parker S, Parker T.

Northampton: Ansell; Smalley, Barron; Blunt, McCoy, Coley; Briscoe, Smith D, Garrett, King Fowler.   **Scorers:** Garrett, Fowler.

Cobblers go two up, Ipswich pull level to 2-2 after 80 minutes, then score twice!

12. March 1949   Division 3 South   County Ground   8,473

NORTHAMPTON TOWN 1   BOURNEMOUTH & BOSCOMBE ATHLETIC 0

Northampton: Ansell; Smalley, Barron; Lowery, McCoy, Coley; Smith W, Smith D, Garrett,King, Fowler.   **Scorer:** Smith W.

Bournemouth: Bird; Cunningham, Sanaghan; Woodward, Stirling, Percival; Stephens, Reid, McGibbon, Blakeman, Hanlon.

Cobblers second win in seven games.

19. March 1949   Division 3 South   Somerset Park   14,869

NEWPORT COUNTY 2   NORTHAMPTON TOWN 0

Newport County: Grant; Bradford, Hayward; Roffi, Wilcox;Newall, Williams, Comley, Parker, Carr, Harper.   **Scorer:** Carr 2.

Northampton: Ansell; Smalley, Barron; Lowery, McCoy, Coley, Smith W, Smith D, Garrett, King, Fowler.

Carr of Newport scores both goals in the first 25 minutes of the game.

26. March 1949   Division 3 South   County Ground   7,425

NORTHAMPTON TOWN 0   BRISTOL ROVERS 1

Northampton: Ansell; Smalley, Barron; Lowery, McCoy, Blunt; Smith W, Smith D, Garrett, King, Fowler.

Bristol Rovers: Weare; Bamford, Fox; Pitt, Warren, McArthur, Petherbridge, Hodges, Lambden, Morgan, Watling.   **Scorer:** Lambden

Coley went down with Flu at the last minute, Blunt drafted in.

2. April 1949   Division 3 South   Elm Park   14,148

READING 1   NORTHAMPTON TOWN 0
Reading: Marks; Clover, Gulliver; Henley, Brice, Green; Fisher, Edelston, Blackman, Glidden, Allison.   **Scorer:** o.g.
Northampton: Ansell; Smalley, Barron; Smith, McCoy, Coley, English, Smith W, Garrett, King, Fowler.
Manager Bob Dennison shuffles the forward line.

6. April 1949   Maunsell Cup (semi final)   London Road.

PETERBOROUGH UNITED 0   NORTHAMPTON TOWN 0
Peterborough: Ferguson; Bryan, Parrott; Cockcroft, Fallon, Woods; Brookbank, Rickards, Robinson,Vaughan, Guest.
Northampton: Ansell, Smalley, Barron; Smith D, McCoy, Coley; English, Hughes, Freiman, Garrett, Fowler.
Peterborough players argue with the referee over a decision, game held up 10 minutes.

8. April 1949   Division 3 South   County Ground   10,194

NORTHAMPTON TOWN 0   SWANSEA TOWN 1
Northampton: Ansell; Smalley, Barron; Smith D, McCoy, Coley; English, Smith W, Briscoe, Garrett, Fowler.
Swansea: Canning, Elwell, Keane: Paul, Weston, Burns; O'Driscoll, McGrory, Richards, Lucas, Scrine.   **Scorer:** Richards.
Promotion almost assured for Swansea

15. April 1949   Division 3 South   Goldstone Ground   18,271

BRIGHTON & HOVE ALBION 0   NORTHAMPTON TOWN 0
Brighton: Baldwin, Tennant, Willense; Willard, Whent, Daniels, Roberts, Lancelotte, McCurley, McNichol, Mansell.
Northampton: Ansell; Smalley, Barron; Smith, McCoy, Coley; English, King, Briscoe, Garrett, Fowler.
Tommy was injured during the game and taken off.

1949- 1950

8. October 1949   Division 3 South   County Ground   13,773

NORTHAMPTON TOWN 1   IPSWICH TOWN 2
Northampton: Ansell; Smalley, Southam; Candlin, McCoy, Coley; King, Smith, McCulloch, Murphy, Fowler.   **Scorer:** King
Ipswich: Brown; Bell, Mitchell; Baird, Smith, Parker T: Brown, Jennings, Parker S, Little, O'Brien.   **Scorers:** O'Brien, Parker S.
Tommy's first league game for nearly 6 months.

15. October 1949   Division 3 South   St. James Park   8,353

EXETER CITY 1   NORTHAMPTON TOWN 3
Exeter: Singleton; Johnstone, Rowe; Doyle, Davey, Greenwood; Hutchings, Harrower, Smith, McLelland, Regan.   **Scorer:** Regan
Northampton: Ansell; Smalley, Southam; Candlin, McCoy, Coley; Smith D, Garrett, McCulloch, Murphy, Fowler.   **Scorers:** McCulloch 2, Murphy.
The Cobblers third away win of the season.

22. October 1949   Division 3 South   County Ground   11,950

NORTHAMPTON TOWN 3   LEYTON ORIENT 0

Northampton: Ansell; Smalley, Southam; Candlin, McCoy, Coley; Smith, Garrett, McCulloch, Murphy, Fowler.   **Scorer:** Garrett, McCulloch, Murphy.
Leyton Orient: Gerula; Banner, Walton; Taylor, Rooney, Trailer; Neary, Bacon, Sherratt, Dryden, Wood.
All three goals were laid on by Dave Smith.

---

29. October 1949   Division 3 South   Elm Park   18,636

READING 3   NORTHAMPTON TOWN 1

Reading: Marks; Wicks, Gaunt; Henley, Brice, Reeves; Fisher, Edelston, Blackman, Allen, Amor.   **Scorers:** Allen, Edelston, Amor.
Northampton: Ansell; Smalley, Southam; Candlin, McCoy, Hughes; Smith D, Garrett, McCulloch, Murphy, Fowler.   **Scorer:** McCulloch
Candlin protested Reading's first goal so strongly, he was booked!

---

5. November 1949   Division 3 South   County Ground   9,722

NORTHAMPTON TOWN 0   WATFORD 0

Northampton: Ansell; Smalley, Southam; Candlin, McCoy, Hughes; Smith, Garrett. McCulloch, Murphy, Fowler.
Watford: Morton; Eggleston, Harper; Paton, Oliver, Fisher; Jones, Worthington, Thomas, Brown, Hartburn.
Bert Mitchell returns to full fitness, and replaces Tommy for the next game.

---

11. April 1950   Division 3 South   County Ground   11,167

NORTHAMPTON TOWN 3   NORWICH CITY 1

Northampton: Ansell; Smalley, Barron; Candlin, Collins, Coley; Mitchell, Dixon, McCulloch, Murphy, Fowler.   **Scorers:** Murphy 2, Coley.
Norwich: Nethercott; Duffey, Lewis; Pickwick, Low, Ashman; Hollis, Kinsey, Owen, Dutton, Dolby.   **Scorer:** Hollis
Tommy plays his first game for 5 months, Ben Collins plays his first game of the season.

---

15. April 1950   Division 3 South   County Ground   9,622

NORTHAMPTON TOWN 2   BRISTOL ROVERS 0

Northampton: Ansell; Smalley, Barron; Candlin, Collins, Coley; Mitchell, Dixon, McCulloch, Murphy, Fowler.   **Scorers:** Mitchell (p), Fowler.
Bristol Rovers: Lilley; Barford, Fox; Pitt, Warren, McCourt, Tippett, Bradford, Parsons, Watkins, Pethbridge.
Adam McCulloch injured during the game.

---

22. April 1950   Division 3 South   Southend Stadium   13,195

SOUTHEND UNITED 1   NORTHAMPTON TOWN 2

Southend: Hankey, Lindsay, Walton; Wallbank, Sheard, French; Davies, McAlinden, Wakefield, Stubbs, Clough.   **Scorer:** McAlinden (p)
Northampton: Ansell; Smalley, Barron; Candlin, Collins, Coley; Mitchell, Dixon, Garrett, Murphy, Fowler.   **Scorers:** Garrett, Murphy.
Notts County also won and are guaranteed the Third Division South championship.

---

27. April 1950   Division 3 South   Meadow Lane   31,843

NOTTS COUNTY 2   NORTHAMPTON TOWN 0

Notts County: Smith; Deans, Rigby; Chapman, Baxter, Adamson; Broome, Sewell, Lawton, Evans, Johnston.   **Scorer:** Lawton 2
Northampton: Ansell; Smalley, Barron; Candlin, Collins, Coley; Mitchell, Dixon, Garrett, Murphy, Fowler.
That man 'Lawton' grabs a brace of goals.

29. April 1950   Division 3 South   County Ground   9,971
NORTHAMPTON TOWN 5   NOTTS COUNTY 1
Northampton: Ansell; Smalley, Barron; Candlin, Collins, Coley; Mitchell, Dixon, Garrett, Murphy, Fowler.   **Scorers:** Mitchell 2, Dixon 2, Garrett.
Notts County: Smith; Deans, Rigby; Chapman, Baxter, Adamson. Broome, Simpson, Evans W, Evans F, Johnston.   **Scorer:** Broome
Sweet revenge! Bert Mitchell missed scoring a hat trick when he missed a penalty.

1. May, 1950   Division 3 South   Eastville Stadium   11,679
BRISTOL ROVERS 0   NORTHAMPTON TOWN 0
Bristol Rovers: Lilley; Bamford, Fox; Pitt, Warren, McCourt; Tipett, Bradford, Parsons, Hodges, Lockier.
Northampton: Ansell; Smalley, Barron; Candlin, Collins, Coley; Mitchell, Dixon, Garrett, Murphy, Fowler.
Cobblers finish second, Southend Third, same points, but goal average is better.

4. May. 1950   Bill Barron Testimonial   County Ground
NORTHAMPTON TOWN v COMBINED LEAGUE X1
Northampton: Herod (Stoke); Smalley, Barron; Candlin, Franklin (stoke), Coley; Mitchell, Dixon, Garrett, Murphy, Fowler.
Combined: Wood (Coventry); Frame (Leicester), Aherne (Luton); Barratt (Coventry), Brice (Reading), Lawler (Fulham). Adam (Leicester), Broome (Notts C.), Rowley (Fulham), Stobbart (Luton), Johnston (Notts C).

1950-1951

23. March. 1951   Division 3 South   Goldstone Ground   15, 511
BRIGHTON & HOVE ALBION 5   NORTHAMPTON TOWN 1
Brighton: Baldwin: Wilkins, Mansell; Willard, McCoy, Wilson; Reed, McNicol, McCurley, Bennett, Keene.   **Scorers:** McCurley 2, Bennett, Keene, Wilkins (p)
Northampton: Feehan; Southam, Woollard; Davie, Duckhouse, Hughes; Smith, Dixon, McCulloch, Garrett, Fowler.   **Scorer:** o.g.
Tommy returns, Bert Mitchell out with food poisoning. McCoy the ex-Cobblers player.

24. March. 1951   Division 3 South   Priestfield Stadium 10,657
GILLINGHAM 3   NORTHAMPTON TOWN 1
Gillingham: Gage; Marks, Lewin; Boswell, Kingsnorth, Ayres; Carr, Lewis, Thomas, Russell, Veck.   **Scorers:** Carr, Lewis, Thomas.
Northampton: Feehan; Smalley, Southam; Davie, Duckhouse, Hughes, Smith, Dixon, McCulloch, Garrett, Fowler.   **Scorer:** Fowler.
Tommy opens his account, but the club have now won just one game in the last ten.

27. March. 1951   Division 3 South   County Ground   8,966
NORTHAMPTON TOWN 0   BRIGHTON & HOVE ALBION 0
Northampton: Freeman; Southam, Barron; Davie, Duckhouse, Hughes; Mitchell, Dixon, McCulloch, Garrett, Fowler.
Brighton: Baldwin; Wilkins, Marshall; Willard, McCoy, Wilson; Tenant, McNichol, Garbutt, Bennett, Keene,
Both goalkeepers injured, amateur Neville Freeman plays between the posts.

31. March. 1951   Division 3 South   County Ground   6,260

NORTHAMPTON TOWN 0   BOURNEMOUTH & BOSCOMBE ATHLETIC 1

Northampton: Feehan; Southam, Barron; Hughes, Duckhouse, Coley; Mitchell, Dixon, McCulloch, Davie, Fowler.

Bournemouth: Bird; Cunningham, Drummond; Wodward, Cripon, Lewis; Cross, McGibbon, Cheney, Marsh, Boxhall.   **Scorer:** Boxhall.

Davie moved in to the forward line, as Tommy's partner. He looked out of position.

5. April. 1951   Division 3 South   County Ground   6,425

NORTHAMPTON TOWN 1   NEWPORT COUNTY 4

Northampton: Feehan; Southam, Barron; Hughes, Duckhouse, Coley; Mitchell, Dixon, McCulloch, Davie, Fowler.   **Scorer:** Fowler

Newport County: Pope, Staples, Hayward; Stroud, Wilcox, Newall; Birch, Beattie, Parker, Shergold, Moore.   **Scorer:** Moore 2, Hayward, Parker.

Cobblers have picked up just two points from the last five games.

7. April. 1951   Division 3 South   St. James Park   6,141

EXETER CITY 1   NORTHAMPTON TOWN 0

Exeter: Singleton; Johnstone, Rowe; Fallon, Doyle, Davey; Hutchings, Smart, Dare, Mackay, McClleland.   **Scorer:** Smart.

Northampton: Feehan; Smalley, Barron; Davie, Duckhouse, Maxwell; Mitchell, Dixon, McCulloch, Hughes, Fowler.

Cobblers make four changes, giving Maxwell his debut.

9. April. 1951   Division 3 South   Home Park   7,515

PLYMOUTH ARGYLE 4   NORTHAMPTON TOWN 1

Plymouth: Major; Ratcliffe, Jones; McShane, Robertson, Porteous; Astall, Dobbie, Tadman, Rattray, Govan.   **Scorer:** Astall, Dobbie, Tadman, Govan.

Northampton: Feehan; Smalley, Barron; Davie, Duckhouse, Maxwell; Mitchell, Dixon, McCulloch, Hughes, Fowler.   **Scorer:** McCulloch.

Plymouth had only lost one of their last eight games.

14. April. 1951   Division 3 South   County Ground   7,342

NORTHAMPTON TOWN 1   SOUTHEND UNITED 1

Northampton: Feehan, Smalley, Barron; Hughes, Duckhouse, Davie; Mitchell, Mulgrew, McCulloch, Dixon, Fowler.   **Scorer:** McCulloch

Southend: Coombs; Loughran, Anderson; French, Stirling, Lawler; Sibley, McAlinden, Grant, Stubbs, Tippett.   **Scorer:** Sibley.

Cobblers first point in five games, Tommy Mulgrew makes his debut.

19. April. 1951   Division 3 South   County Ground   6,796

NORTHAMPTON TOWN 1   BRISTOL ROVERS 1

Northampton: Feehan; Smalley, Barron; Hughes, Duckhouse, Davie; Mitchell, Mulgrew, McCulloch, Dixon, Fowler. **Scorer**; Hughes

Bristol Rovers: Hoyle; Bamford, Watkin; Pitt, Warren, Sampson, Pethbridge, Bradford, Lambden, Roost, Watling.   **Scorer:** Watling

It is now eleven games without a win for the Cobblers.

21. April. 1951.   Division 3 South   Elm Park   13,401

READING 2   NORTHAMPTON TOWN 0

Reading: Marks; Moyse, Wicks; McLean, Brice, Johnston; Simpson, Edelston, Blackman, Henley, Amor.   **Scorers:** Amor, Henley

Northampton: Feehan; Smalley, Barron; Davie, Duckhouse, Hughes; Mitchell, Mulgrew, McCulloch, Dixon, Fowler.

Brice of Reading is also the Northamptonshire County Cricket Club player

25. April. 1951   Division 3 South   City Ground   27,244
NOTTINGHAM FOREST 2   NORTHAMPTON TOWN 2
Nottingham Forest: Walker; Whare, Thomas; Burkitt, Gager, Morley; Scott, Johnson, Ardon, Capel, Collingridge.   **Scorer:** Johnson 2
Northampton: Feehan; Smalley, Southam; Hughes, Duckhouse, Davie; Mitchell, Mulgrew, McCulloch, Garrett, Fowler.   **Scorers:** Mulgrew, Fowler.
A good result for the Cobblers against the runaway league leaders.

27. April. 1951   Maunsell Cup (Semi Final)   County Ground
NORTHAMPTON TOWN 3   PETERBOROUGH UNITED 1
Northampton: Feehan; Smalley, Southam; Hughes, Duckhose, Davie; Mitchell, Burns, McCulloch, Garrett, Fowler.   **Scorers:** McCulloch 2, Garrett.
Peterborough: Moulson; Bryan, Parrott; Woods, Machin, Pycroft; Dowson, Bee, Robinson, Martin, Clarke.   **Scorer:** Dowson
Cobblers win through to final of the competition.

28. April. 1951   Division 3 South   County Ground   6,342
NORTHAMPTON TOWN 1   PLYMOUTH ARGYLE 3
Northampton: Feehan; Smalley, Southam; Hughes, Duckhouse, Davie; Mitchell, Mulgrew, McCulloch, Dixon, Fowler.   **Scorer:** McCulloch.
Plymouth: Major; Ratcliffe, Jones, Douglas , Chisholm, Porteous; Astall, Dewis, Tadman, Rattray, Govan.   **Scorers:** Astall, Dewis, Govan
The Cobblers sixth home defeat of the season.

7. May 1951   Maunsell Cup (Final)   Occupation Road
CORBY TOWN 1   NORTHAMPTON TOWN 3
Corby: line up not available
Northampton: line up not available.   **Scorers:** Mitchell 2, Hughes.
The Cobblers win the Maunsell Cup for the Tenth time.

1951 - 1952

11. September 1951   Division 3 South   Southend Stadium 6,690
SOUTHEND UNITED 2   NORTHAMPTON TOWN 0
Southend: Scannell; Loughran, Anderson; French, Sheard, Lawler; Thompson, McAllinden, Wakefield, Grant, Lowkes; **Scorers**; French, Grant.
Northampton: Ansell; Connell, Wilson; Candlin, Duckhouse, Davie; English, Payne, O'Donnell, Ramscar, Fowler.
Tommy's first game of the season, replaces the injured Starocsik.

15. September. 1951   Division 3 South   Plainmoor   7,627
TORQUAY UNITED 1   NORTHAMPTON TOWN 2
Torquay: Webber; Lewis, Winters; Towers, McGuiness, Topping; Shaw, Brown, Calland, Edds, Reid.   **Scorer:** Topping
Northampton: Ansell; Collins, Wilson; Candlin, Duckhouse, Hughes; English, Payne. O'Donnell, Ramscar, Fowler.   **Scorer:** O'Donnell 2
Ben Collins and Gwyn Hughes play their first game of the season.

20. September. 1951   Division 3 South   County Ground   10,466
NORTHAMPTON TOWN 4   SOUTHEND UNITED 3
Northampton: Ansell; Collins, Wilson: Candlin, Duckhouse, Hughes; English, Payne,
O'Donnell, Ramscar, Fowler.   **Scorers:** English 2, Hughes, Ramscar
Southend: Scannell; Loughran, Anderson; French, Stirling. Lawler ,Thompson,
McAlinden, Stubbs, Grant, Butler.   **Scorers:** Lawler, Thompson, Stubbs.
Tommy laid on two of the Cobblers goals.

22. September 1951   Division 3 South   County Ground   12,782
NORTHAMPTON TOWN 2   GILLINGHAM 1
Northampton: Ansell; Collins, Wilson; Candlin, Duckhouse, Hughes; English. Payne,
O'Donnell, Ramscar, Fowler.   **Scorers:** Fowler, English.
Gillingham: Riggs; Marks, Lewin; Boswell, Niblett, Ayres; Hillman, Lewis, Thomas,
Russell, Briggs.   **Scorer:** Briggs.
Tommy gives the Cobblers the lead, Jack English scores the winner

27. September 1951   Division 3 South   County Ground   8,082
NORTHAMPTON TOWN 3   PORT VALE 1
Northampton: Ansell; Collins, Wilson; Candlin, Duckhouse, Hughes; English. Payne,
O'Donnell, Ramscar, Fowler.   **Scorers:** Fowler 2, English
Port Vale: Heppell, Hamlett, Potts, Turner, Hayward, Powell; Askey, Polk, Pinchbech,
Mullard, Bennett.   **Scorer:** Mullard.
Cobblers moves up to 8th. place.

29. September 1951   Division 3 South   Goldstone Ground   15,861
BRIGHTON & HOVE ALBION 2   NORTHAMPTON TOWN 0
Brighton: Baldwin, Tennant, Mansell; Willard, McCoy, Wilson; Reed, McNichol,
Bennett, Sirrell, Keene.   **Scorer:** Sirrell 2
Northampton: Ansell; Collins, Wilson; Candlin, Duckhouse, Hughes; English, Payne,
O'Donnell, Ramscar, Fowler.
O'Donnell injured during the game.

6. October 1951.   Division 3 South   Eastville Stadium   20,905
BRISTOL ROVERS 2   NORTHAMPTON TOWN 2
Rovers: Hoyle; Bamford, Fox; Pitt, Warren, Sampson; Pethbridge, Bradford, Lambden,
Roost, Watling;   **Scorer:** Bradford 2
Northampton: Ansell; Collins, Wilson; Candlin, Duckhouse, Hughes; English, Payne,
McCulloch, Ramscar, Fowler.   **Scorers:** McCulloch, Fowler.
Tommy becomes the Club's second top scorer to Jack English.

13. October 1951   Division 3 South   County Ground   14,661
NORTHAMPTON TOWN 3   PLYMOUTH ARGYLE 1
Northampton: Ansell; Collins, Wilson; Candlin, Duckhouse, Hughes; Starocsik,
English, McCulloch, Ramscar, Fowler,   **Scorer:** English 2 , Ramscar
Plymouth: Shortt; Racliffe, Jones; Douall, Chisholm, McShane; Astell, Dews, Tadman,
Rattary, Govan.   **Scorer:** Chisholm.
Plymouth were second, the Cobblers third.

20. October. 1951   Division 3 South   Carrow Road.   28,078
NORWICH CITY 2   NORTHAMPTON TOWN 1
Norwich: Nethercott; Duffy. Lewis; Pickwick, Foulkes, Ashman; Gavin, Ackerman,
Hollis, Bradley, Docherty.   **Scorers:** Hollis, Docherty
Northampton: Ansell; Collins, Wilson; Candlin, Duckhouse, Hughes; Starocsik,
English, McCulloch, Ramscar, Fowler.   **Scorer:** Ramscar.
Had the Cobblers won, they would have gone top of the division.

27. October 1951   Division 3 South   County Ground   12,943
NORTHAMPTON TOWN 3   EXETER CITY 1
Northampton: Feehan; Collins, Wilson; Candlin, Duckhouse, Hughes;English, Payne,
McCulloch, Ramscar, Fowler.   **Scorers:** English, Fowler, Ramscar.
Exeter: Lear; Warren, Rowe, Fallon, Goddard, Davey, Regan. Smart, Smith, Mackay,
McClelland.   **Scorer:** Smart.
Cobblers seventh consecutive home win.

3. November 1951   Division 3 South   Layer Road   10,326
COLCHESTER UNITED 2   NORTHAMPTON TOWN 5
Colchester: Wright; Harrison, Rowlands; Bearryman, Stewart, Elder; Jones, Scott,
Keeble, Cullum, Church.   **Scorers:** Church, Keeble.
Northampton: Feehan; Collins, Wilson; Candlin, Duckhouse, Hughes; English,
Payne, McCulloch, Ramscar. Fowler.   **Scorers:** Ramscar 2, English 2, McCulloch.
Most goals Cobblers scored away from home, since 1928.

10. November. 1951   Division 3 South   County Ground   14,845
NORTHAMPTON TOWN 5   CRYSTAL PALACE 2
Northampton: Feehan, Collins, Wilson; Candlin, Duckhouse, Hughes, English;
Payne, McCulloch, Ramscar, Fowler.   **Scorers:** McCulloch 2, Ramscar 2,(p) English
Palace: Anderson; Scott, McDonald; McGeachie, Briggs, Price; Broughton, Rainford,
Evans, Burgess, Devonshire.   **Scorer:** Burgess 2.
With ten goals in two games, the Cobblers go third.

17. November 1951   Division 3 South   County Ground (Swindon)   11,226
SWINDON TOWN 1   NORTHAMPTON TOWN 1
Swindon: Uprichard; Hunt, Gulliver; Kaye, Hudson, Batchelor; Lunn, Onslow, Owen,
Betteridge, Bain.   **Scorer:** Owen
Northampton: Feehan; Collins, Wilson; Candlin, Duckhouse, Hughes; English,
Payne, McCulloch, Ramscar, Fowler.   **Scorer:** Ramscar (p)
Freddie Ramscar scores his second penalty in as many games.

24. November 1951   F.A. Cup (Round 1)   Carrow Road   27,120
NORWICH CITY 2   NORTHAMPTON TOWN 3
Norwich: Nethercott; Morgan, Lerwis; Pickwick, Holmes, Ashman; Gavin, Kinsey,
Hollis, Ackerman, Docherty.   **Scorers:** Kinsey (p), Hollis, Ackerman
Northampton: Feehan; Collins, Wilson; Candlin, Duckhouse, Hughes; Smith, Payne,
McCulloch, Ramscar , Fowler.   **Scorers:** Ramscar (p), Payne.
Cobblers go out at the first hurdle, for the first time since 1938.

1. December 1951   Division 3 South   Fellows Park   7,671
WALSALL 3   NORTHAMPTON TOWN 0
Walsall: Lewis; Holding, Green; Dean, Russon, Watters; Bowen, O'Neill, Bridgett,
Evans, Giles.   **Scorers:** Bowen, O'Neil, Bridgett.
Northampton: Feehan; Collins, Wilson; Candlin, Duckhouse, Hughes; Starocsik,
Payne, McCulloch, Ramscar, Fowler.
Cobblers biggest defeat since April.

8. December 1951   Division 3 South   County Ground   13,715
NORTHAMPTON TOWN 6   SHREWSBURY TOWN 0
Northampton: Wood; Collins, Wilson; Candlin, Duckhouse, Hughes; English, Payne,
McCulloch, Ramscar, Fowler.   **Scorers:** McCulloch 2, English, Payne, Ramscar, Fowler.
Shrewsbury: Egglesthorpe; Ashworth, Lewis; Bullins, Depear, Crutchley; Reagan,
Ayton, Williams, Brown, Roberts.
Alf Wood, ex war time guest makes his league debut for the Cobblers.

15. December 1951   Friendly   County Ground

NORTHAMPTON TOWN 1   CARLISLE UNITED 1
Northampton: Wood; Collins, Wilson; Candlin, Duckhouse, Hughes; English, Payne,
McCulloch, Ramscar, Fowler.   **Scorer:** Ramscar
Carlisle: Godwin; McIntosh, Scott; Kinloch, Waters, Stokoe; Steen, Whitehouse,
Ashman, Duffett, Caton.   **Scorer:** Ashman.
Both clubs out of the F.A. Cup so played this friendly.

22. December. 1951   Division 3 South   Vale Park   8,973

PORT VALE 0   NORTHAMPTON TOWN 0
Port Vale: King; Turner, Hayward; Todd, Cheadle, Polk; Hulligan, Mullard, Barber,
Cunliffe, Bennett.
Northampton: Wood; Collins, Wilson; Candlin, Duckhouse, Hughes; English, Payne,
McCulloch, Ramscar, Fowler.
Cobblers first 0-0 draw away from home for a year.

25. December   1951 Division 3 South   Vicarage Road   7,847

WATFORD 2   NORTHAMPTON TOWN 4
Watford: Saphin; Eastway, Jones; Eggleston, Meadows, Paton; Cook, Brown,
Thompson, Haigh, Collins.   **Scorers:** Thompson, Haigh.
Northampton: Wood; Collins, Wilson; Candlin, Duckhouse, Hughes; English, Payne,
McCulloch, Ramscar, Fowler.   **Scorers:** McCulloch 2, English, o.g.
Poor attendance for a Christmas Day match.

26. December 1951   Division 3 South   County Ground   18,295

NORTHAMPTON TOWN 1   WATFORD 4
Northampton: Wood; Collins, Wilson; Candlin, Duckhouse, Hughes; English, Payne,
McCulloch, Ramscar, Fowler.   **Scorer:** Payne.
Watford: Saphin; Eastway, Jones; Eggleston, Meadows, Nolan; Cook, Brown,
Thompson, Haigh, Collins.   **Scorers:** Thompson 3. Cook.
Sweet revenge for Watford.

29. December 1951   Division 3 South   Ashton Gate   18,733

BRISTOL CITY 2   NORTHAMPTON TOWN 0
Bristol City: Sullivan; Guy, Bailey; Peacock, Roberts, Tovey; Masters, Eisentrager,
Atyeo, Williams. Rogers.   **Scorers:** Eisentranger, Rogers.
Northampton: Wood; Collins, Connell; Candlin, Duckhouse, Dodgin; English, Payne,
McCulloch, Ramscar, Fowler.
Norman Dodgin makes his debut for Northampton.

5. January 1952   Division 3 South   Portman Road   10,071

IPSWICH TOWN 3   NORTHAMPTON TOWN 2
Ipswich: Parry; Feeney, Deacon; Murchison, Rose, Parker; Green, Myles, Garney,
Elsworthy, Roberts.   **Scorers:** Roberts 2, Parker.
Northampton: Wood; Connell, Collins; Candlin, Duckhouse, Dodgin; English, Payne,
Pinchbech, Ramscar, Fowler.   **Scorer:** Pinchbech, Fowler
Cliff Pinchbech scores on his Cobblers debut.

12. January 1952   Division 3 South   County Ground   13,317

NORTHAMPTON TOWN 1   MILLWALL 1
Northampton: Wood; Collins, Connell; Candlin, Duckhouse, Dodgin; English, Payne,
Pinchbech, Ramscar, Fowler.   **Scorers:** English.
Millwall: Hinton; Jardine, Fisher; Short, Bowler, Reeves; Johnson, Neary, Monkhouse,
Morgan, Hartburn.   **Scorer:** Johnson.
Match refereee by the Reverend Davies,

19. January 1952   Division 3 South   County Ground   10,535

NORTHAMPTON TOWN 2   TORQUAY UNITED   4

Northampton: Wood; Collins, Connell; Davie, Duckhouse, Hughes; English, Smith J,
McCulloch, Ramscar, Fowler.   **Scorer:** English, Fowler.
Torquay: Webber G: Topping, Callard; Lewis, Webber E, Brown; Shaw, Collins,
Northcott, Reid, Edds.   **Scorers:** Callard 2, Collins 2.
Manager Dennison makes wholesale changes.

24. January 1952   Division 3 South   County Ground   4,490

NORTHAMPTON TOWN 6   ALDERSHOT 2

Northampton: Wood; Collins, Connell; Davie, Croy, Hughes; English, Smith,
Pinchbech, Ramscar, Fowler.   **Scorers:** Pinchbech 2, Ramscar 2, English. Fowler.
Aldershot: Houston; Rogers, Kirston; Taggart, Billington, Rennie; Hobbs, Laird, Raine,
MaCauley, Flint.   **Scorers:** Raine, Flint.
Pinchbech is carried off, Flint of Aldershot is sent off, attendance poor, Thursday game.

26. January 1952   Division 3 South   Priestfield Stadium   9,625

GILLINGHAM 2   NORTHAMPTON TOWN 1

Gillingham: Rigg; Marks, Murray; Boswell, Niblett, Forrester. Russell, Burtenshaw,
Thomas, Lewis, Briggs.   **Scorers:** Burtenshaw, Lewis
Northampton: Wood; Collins, Connell; Davie, Croy, Hughes; English, Smith,
O'Donnell, Ramscar, Fowler.   **Scorers:** O'Donnell
Third consecutive away defeat.

2. February 1952   Division 3 South   Elm Park   15,932

READING 2   NORTHAMPTON TOWN 0

Reading: Marks; Moyse, Wicks; Lewis, Brice, Johnson, Grieve, Edelston, Blackman,
Henley, Bambridge.   **Scorers:** Lewis, Henley.
Northampton: Wood; Collins, Connell;Davie, Candlin, Hughes; English, Smith,
O'Donnell, Ramscar, Fowler.
Tommy's last game for two months.

14. April . 1952   Division 3 South   Dean Court   9,933

BOURNEMOUTH & BOSCOMBE ATHLETIC 3   NORTHAMPTON TOWN 0

Bournemouth: Bird; Cunningham, Drummond; Woodward, Neave, Casey; Stroud,
Cheney, Cross, Gaynor, Tippett;   **Scorers:** Cheney, Cross, Gaynor.
Northampton: Feehan; Collins, Southam; Davie, Candlin, Hughes; Starocsik, Payne,
Adams, Ramscar, Fowler.
Tommy returns as the forward line is shuffled to find a scoring combination.

15. April. 1952   Division 3 South   County Ground   9,524

NORTHAMPTON TOWN 5   BOURNEMOUTH & BOSCOMBE ATHLETIC 3

Northampton: Feehan; Collins, Southam; Davie, Candlin, Hughes; Starocsik, English,
O'Donnell, Ramscar, Fowler.   **Scorers:** Ramscar 3, O'Donnell, English.
Bournemouth: Bird; Cunningham, Drummond; Woodward, Neave, Casey; Stroud,
Cheney, Cross, Gaynor, Tippett.   **Scorers:** Cheney, Cross, Gaynor
Jack Cross is sent off for striking Sonny Feehan.

19. April. 1952   Division 3 South   County Ground   8,311

NORTHAMPTON TOWN 4   WALSALL 1

Northampton: Feehan; Collins, Southam; Davie, Croy, Hughes; Starocsik, English,
O'Donnell, Ramscar, Fowler.   **Scorers:** O'Donnell 2, English, Fowler.
Walsall: Chilvers; Jones, Montgomery, Dean, Green, Walters; Bowen, Devlin, Winter,
Evans, Giles.   **Scorer:** Devlin (p)
Tommy scores his 10th goal of the season.

21. April 1952   Maunsell Cup (Semi Final)   Occupation Road
CORBY TOWN 1   NORTHAMPTON TOWN 1
Corby: Mackin, Poole, Hammell; Horne, Wards, Smith; Storey, Garvey, Middlemas,
Haddrick, Akers.   **Scorer:** unknown
Northampton: Feehan; Collins, Southam; Davie, Croy, Hughes; Starocsik, English,
O'Donnell, Ramscar, Fowler.   **Scorer:** unknown
Thirty minutes extra time played.

23. April. 1952   Maunsell Cup (Semi Final Replay)   County Ground   2,823
NORTHAMPTON TOWN 1   CORBY TOWN 0
Northampton: Feehan; Collins, Southam; Davie, Croy, Hughes; Starocsik, English,
O'Donnell, Ramscar, Fowler.   **Scorer:** Starocsik.
Corby: Mackin; Poole, Hammell; Horne, Wards, Smith; Storey, Garvey, Middlemas,
Haddrick, Akers.
Horne and Garvey of Corby, both ex-Cobblers.

24. April 1952   Division 3 South   County Ground   6,907
NORTHAMPTON TOWN 4   LEYTON ORIENT 0
Northampton: Feehan; Collins, Southam; Davie, Candlin, Hughes; Starocsik, English,
O'Donnell, Ramscar, Fowler.   **Scorers:** Ramscar 2, English, O'Donnell.
Leyton Orient: Welton; Evans, Banner. Blizzard, Aldous, Deverall; Woan, Pope, Harris,
Rees, Blatchford.
Cobblers third win in three games.

26. April. 1952   Division 3 South   Gay Meadow   9,514
SHREWSBURY TOWN 3   NORTHAMPTON TOWN 1
Shrewsbury: Egglestone; Malpin, Potter; Bullions, Ashworth, Butler, Regan, Jackson,
McCulloch, Brown, Roberts.   **Scorers:** Jackson, McCulloch, Brown.
Northampton: Feehan; Collins, Southam; Davie, Candlin, Hughes; Starocsik, English,
O'Donnell, Ramscar, Fowler.   **Scorer:** O'Donnell.
Adam McCulloch of Shrewsbury, is ex-Cobbler.

28. April 1952   Hughes/Fowler Benefit   County Ground
NORTHAMPTON TOWN 5   COMBINED LEAGUE X1 0
Northampton: Wood; Collins, Southam; Davie, Candlin, Burgess (Spurs); Starocsik,
English, O'Donnell, Ramscar, Fowler.
League XI: Feehan (Cobblers); Withers (Spurs), Jones (Luton); Nicholson (Spurs),
Owen (Luton), Hughes (Cobblers), Mitchell (Luton), Harmer (Spurs), Lowerie (Coventry),
Bailey (Spurs), Lockhart (Coventry).
Both Hughes and Fowler receive over £100 each.

30. April 1952   Division 3 South   The Den   10,389
MILLWALL 2   NORTHAMPTON TOWN 1
Millwall: Hinton; Jardine, Fisher; Short, Bowler, Reeves; Johnson, Saward, Neary,
Morgan, Hartburn.   **Scorers:** Saward, Hartburn.
Northampton: Feehan; Collins, Southam; French, Candlin, Dodgin; Starocsik, Payne,
O'Donnell, Ramscar, Fowler.   **Scorer:** Ramscar
Fourth consecutive away defeat for the Cobblers

1. May. 1952   Maunsell Cup (Final)   Rockingham Road   8,082
KETTERING TOWN 4   NORTHAMPTON TOWN 0
Kettering: Pickering; Johnston, Tart; Scott, Waddell, McCauley; Potts, Stenhouse,
Gallagher, Whent, Reynolds.   **Scorers:** Stenhouse, Gallagher, Whent, Reynolds.
Northampton: Feehan; Collins, Southam; Davie, Candlin, Hughes; English, Payne,
O'Donnell, Ramscar, Fowler.
James Potts is an ex Cobbler.

3. May. 1952   Division 3 South   Selhurst Park   7,214
CRYSTAL PALACE 3   NORTHAMPTON TOWN 3
Crystal Palace: Anderson; Edwards, McDonald; McGeachie, Briggs, Nelson; Broughton, Rainford, Marsden, Hancox, Bennett.   **Scorers:** Marsden 2, Rainford
Northampton: Feehan; Collins, Southam; Davie, Candlin, Hughes; Starocsik, English, O'Donnell, Ramscar, Fowler.   **Scorers:** Starocsik, O'Donnell, Ramscar
Last game of the season, Cobblers finish 8th.

1952 - 1953

21. August 1952   Division 3 South   Dean Court   14,771
BOURNEMOUTH & BOSCOMBE ATHLETIC 0   NORTHAMPTON TOWN 1
Bournemouth: Godwin; Cunningham. Drummond; Woodward, Hughes, Neave, Harrison, Haddington, Cheney, Eyre, Tippett.
Northampton: Wood; Southam, Patterson; Candlin, McLain, Davie; English, Ramscar, O'Donnell, Mulgrew, Fowler.   **Scorer:** English
Ron Patterson and Tommy McLain make their Cobblers debuts

27. August 1952   Division 3 South   St. James Park   12,729
EXETER CITY 2   NORTHAMPTON TOWN 0
Exeter: Kelly; Walton, Rowe; Booth, Goddard, Fallon; Mitchell, Knight, Dailey, Murphy, Regan.   **Scorers:** Knight, Dailey.
Northampton: Wood; Southam, Patterson; Davie, Candlin, McLain; English, Mulgrew, O'Donnell, Ramscar, Fowler.
Exeter's Eddie Murphy is one of Tommy's ex-team mates at Northampton.

30. August 1952   Division 3 South   County Ground   13,611
NORTHAMPTON TOWN 4   SOUTHEND UNITED 3
Northampton: Wood; Southam, Patterson; Davie, Candlin McLain; English, Mulgrew, O'Donnell, Ramscar, Fowler.   **Scorers:** Ramscar (2, 1 p) Fowler 2
Southend: Scannell; Loughlan, Anderson; French, Sheard, Lawler; Sibley, McAlinden, Wakefield, Grant, Stubbs.   **Scorers:** Wakefield, Grant, o.g.
Alf Wood saves a penalty, Grant of Southend is sent off.

4. September 1952   Division 3 South   County Ground   11,988
NORTHAMPTON TOWN 3   EXETER CITY 1
Northampton: ;Wood; Southam, Patterson; Davie, Candlin, McLain; English, Edelston, O'Donnell, Ramscar, Fowler.   **Scorers:** Edelston, O'Donnell, Ramscar
Exeter: Kelly; Walton, Rowe; Booth, Goddard, Fallon; Mitchell, Knight, Dailey, Murphy, Regan.   **Scorer:** Regan.
Maurice Edelston scores for the Cobblers within 10 seconds of his debut,

7. September 1952   Division 3 South   Vicarage Road   21,959
WATFORD 2   NORTHAMPTON TOWN 1
Watford: Saphin; Gallogly, Croker; Eggleston, Phipps, Mitchell; Cook; Bowie, Thompson, Patterson, Collins.   **Scorers:** Bowie, Thompson.
Northampton: Wood; Southam, Patterson; Davie, Candlin, McLain; English, Edelston, O'Donnell, Ramscar, Fowler.   **Scorers:** English
Cobblers had more of the game, but lost.

11. September 1952   Division 3 South   County Ground   13,280
NORTHAMPTON TOWN 3   COVENTRY CITY 1
Northampton: Wood; Southam, Patterson; Davie, Candlin, McLain; English, Edelston, O'Donnell, Ramscar, Fowler.   **Scorers:** English, Edelston, O'Donnell.
Coventry: Gilbert; McDonnell, Mason; Harvey, Kirk, Cook; Warner, Dorman, Harrison, Hill, Lockhart   **Scorer:** Hill
Cobblers forward line is excellent.

13. September 1952   Division 3 South   County Ground   14,342
NORTHAMPTON TOWN 5   BRIGHTON & HOVE ALBION 3
Northampton: Wood; Southam, Patterson; Davie, Candlin, McLain; English, Edelston, O'Donnell, Ramscar, Fowler.   **Scorers:** O'Donnell 3, Edelston 2
Brighton: Ball; Tennant, Mansell; McIvern, McCoy, South; Reed, Bennett, Owers, Leadbetter, Keene.   **Scorer:** Tennant (p), Bennett, Owers.
Two old faces return, Tim McCoy is Brighton's captain, and Reverend Davis is referee

15. September. 1952   Division 3 South   Highfield Road   18,217
COVENTRY CITY 1   NORTHAMPTON TOWN 1
Coventry: Taylor; Timmins, Mason; Cook, McConnell, Simpson; Lewis, Dorman, Kirk, Hill, Lockhart.   **Scorer:** Dorman
Northampton: Wood; Southam, Patterson, Davie, Candlin, McLain; English. Edelston, O'Donnell, Ramscar , Fowler.   **Scorer:** Ramscar (p)
Many Cobblers supporters in the crowd,

20. September 1952   Division 3 South   Somerset Park   10,479
NEWPORT COUNTY 4   NORTHAMPTON TOWN 1
Newport County: Fearnley; Staples, Haines; Newall, Wilcox, Waite; Birch, Nelson, Parker, Shergold, Moore.   **Scorers:** Parker 2 (1 p), Moore 2.
Northampton: Wood; Southam, Patterson; Davie, Collins, McLain; English, Edelston, O'Donnell, Ramscar, Fowler.   **Scorer:** O'Donnell.
Ramscar limped off during the second half.

25. September 1952   Division 3 South   County Ground   8,746
NORTHAMPTON TOWN 3   SWINDON TOWN 1
Northampton: Wood; Southam, Patterson; Davie, Collins, McLain; English, Edelston, O'Donnell, Ramscar, Fowler.   **Scorers:** Edelston 2, Fowler.
Swindon: Uprichard; Hunt, Radford; Cryle, Hudson, Gray; Ryder, Owen, Johnson, Betteridge, Williams.   **Scorer:** Cryle.
Tenth home game since the Cobblers last defeat

27. September 1952   Division 3 South   County Ground   12,805
NORTHAMPTON TOWN 5   CRYSTAL PALACE 1
Northampton: Wood; Southam, Patterson; Davie, Collins, Mclain; English, Edelston, O'Donnell, Ramscar, Fowler.   **Scorers:** English 2, Edelston, Fowler, Southam.
Crystal Palace: Anderson; George, Edwards, Price, Briggs, Chilvers; Devonshire, Rainford, Marsden, Thomas, Bennett.   **Scorer:** Bennett
Freddie Ramscar misses a penalty.

1. October. 1952   Division 3 South   Plainmoor   4,784
TORQUAY UNITED 3   NORTHAMPTON TOWN 0
Torquay: Webber G: Topping, Calland; Lewis, McGuiness, Towers; Shaw, Thomas, Webber E, Collins, Edds.   **Scorers:** Collins 2 (1p), Webber E.
Northampton: Wood; Southam, Patterson; Hughes, Collins, McLain; English, Edelston, O'Donnell, Ramscar, Fowler.
For the second game in succession the Cobblers have a penalty awarded against them.

4. October. 1952   Division 3 South   Ashton Gate   21,795
BRISTOL CITY 2   NORTHAMPTON TOWN 3
Bristol City: Morgan; Guy, Stone; Peacock, Roberts, Tovey; Eisentranger, Atyeo, Rodgers, Williams, Boxley. **Scorers:** Eisentranger, Rodgers.
Northampton: Wood, Southam, Patterson; Hughes, Collins, McClain; English, Edelston, O'Donnell, Ramscar, Fowler. **Scorers:** English, O'Donnell, o.g.
Alf Wood saves a penalty.

---

11. October 1952   Division 3 South   County Ground   19,064
NORTHAMPTON TOWN 2   BRISTOL ROVERS 2
Northampton: Wood; Southam, Patterson; Hughes, Collins, McLain; English, Edelston, O'Donnell, Ramscar, Fowler. **Scorers:** McLain, English.
Bristol Rovers: Hoyle, Bamford, Fox; Pitt, Warren, Sampson; McIlvenny, Bush, Lambden, Bradford, Pethbridge. **Scorers:** Bradford, Pethbridge.
First point the Cobblers dropped at home this season.

---

17. October 1952.   Division 3 South   The Den   22,948
MILLWALL 1   NORTHAMPTON TOWN 2
Millwall: Finlayson; Fisher, Shortt; Bowler, Sawford, Mansfield; Stobhart, Jardine, Neary, Morgan, Hartburn. **Scorer:** Hartburn.
Northampton: Wood; Southam, Patterson; Hughes, Collins, McLain; English, Edelston, O'Donnell, Ramscar, Fowler. **Scorers:** Ramscar, English.
One of only two home defeats Millwall were to suffer that season.

---

25. October 1952   Division 3 South   County Ground   3,689.
NORTHAMPTON TOWN 3   GILLINGHAM 1
Northampton: Wood; Southam. Patterson; Hughes, Collins, McLain; English, Edelston, O'Donnell, Ramscar, Fowler. **Scorers:** English, Edelston, Ramscar.
Gillingham: Rigg, Marks, Lewis, Boswell, Niblett, McKee; Long, Borgin, Scarth, Lambert, Forrester. **Scorer:** Boswell.
Tommy laid on two of the goals.

---

31. October 1952   Division 3 South   Fellows Park   8,420
WALSALL 1   NORTHAMPTON TOWN 5
Walsall: Lewis; Freeman, Walters; Dean, Green, Driver; Morris, Bowen, Bridgett, Duggin, Giles. **Scorer:** Giles
Northampton: Wood; Southam, Patterson; Hughes, Candlin, McLain; English, Edelston, O'Donnell, Ramscar, Fowler. **Scorers:** O'Donnell 2, English, Edelston, Ramscar.
Cobblers biggest away win for over a year.

---

8. November 1952   Division 3 South   County Ground   13,988
NORTHAMPTON TOWN 3   SHREWSBURY TOWN1
Northampton: Wood; Southam, Patterson; Hughes, Candlin, McLain; English, Edelston, O'Donnell, Ramscar, Fowler. **Scorers:** Edelston 2, English
Shrewsbury Town: Birkett; Halpin, Lewis; Beynon, Ashworth, Butler; Fisher, Keery, McCulloch, Jackson, Reagan. **Scorer:** Regan
Adam McCulloch, the Shrewsbury forward, is Tommys ex-Cobblers team mate.

---

15. November 1952   Division 3 South   Loftus Road   14,661
QUEENS PARK RANGERS 2   NORTHAMPTON TOWN 2
Q. P. R: Brown; Poppitt, Ingham; Nicholas, Spence, Parsons; Mountford, Gilberg, Addinall, Cameron, Shepherd **Scorers:** Shepherd, Gilberg.
Northampton: Wood; Southam, Patterson; Hughes, Candlin, McLain; English, Edelston, O'Donnell, Ramscar, Fowler. **Scorers:** Edelston, O'Donnell.
Cobblers Seventh league game without defeat.

22. November 1952   F.A. Cup (Round 1)   Claremont Road   9,000
HENDON 0   NORTHAMPTON TOWN 0
Hendon: Ivey; Fisher, Lane, Topp, Adams, Austin; Avis, Phebey, Stroud, Richards, Benfield.
Northampton: Wood, Southam, Patterson; Hughes, Candlin, McLain; English, Edelston, O'Donnell, Ramscar, Fowler.
Tommy and Jack both had excellent games, but could not find the back of the net.

27. November 1952   F.A. Cup (Round 1 replay)   County Ground   6,100
NORTHAMPTON TOWN 2   HENDON 0
Northampton: Wood, Southam, Patterson: Hughes, Candlin, McLain,; English, Edelston, O'Donnell, Ramscar, Fowler.   **Scorers:** Ramscar, Fowler.
Hendon: Ivey; Fisher, Lane; Topp, Adams, Austin; Avis, Phebey, Stroud, Richardson, Benfield.
Tommy scores his first F.A. Cup goal for the Cobblers in peace time football

29, November. 1952   Division 3 South   Recreation Ground 3,263
ALDERSHOT 2   NORTHAMPTON TOWN 1
Aldershot: Brown, Rogers, Jefferson; Reddie, Billington, Cropley; Wright, Alison, Bonnar, Durkin, Flint.   **Scorers:** Alison, Durkin.
Northampton: Wood; Southam, Patterson; Hughes, Candlin, McLain; English, Baxter,O'Donnell, Ramscar, Fowler.   **Scorer:** Fowler.
Larry Baxter makes his debut, its two goals in two games for Tommy.

6. December 1952   F.A. Cup (Round 2)   County Ground (Swindon)   12,936
SWINDON TOWN 2   NORTHAMPTON TOWN 0
Swindon: Burton; Hunt, Radford; Betteridge, Hudson, Prouton; Lunn, Millar, Owen, Ryden, Baker.   **Scorers:** Millar, Owen.
Northampton: Wood; Southam. Patterson; Hughes, Candlin, McLain; English, Edelston, O'Donnell, Ramscar, Fowler.
After nine league and cup games without defeat, its now two losses in a row.

13. December 1952   Division 3 South   Carrow Road   21,093
NORWICH CITY 1   NORTHAMPTON TOWN 2
Norwich: Nethercott; Morgan, Lewis; Dutton, Foulkes, Ashman; Gavin, Johnston, Ackerman, Kinsey, Adams.   **Scorer:** Johnston.
Northampton: Wood; Southam, Patterson; Hughes, Candlin, Mclain. English, Edelston, O'Donnell, Ramscar, Fowler.   **Scorer:** English 2
Gavin sent off, Patterson, carried off. McLain booked, carried off, returns then sent off.

20. December 1952   Division 3 South   County Ground   8,649
NORTHAMPTON TOWN 5   BOURNEMOUTH & BOSCOMBE ATHLETIC 1
Northampton: Wood; Southam, Patterson; Hughes, Candlin, Dodgin; English, Edelston, O'Donnell, Ramscar, Fowler.   **Scorers:** O'Donnell 3, Ramscar 2
Bournemouth: Godwin; Drummond, Fisher; Gaynor, Hughes, Neave ; Stroud, Eyre, Fidler, Cheney, Harrison.   **Scorers:** Fidler.
Norman Dodgin replaced the injured Tommy McLain.

26. December 1952   Division 3 South   County Ground   19,242
NORTHAMPTON TOWN 6   READING 1
Northampton: Wood; Southam, Patterson; Hughes, Candlin, Dodgin; English, Edelston,O'Donnell, Ramscar, Fowler.   **Scorers:** English 2,O'Donnell 2, Edelston, Ramscar
Reading: McBride; Moyse, Reeves; Johnson, Smith, Wicks; Anderton. Simpson, Blackman, Bainbridge, Hinshelwood.   **Scorer;** Simpson.
Reading scored after 18 minutes, Cobblers equalised on the hour, then five in 20 minutes

3. January 1953   Division 3 South   Southend Stadium 7,425

SOUTHEND UNITED 3   NORTHAMPTON TOWN 1
Southend: Scannell; Loughran, Duggins; Burns, Stirling, Lawler, Sibley, McAlinden,
Marsden, Grant, Thompson.   **Scorers:** Sibley 2, Grant.
Northampton: Wood; Southam, Patterson; Hughes, Candlin, McLain; English,
Edelston, O'Donnell, Adams, Fowler.   **Scorer:** O'Donnell.
Tommy McLain returns, Freddie Ramscar drops out injured, Don Adams replaces him.

10. January 1953   Division 3 South   Brisbane Road   7,826

LEYTON ORIENT 0   NORTHAMPTON TOWN 1
Orient: Groombridge; Evans, Banner; Blizzard, Aldous, Deverall; Pacey, Charlton,
Harris, Brown, Blatchford.
Northampton: Wood; Southam, Patterson; Hughes, Candlin, McLain; English,
Edeldston, O'Donnell, Ramscar, Fower.   **Scorer:** English.
Cobblers keep in touch with the league leaders.

17, January 1953   Division 3 South   County Ground   13,250

NORTHAMPTON TOWN 4   WATFORD 1
Northampton: Wood; Southam, Patterson; Hughes, Candlin, McLain; English,
Edelston. O'Donnell, Ramscar, Fowler.   **Scorers:** O'Donnell 2, English, Edelston
Watford: Underwood; Galloghy, Jones; Kelly, Phipps, Mitchell; Paton, Meadows, Reid,
Evans, Collins.   **Scorer:** Reid.
Now 16 league games since the Cobblers suffered a home defeat.

24. January 1953   Division 3 South   Goldstone Ground 18,750

BRIGHTON & HOVE ALBION 1   NORTHAMPTON TOWN 1
Brighton: Medhurst; Tennant, Mclafferty, McIlvenny, South, Wilson, Reid, Bennett,
Addinall, Gilberg, Howard.   **Scorer:** Tennant (p)
Northampton: Wood; Southam, Patterson; Hughes, Candlin, Dodgin ; Starocsik,
Edelston, O'Donell, Ramscar, Fowler.   **Scorer:** Starocsik
Both Jack English and reserve right winger Raynes were attending their fathers' funerals

31. January 1953   Division 3 South   County Ground   9,868

NORTHAMPTON TOWN 3   LEYTON ORIENT 1
Northampton: Wood; Southam, Patterson; Hughes, Candlin, Dodgin; English, McLain,
O'Donnell, Ramscar, Fowler.   **Scorers:** Ramscar 2, Fowler.
Leyton Orient: Groombridge; Evans, Charlton; Blizzard, Aldous, Deverall, Blatchford,
Rees, Pacey, Brown, Poulton.   **Scorer:** Pacey.
McLain returns as a forward, and English takes his place back on the right wing.

6. February 1953   Division 3 South   County Ground   11,977

NORTHAMPTON TOWN 5   NEWPORT COUNTY 0
Northampton: Wood; Southam, Patterson; Hughes, Candlin, Dodgin; English,
Edelston, O'Donnell, Ramscar, Fowler.   **Scorers:** English 2, Ramscar, 2, Edelston.
Newport County: Fearnley; Barton, White; Newall, Wilcox, Haines; Birch, Beattie,
Parker, Shergold, Moore.
Freddie Ramscar missed a penalty, and the chance of a hat trick

14. February 1953   Divison 3 South   Selhurst Park   6.409

CRYSTAL PALACE 4   NORTHAMPTON TOWN 3
Crystal Palace: Anderson; George, McDonald,Grimshaw, Higgins, Chilvers; Fell,
Hancox, Thomas, Burgess, Devonshire.   **Scorers:** Burgess 3, Thomas
Northampton: Wood, Southam, Patterson; Hughes, Candlin, Dodgin; English, Adams,
O'Donnell, Ramscar, Fowler   **Scorers:** O'Donnell 2, Adams.
Don Adams scores, he was a late replacement for Edelston who cried off injured.

21. February 1953   Division 3 South   County Ground   15,291

NORTHAMPTON TOWN 0   BRISTOL CITY 2
Northampton: Wood; Southam,Patterson; Hughes, Candlin, Dodgin; English, Baxter,
O'Donnell, Ramscar, Fowler
Bristol City: Cook; Guy, Bailey; Peacock, White, Tovey, Eisentranger, Atyeo,
Rodgers, Williams, Regan.   **Scorer:** Regan 2 (1 p)
Edelston injured, McLain ill, Adams dropped, Tommy and O'Donnell stars of the side.

28. February 1953   Division 3 South   Eastville Stadium   31,115

BRISTOL ROVERS 1   NORTHAMPTON TOWN 1
Bristol Rovers: Radford; Bamford, Fox; Pitt, Warren, Sampson; McIlvenny, Bush,
Lambden, Bradford, Pethbridge.   **Scorer:** Bradford
Northampton: Wood; Southan, Patterson; Hughes, Candlin, Dodgin; English, Baxter,
O'Donnell, Ramscar, Fowler.   **Scorer:** Ramscar.
Top of the table clash. Tommy makes the goal for Freddie Ramscar

7. March. 1953   Division 3 South   County Ground   13,687

NORTHAMPTON TOWN 1   MILLWALL 1
Northampton: Wood; Southam, Patterson; Hughes, Collins, Dodgin; English,
Edelston, O'Donnell, Ramscar, Fowler.   **Scorer:** O'Donnell
Millwall: Finlayson, Jardine, Fisher; Shortt, Bowler, Saward; Johnson, Smith,
Monkhouse, Neary, Hartburn.   **Scorer:** Neary.
Another top of the table clash, Ben Collins replaced the injured Candlin.

14. March. 1953   Division 3 South   Priestfield Stadium   10,250

GILLINGHAM 1   NORTHAMPTON TOWN 1
Gillingham: Rigg; Marks, Lewin; Boswell, Niblett, Forrester; Lewis, Scarth, King,
Sowden, Long.   **Scorer:** King
Northampton: Wood; Southam, Patterson; Hughes, Collins, Dodgin; English,
Edelston, O'Donnell, Ramscar, Fowler.   **Scorer:** Ramscar.
The Cobblers third consecutive 1-1 draw.

21. March, 1953.   Division 3 South   County Ground   9,717

NORTHAMPTON TOWN 2   WALSALL 1
Northampton: Wood; Southam, Patterson; Hughes, Collins, Dodgin; English,
Edelston, O'Donnell, Ramscar, Fowler.   **Scorers:** O'Donnell, Ramscar.
Walsall: Chilvers; Rowe, Walters; Dean, Horne, Green; Bowen, Wright, McIntosh,
Hughes, Giles.   **Scorer:** McIntosh
Cobblers first home win since 7th February.

28. March 1953   Division 3 South   Gay Meadow   7,329

SHREWSBURY TOWN 2   NORTHAMPTON TOWN 4
Shrewsbury: Birkett; Bannister, Lewis; Bullions, Ashworth, Crutchley; Fisher, Jackson,
Marsden, Stewart, Brown.   **Scorers:** Jackson, Stewart.
Northampton: Wood; Southam, Patterson; McLain, Collins, Dodgin; English, Baxter,
O'Donnell, Ramscar, Fowler.   **Scorers:** O'Donnell 2, English, Ramscar.
First away win since January.

4. April. 1953   Division 3 South   County Ground   12,546

NORTHAMPTON TOWN 4   QUEENS PARK RANGERS 2
Northampton: Wood; Southam, Patterson; McLain, Collins, Dodgin; English, Baxter,
O'Donnell, Ramscar, Fowler.   **Scorers:** Fowler, Baxter, English, Dodgin.
Q.P.R.: Brown; Powell G, Ingham; Nicholas, Powell M, Chapman; Mountford, Smith,
Tomkeys, Cameron, Shepherd.   **Scorers:** Tomkeys, Cameron.
Larry Baxter opens his account for the Cobblers.

6. April. 1953   Division 3 South   Portman Road   12,048

IPSWICH TOWN 1   NORTHAMPTON TOWN 1

Ipswich: Parry; Ackers, Feeney; Myles, Clarke, Murchinson; Gaynor, Elsworthy, Brown, Parker, Ball.   **Scorer:** Elsworthy.

Northampton: Wood; Southam. Patterson; McLain, Collins, Dodgin; English, Edelston, O'Donnell, Ramscar, Fowler.   **Scorer:** Ramscar.

On Saturday Norman Dodgin scored for the Cobblers, today, he was carried off.

7. April. 1953   Division 3 South   County Ground   12,307

NORTHAMPTON TOWN 2   IPSWICH TOWN 0

Northampton: Wood; Southam, Patterson; Candlin, Collins,McLain; English, Edelston, O'Donnell, Ramscar, Fowler.   **Scorers:** McLain, Fowler.

Ipswich: Parry; Ackers, Feeney; Myles, Clarke, Murchinson; Gaynor, Elsworthy, Brown, Dobson, Ball.

Maurice Candlin returns to the side

11. April. 1953   Division 3 South   County Ground (Swindon)   9,564

SWINDON TOWN 3   NORTHAMPTON TOWN 0

Swindon: Burton; Hunt, Elwell; Johnston, Batchelor, Williams; Lunn, Betteridge, Owen, Miller, Bain.   **Scorers:** Miller, Bain(p), Owen

Northampton: Wood; Southam, Patterson; Candlin, Collins, McLain; English, Baxter, O'Donnell, Ramscar, Fowler.

Eight consecutive games without defeat, come to an end.

13. April 1953   Division 3 South   Elm Park   9,020

READING 2   NORTHAMPTON TOWN 0

Reading: Marks; Moyse, Smith; Robshaw, Wicks, Lewis; Grieve, Uphill, Blackman, McLean, Reeves.   **Scorers:** McLean, Blackman.

Northampton: Wood; Southam, Patterson; Candlin, Collins, McLain; English, Edelston, O'Donnell, Ramscar, Fowler.

Edelston replaces Baxter, to play against his old club.

16. April. 1953   Division 3 South   County Ground   7,982

NORTHAMPTON TOWN 2   COLCHESTER UNITED 0

Northampton: Wood; Southam, Patterson; Hughes, Candlin, McLain; English, Baxter, O'Donnell, Ramscar, Fowler.   **Scorers:** O'Donnell 2

Colchester: Wright; Harrison, Rooks; Berryman, Stewart, Elder; McCurley, Scott, Edwards, Barton, Shrubb.

Baxter returns again, vice Edelston.

18. April. 1953   Division 3 South   County Ground   10,040

NORTHAMPTON TOWN 4   ALDERSHOT 0

Northampton: Wood; Southam, Patterson; Hughes, Collins, Upton; English, Baxter, O'Donnell, Ramscar, Fowler.   **Scorers:** Ramscar 2, O'Donnell, Hughes.

Aldershot: Jackson; Jefferson S, Jefferson A, Alison, Laird, Wools; Wright, Lacey, McCulloch, Menzies, Flint.

Frank Upton makes his Cobblers debut, six on injury list, Adam McCulloch is ex Cobbler.

23. April. 1953   Division 3 South   County Ground   11,510

NORTHAMPTON TOWN 3   TORQUAY UNITED 3

Northampton: Wood; Southam, Patterson; Hughes, Croy, Upton; English, Baxter, O'Donnell, Ramscar, Fowler.   **Scorers:** English, O'Donnell, Fowler.

Torquay: Hayes; Parfitt, Drinkwater; Lewis, Webber, Norman; Shaw, Collins, Marchant, Mills, Edds.   **Scorers:** Collins, Marchant, Edds.

Promotion is no longer in the Club's hands, they must rely on the results of other matches

25. April 1953   Division 3 South   Layer Road   8,122

COLCHESTER UNITED 1   NORTHAMPTON TOWN 2

Colchester: Wright; Harrison, Rookes; Berryman, Stewart, Elder; Aitchinson, Scott, Edwards, Barton, Rice. **Scorer:** Barton

Northampton: Wood; Southam, Patterson; Hughes, Collins, Upton; English, Baxter, O'Donnell, Ramscar, Fowler. **Scorers:** Fowler, English.

Bristol Rovers win their game to assure themselves promotion.

27. April 1953   Jack English Benefit   County Ground

NORTHAMPTON TOWN v ALF RAMSEY X1

Northampton: Wood; Southam, Patterson; Hughes, Collins, Upton; English, Baxter, O'Donnell, Ramscar, Fowler

Alf Ramsey XI: line up not available.

Alf Ramsey was in the R.A.F. with Jack English

30. April 1953   Division 3 South   County Ground   9,555

NORTHAMPTON TOWN 3   NORWICH CITY 3

Northampton: Wood; Southam, Patterson; Hughes, Croy, Upton; English, Baxter, O'Donnell, Ramscar, Fowler. **Scorers:** English, Baxter, Fowler

Norwich: Nethercott; Proctor, Lewis; Foulkes, Houlkes, Ashman; Gavin, Johnson, Ackerman, Coxon, Adams. **Scorers:** Ashman, Johnson, Ackerman

Cobblers finish in third position

1953- 1954

20. August. 1953   Division 3 South   Selhurst Park   13,935

CRYSTAL PALACE 2   NORTHAMPTON TOWN 2

Crystal Palace: Bailey; George, McDonald; Willard, Briggs, Andrews; Fell, Thomas, Randall, Foulds, Downs. **Scorers:** Thomas, Foulds

Northampton: Wood; Marston, Patterson; Hughes, Walsh, McLain; English, Edelston, O'Donnell, Ramscar. Fowler. **Scorer:** English 2

Cobblers give debuts to Maurice Marston and Bill Walsh, both signed from Sunderland

22. August 1953   Division 3 South   Southend Stadium   10,295

SOUTHEND UNITED 2   NORTHAMPTON TOWN 0

Southend: Threadgold; Anderson, Duggin; Duthie, Parfitt, Lawler; Sibley, McAlinden, McDonald, Grant, Baimbridge. **Scorer:** Sibley 2

Northampton: Wood; Marston, Patterson; Hughes, Walsh, McLain; English, Edelston, O'Donnell, Ramscar, Fowler.

Fourth consecutive defeat for the Cobblers at Southend stadium.

26. August 1953   Division 3 South   Dean Court   14,409

BOURNEMOUTH & BOSCOMBE ATHLETIC 2   NORTHAMPTON TOWN 1

Bournemouth: Goodwin; Cunningham, Drummond; Woodward, Thomas, Neave, Hughes, Buchanan, Cross, Cheney, Harrison. **Scorer:** Cross 2

Northampton: Wood; Marston, Patterson; Hughes, Walsh, McLain; English, Baxter, O'Donnell, Ramscar, Fowler. **Scorer:** English.

With just one point from three games, the Cobblers drop into the bottom four.

29. August 1953   Division 3 South   Goldstone Ground   16,709

BRIGHTON & HOVE ALBION 3   NORTHAMPTON TOWN 2

Brighton: Gill; Tennant, Langley; McNeil, McCoy, Wilson; Bennett, Sirrell, Addinal, Leadbetter, Foreman.. **Scorers:** Leadbetter 2, Foreman

Northampton: Wood; Marston, Patterson; Smith, Walsh, Hughes, English, Baxter, O'Donnell, Ramscar, Fowler. **Scorers:** O'Donnell, Ramscar

Tim McCoy is the ex-Cobbler player.

3 September. 1953   Division 3 South   County Ground   12,618

NORTHAMPTON TOWN 2   BOURNEMOUTH & BOSCOMBE ATHLETIC 1

Northampton: Wood; Marston, Patterson; Smith, Walsh, Hughes; English, Baxter, O'Donnell, Ramscar, Fowler. **Scorer:** English 2.

Bournemouth: Godwin; Thompson, Drummond, Woodward, Harding, Neave; Waugh, Buchanan, Cross, Cheney, Harrison. **Scorer:** Cross.

Cobblers first win of the season.

5 September 1953   Division 3 South   County Ground   13,831

NORTHAMPTON TOWN 4   WATFORD 1

Northampton: Wood; Marston, Patterson; Smith, Walsh, Hughes; English, Edelston, O'Donnell, Ramscar, Fowler. **Scorer:** English 3, O'Donnell.

Watford: Underwood; Oelofse, Bewley, Kelly, Phipps, Mitchell; Cook, Bowie, Wilson, Meadows, Paton. **Scorer:** Paton.

Jack English scores his first hat trick, Freddie Ramscar has two penalties saved.

7. September 1953   Division 3 South   The Den   11,909

MILLWALL 1   NORTHAMPTON TOWN 0

Millwall: Finlayson; Jardine, Fisher. Hendon, Bowles, Saward; Haylett, Neary, Shepherd, Stobbart, Monkhouse. **Scorer:** Neary

Northampton: Wood; Marston, Patterson; Smith, Walsh, Hughes; English, Edelston, O'Donnell, Ramscar, Fowler.

Millwall's first win of the season.

12. September 1953   Division 3 South   Plainmoor   8,148

TORQUAY UNITED 1   NORTHAMPTON TOWN 1

Torquay: Hayes; Parfitt, Calland R: Lewis, Webber, Norman; Shaw, Thomas. Collins, Mills, Edds. **Scorer:** Edds.

Northampton: Wood; Marston, Patterson; Smith, Walsh, Hughes; English, Edelston, O'Donnell, Ramscar, Fowler. **Scorer:** English.

Cobblers go 14th.

17. September 1953   Division 3 South   County Ground   10,131

NORTHAMPTON TOWN 4   MILLWALL 2

Northampton: Wood; Marston, Patterson; Smith, Walsh, Hughes; English, Edelston, O'Donnell, Ramscar, Fowler. **Scorers:** English 3, Edelston.

Millwall: Finlayson; Jardine, Fisher; Haydon, Bowler, Saward; Johnson, Shepherd, Neary, Monkhouse, Hartburn. **Scorers:** Shepherd, Hartburn.

Patterson and Neary sent off, Saward carried off.

19. September 1953   Division 3 South   County Ground   13,138

NORTHAMPTON TOWN 1   NEWPORT COUNTY 0

Northampton: Wood; Marston, Patterson; Smith, Walsh, Hughes; English, Edelston, O'Donnell, Ramscar, Fowler. **Scorer:** English.

Newport County: Hughes; Staples, Barton; Wilcox C, Wilcox R, Newall; Birch, White, Parker, Shergold, Morrey.

Tommy centred for Jack English's goal.

21. September 1953   Division 3 South   County Ground   8,778

NORTHAMPTON TOWN 1   READING 1

Northampton: Wood; Marston, Patterson; Smith, Walsh, Hughes; English, Edelston, O'Donnell, Ramscar, Fowler.. **Scorer:** Fowler (p)

Reading: Hall; Livingston, Smith; Davis, Wicks, Leach; Simpson, Hinshelwood, Blackman, Uphill, Docherty. **Scorer:** Hinshelwood

Tommy, now the club penalty taker, converts his first spot kick.

---

26. September 1953   Division 3 South   County Ground   12,096

NORTHAMPTON TOWN 1   GILLINGHAM 1

Northampton: Wood; Marston, Patterson; Smith, Walsh, Hughes; English, Edelston, O'Donnell, Ramscar, Fowler. **Scorer:** English.

Gillingham: Riggs; Marks, Lewin; Boswell, Niblett, Forester; Durkin, Evans, Scarth, Morgan, Long. **Scorer:** Morgan.

Jack English becomes top scorer in Div. 3 South with 14 goals.

---

30. September 1953   Division 3 South   Elm Park   8,755

READING 2   NORTHAMPTON TOWN 0

Reading: Hall; Livingston, Smith; Davis, Wicks, Leach; Simpson, Hinshelwood, Blackman, Uphill, Quinton. **Scorer:** Blackman, Uphill.

Northampton: Wood; Marston, Patterson; Smith, Walsh, Hughes; English, Baxter, O'Donnell, Starocsik, Fowler.

Edelston and Ramscar are dropped for Baxter and Starocsik.

---

3. October 1953   Division 3 South   Highfield Road   17,540

COVENTRY CITY 0   NORTHAMPTON TOWN 0

Coventry: Taylor; Jones, Kirk; Jamieson, McDonnell, Austin; Nutt, Bradbury, Dutton, Hill P., Hill J.

Northampton: Wood; Marston, Patterson; Smith, Walsh, Hughes; English, Baxter, O'Donnell, Ramscar, Fowler.

Ramscar returns, replacing Starocsik.

---

10. October 1953   Division 3 South   Loftus Road   13,300

QUEENS PARK RANGERS 1   NORTHAMPTON TOWN 1

Q.P.R: Gullans; Woods, Ingham; Nicholas, Powell, Angell; Tonkys, Quinn, Clayton, Smith, Shepherd. **Scorer:** Shepherd.

Northampton: Wood; Marston, Patterson; Smith, Walsh, Hughes, English, B axter, O'Donnell, Ramscar, Fowler. **Scorer:** Fowler

All the Cobblers forward line played well.

---

17. October 1953   Division 3 South   County Ground   14,403

NORTHAMPTON TOWN 3   SOUTHAMPTON 0

Northampton: Wood; Marston; Patterson; Smith, Walsh, Hughes; English, Anderson, O'Donnell, Ramscar, Fowler. **Scorers:** O'Donnell, Fowler, o.g.

Southampton: Christie, Ellington, Day; Gregory, Wilkins, Clements; Horton, Williams, Day, Walker, Digby.

John Anderson makes his Cobblers debut in place of Larry Baxter.

---

24. October. 1953   Division 3 South   Layer Road   7,599

COLCHESTER UNITED 1   NORTHAMPTON TOWN 1

Colchester: Wright; Harrison, Lewis; Bearryman, Stewart, Elder;Grice, Barlow, McCurley, McKim, Church. **Scorer:** Elder (p)

Northampton: Wood; Marston, Southam; Smith, Walsh, Hughes; English, Anderson, Cross, Ramscar, Fowler. **Scorer:** Cross.

Jack Cross makes his debut, Ron Patterson injured, Jack Southam takes his place .

31. October. 1953   Division 3 South   County Ground   12,450
NORTHAMPTON TOWN 6   CRYSTAL PALACE 0
Northampton: Wood; Marston, Patterson; Smith, Collins, Hughes; English, Anderson, Cross, Ramscar, Fowler.   **Scorers:** English 3, Anderson, Cross, Ramscar.
Crystal Palace: Bailey; George, McDonald; Willard, Briggs, Moss; Fell, Thomas, Choules, Foulds, Downs.
Bill Walsh out injured, Ben Collins replaces him as both centre half and captain.

7. November 1953   Division 3 South   Ashton Gate   17,380
BRISTOL CITY 2   NORTHAMPTON TOWN 1
Bristol City: Cook; Guy, Bailey; Peacock, Roberts, Williams; Eisentrager, Atyeo, Rogers, Micklewright, Bayley.   **Scorers:** Atyeo, Rogers.
Northampton: Wood; Marston. Patterson; Smith, Collins, Hughes; English, Anderson, Cross, Ramscar, Fowler.   **Scorer:** Smith.
Ron Patterson returns, Cobblers first defeat for five games.

14.November 1953   Division 3 South   County Ground   11,695
NORTHAMPTON TOWN 6   ALDERSHOT 2
Northampton: Wood; Marston, Patterson; Smith, Collins, Hughes; English, Anderson, O'Donnell, Ramscar, Fowler.   **Scorers:** Anderson 2, English, O'Donnell, Ramscar,Fowler
Aldershot: Jackman; Raine, Wood ; Cropley, Reddie, Alison; Gaynor, Hobbs, Lacey, McCulloch, Flint.   **Scorers:** Wood (p), Gaynor.
Jack Cross out with flu, Willie O'Donnell returns. Adam McCulloch is an ex-Cobbler.

21. November 1953   F. A. Cup (Round 1)   County Ground   16,302
NORTHAMPTON TOWN 3   LLANELLY 0
Northampton: Wood; Marston, Patterson; Smith, Collins, Hughes; English, Anderson, Cross, Ramscar, Fowler.   **Scorer:** Cross, Ramscar (p), Fowler.
Llanelly: Annetts; Maxwell, Roberts; Davies, Newale, Whitelaw; O'Driscoll, Lore, Neilson, Miller, Ange.
Jack Cross returns, ex-Cobbler Robert Maxwell was in the Llanelly side.

28. November 1953   Division 3 South   County Ground   12,561
NORTHAMPTON TOWN 5   WALSALL 1
Northampton: Wood; Marston. Patterson; Smith, Collins, Hughes; English, Anderson, Cross, Ramscar, Fowler.   **Scorers:** Cross 3, Ramscar 2
Walsall: Chilvers; Horne, Flavell; Green, Brickett, Russell; Morris, Jones, Holding, Alsop, Grubb.   **Scorer:** Green.
Gilbert Alsop was a wartime guest for the Cobblers

5. December 1953   Division 3 South   Gay Meadow   7,825
SHREWSBURY TOWN 2   NORTHAMPTON TOWN 4
Shrewsbury: McBride; Bannister, Parr; Bullion, Candlin, Beynor; Fisher, Jackson, Hudson, Brennan, McCue.   **Scorers:** Brennan, McCue.
Northampton: Wood; Southam, Marston; Smith, Collins, Hughes; English, Edelston, Cross, Ramscar, Fowler.   **Scorers:** Edelston, Cross, Ramscar, o.g.
Ron Patterson and John Anderson injured, Maurice Candlin, is ex-Cobblers.

12. December 1953   F.A. Cup (Round. 2)   County Ground   18,772
NORTHAMPTON TOWN 1   HARTLEPOOL UNITED 1
Northampton: Wood; Marston, Southam; Smith, Collins, Hughes; English, Edelston, Cross, Ramscar, Fowler.   **Scorer:** Ramscar
Hartlepool: Brown; Willetts, Thompson; Newton, Moore, Stamper, Linacre, Richardson, Wilson, McGuigin, Harding.   **Scorer:** Harding
First ever meeting between the two sides.

15. December 1953   F.A.Cup (Round 2 replay)   Victoria Ground   12,169

HARTLEPOOL UNITED 1   NORTHAMPTON TOWN 0
Hartlepool: Brown; Willetts, Thompson; Newton, Moore, Stamper; Linacre, Richardson, Johnson, McGuigan, Wilder.   **Scorer:** Linacre.
Northampton: Wood; Southam, Patterson; Hughes, Collins, McLain; English, Edelston, O'Donnell, Ramscar, Fowler.
Ron Patterson returns.

19. December 1953   Division 3 South   County Ground   9,181

NORTHAMPTON TOWN 5   SOUTHEND UNITED 0
Northampton: Wood; Southam, Patterson; Hughes, Collins, McLain; English, Anderson, O'Donnell, Ramscar, Fowler.   **Scorer:** English 4, McLain.
Southend United: Threadgold; Young, Anderson; Lawler, Pavitt, Bridge, Lockhart, McAlinden, Grant, Thompson, Bainbridge.
Jack English scores four goals, including a six minute hat trick.

25. December 1953   Division 3 South   County Ground   13,809

NORTHAMPTON TOWN 2   LEYTON ORIENT 2
Northampton: Wood; Southam, Patterson; Hughes, Collins, McLain; English, O'Donnell. Cross, Ramscar, Fowler.   **Scorers:** Hughes, English.
Southend United: Groombridge; Evans, Charlton; Blizzard, Dalrous, McMahon; Facey, Pacey, Rees, Morgan, Poulter.   **Scorer:** Rees 2.
Injury to Anderson allows manager Dennison to play O'Donnell and Cross together.

26. December 1953   Division 3 South   Brisbane Road   14,768

LEYTON ORIENT 2   NORTHAMPTON TOWN 0
Leyton Orient: Groombridge; Evans, Charlton; Blizzard, Aldous, McMahon; Facey, Pacey, Rees, Morgan, Poulton.   **Scorer:** Rees, Pacey.
Northampton: Wood; Southam, Patterson; Hughes, Collins, McLain; English, Smith, Cross, Ramscar, Fowler.
Although Anderson is fit again, Smith is selected at inside right,

2. January 1954   Division 3 South   County Ground   10,989

NORTHAMPTON TOWN 4   BRIGHTON & HOVE ALBION 2
Northampton: Wood; Southam. Patterson; Hughes, Collins, McLain; Starocsik, Smith, Cross, Ramscar, Fowler.   **Scorers:** Starocsik, Cross   2 og
Brighton & Hove Albion: Gill; Tennant, Langley; McIlvenny, South, Wilson; Gordon, Munday, Addinall, Leadbetter, Foreman.   **Scorer:** Addinall 2
English, O'Donnell and Edelston all out injured.

9. January 1954   Friendly   County Ground   3,000

NORTHAMPTON TOWN 3   WATFORD 0
Northampton: Wood; Marston, Southam; Hughes, Collins, McLain; Staroscik, Anderson, Cross, Ramscar. Fowler.   **Scorer:** Cross 2, Anderson.
Watford: Bennett; Bewley, Jones; Bateman, Oelofse, Mitchell; Cook, Smith, Brown, Jelley, Paton.
Both sides out of the F.A. Cup, played a friendly.

16. January. 1954   Division 3 South   Vicarage Road   13,134

WATFORD 1   NORTHAMPTON TOWN 1
Watford: Bennett; Bewley, Jones; Kelley, Oelofse, Mitchell; Cook, Smith, Brown, Bowie, Paton.   **Scorer:** Bowie (p)
Northampton: Wood; Marston, Southam; Hughes, Collins, McLain; English, Anderson, Cross, Ramscar, Fowler.   **Scorer:** Cross.
Eight minutes of extra time was added to the game in which Watford scored.

23. January 1954   Division 3 South   County Ground   11,162

NORTHAMPTON TOWN 3   TORQUAY UNITED 1

Northampton: Wood; Marston, Southam; Hughes, Collins, McLain; English, Anderson, Cross, Ramscar, Fowler.   **Scorer:** Anderson, Cross, Marston.

Torquay: Hayes; Parfitt, Drinkwater; Lewis, Webber, Norman; Wwings, Collins, Dobbie, Mills, Thomas.   **Scorer:** Dobbie

Cobblers go 6th, 12 points behind leaders Ipswich. Alf Wood made his 100th appearance.

6. February 1954   Division 3 South   Somerset Park   10,221

NEWPORT COUNTY 2   NORTHAMPTON TOWN 0

Newport: Hughes; Haines, Hayward; Thomas, Wilcox, Witcomb; Birch, Lucas, Saward, Graham, Shergold.   **Scorer:** Saward, Graham.

Northampton: Wood; Marston, Patterson; Hughes, Collins, McLain; English, Anderson, O'Donnell, Ramscar, Fowler.

Jack Cross is sold to Sheffield United, the supporters are unhappy.

13. February 1954   Division 3 South   Priestfield Stadium   9,558

GILLINGHAM 2   NORTHAMPTON TOWN 1

Gillingham: Rigg; Marks. Lewis; Boswell, Ayres, Forrester; Scarth, Evans, Morgan, Sowder, Millar.   **Scorers:** Scarth, Sowder.

Northampton: Wood; Marston, Patterson; Hughes, Collins, McLain; English, Anderson, O'Donnell, Ramscar, Fowler.   **Scorer:** English.

Anderson leaves the field suffering from head injuries.

18. February 1954   Division 3 South   County Ground   10,539

NORTHAMPTON TOWN 0   COVENTRY CITY 1

Northampton: Wood; Marston, Southam; Hughes, Collins, McLain; English, Anderson, O'Donnell, Ramscar, Fowler.

Coventry: Taylor, Timmins, Kirk; Simpson, McDonald, Austin; Nutt, Jamieson, Brown, Bradbury, Hill J.   **Scorer:** Nutt.

Cobblers first home defeat of the season.

27. February 1954   Division 3 South   County Ground   8,259

NORTHAMPTON TOWN 2   QUEENS PARK RANGERS 1

Northampton: Wood; Marston, Southam; Hughes, Collins, McLain; English, O'Donnell, Walsh, Ramscar, Fowler.   **Scorer:** English 2

Q.P.R.: Brown; Taylor, Ingham; Nicholas, Powell, Angell; Pounder, Cameron, Clark, Smith, Kernan.   **Scorer:** Clark.

Walsh is tried at centre forward, with little success.

6. March 1954   Division 3 South   The Dell   14,196

SOUTHAMPTON 1   NORTHAMPTON TOWN 0

Southampton: Christie; Oakley, Gregory; Elliott, Clements, McLaughlin, Flood, Walker, Day, Purdie, Hoskis.   **Scorer:** Day.

Northampton: Wood; Marston, Southam; Hughes, Collins, McLain; English, O'Donnell, Walsh, Ramscar, Fowler.

Cobblers drop to 10th.

13. March. 1954   Division 3 South   County Ground   6,821

NORTHAMPTON TOWN 2   SWINDON TOWN 0

Northampton: Wood; Marston, Southam; Hughes, Collins, Upton; English, O'Donnell, McLain, Ramscar, Fowler.   **Scorer:** McLain, Ramscar.

Swindon: Burton; Hunt, Hilton; Cross, Hudson, Johnston; Lambert, Onslow, Johnson, Sampson, Beard.

Tommy McLain becomes the fourth player the Cobblers play at centre forward this term.

20th March 1954　　　Division 3 South　　　Fellows Park　　　10,032

WALSALL 0　NORTHAMPTON TOWN 1
Walsall: Baldwin; Fort, Green; Morris, Russell, Tarrant; Fleck, Lewis, Davis, Dean, Colombo.
Northampton: Wood; Marston, Southam; Hughes, Collins, Upton; English, O'Donnell, McLain, Ramscar, Fowler.　**Scorer:** McLain.
Only the Cobblers second away win this season.

25. March 1954　　　Division 3 South　　　County　Ground　　　5,968

NORTHAMPTON TOWN 1　IPSWICH TOWN 0
Northampton: Wood; Marston, Southam; Hughes, Collins, Upton; English. O'Donnell, McLain, Ramscar, Fowler.　**Scorer:** McLain
Ipswich: Parry; Acres, Feeney;Myles, Rees, Parker; Reed, Crowe, Garneys, Elsworthy, McLuck.
The Cobblers move to 10th.

27. March. 1954　　　Division 3 South　　　County Ground　　　8,283

NORTHAMPTON TOWN 3　BRISTOL CITY 0
Northampton: Wood; Marston, Southam; Hughes, Collins, Upton; English, O'Donnell, McLain, Ramscar, Fowler.　**Scorers:** O'Donnell, English, McLain
Bristol City: Cook; Guy, Bailey; Regan R, Peacock, White; Boxley, Atyeo, Micklewright, Williams, Regan P.
Fourth consecutive game the Cobblers have kept a clean sheet.

3. April 1954　　　Division 3 South　　　Recreation Ground　　　5,728

ALDERSHOT 3　NORTHAMPTON TOWN 1
Aldershot: Brown; Rodgers, Wood;Alison, Billingham, Miller; Gaynor, Menzies, McCulloch, Durkin, Flint.　**Scorers:** Gaynor, Menzies, Durkin.
Northampton: Wood; Marston, Southam; Hughes, Collins, Upton; English, O'Donnell, McLain, Ramscar, Fowler.　**Scorer:** English.
Adam McCulloch is the ex-Cobblers player.

8. April 1954　　　Division 3 South　　　County Ground　　　5,597

NORTHAMPTON TOWN 2　EXETER CITY 2
Northampton: Wood; Marston, Southam; Hughes, Collins, Upton; English, O'Donnell, McLain, Ramscar, Fowler.　**Scorers:** English, Ramscar.
Exeter: Kelley; Walker, Douglas; Mitchell, Davey, Dodgin; Priestley, Elleway, Donaldson, McKay, Park.　**Scorers:** Elleway, Donaldson.
Ex Cobbler, Norman Dodgin, is the Exeter player / manager.

10. April 1954　　　Division 3 South　　　County Ground　　　8,088

NORTHAMPTON TOWN 1　SHREWSURY TOWN 0
Northampton: Wood; Marston, Southam; Smith, Collins, Upton; English, O'Donnell, McLain, Ramscar, Fowler.　**Scorer:** O'Donnell.
Shrewsbury: McBride; Bannister, Parr; Benyon, Candlin, Crutchley; Price, Stamps, Hudson, Jackson, McCue.
Ex Cobbler Maurice Candlin is captain of the Shrewsbury side.

13. April 1954　　　Jack Jennings Benefit　　　County Ground

NORTHAMPTON TOWN 2　COMBINED LEAGUE X1 2
Northampton: Wood; Marston, Patterson; Smith, Collins, Upton; English, Walton (Man U), McLain, Downie (Luton), Fowler.
League XI: Stretton (Luton); Jones (Coventry), Evans (Arsenal); Macauley (Guildford), Pemberton (Luton), Bowen (Arsenal); Matthews (Blackpool), Mortenson (Blackpool), McCormack (Notts C), Bradbury (Coventry), Lewis (Chelsea).

17. April 1954   Division 3 South   St James Park   8,844

EXETER CITY 1   NORTHAMPTON TOWN 0

Exeter: Kelley; Walton, Douglas; Booth, Davey, Mitchell,; Priestley, Knight, Donaldson, Parker, McClelland.   **Scorer:** McClelland.

Northampton: Wood; Marston, Southam; Hughes, Collins, Upton; English, Smith, McLain, O'Donnell, Fowler.

Gwyn Hughes returns, Jack Smith moves in to the forwards, Freddie Ramscar is dropped.

19. April 1954   Division 3 South   Carrow Road   22,961

NORWICH CITY 4   NORTHAMPTON TOWN 1

Norwich: Oxford; Morgan, Lewis; McGrachen, Foulkes, Ashman; Gavin, Brennan, Summers, Woan, Gordon.   **Scorers:** Ashman, Gavin, Brennan, Woan.

Northampton: Wood; Marston, Southam.Hughes, Collins, Upton; English, O'Donnell, McLain, Ramscar, Fowler.   **Scorer:** O'Donnell

Freddie Ramscar returns. Alan Woan makes his Norwich debut, and scores.

20. April 1954   Division 3 South   County Ground   8,906

NORTHAMPTON TOWN 2   NORWICH CITY 0

Northampton: Wood; Marston, Southam; Hughes, Collins, Upton; English, Ramscar, McLain, O'Donnell, Fowler.   **Scorers:** Ramscar, Upton.

Norwich: Oxford; Morgan, Lewis; McGrachan, Foulkes, Ashman; Gavin, Brennan, Summers, Woan, Gordon.

The Cobblers swap their inside forwards, the experiment worked.

24. April 1954   Division 3 South   County Ground   7,344

NORTHAMPTON TOWN 3   COLCHESTER UNITED 0

Northampton: Wood; Marston, Southam; Hughes, Collins, Upton; English, Ramscar, O'Donnell, Anderson, Fowler.   **Scorer:** Anderson, Fowler, English.

Colchester: Wright G: Harrison, Lewis; Berryman, Stewart, Hill; Grice, Dale, Plant, McKim, Wright P.

Colchester will have to apply for re-election after this defeat.

27. April 1954   Ben Collins Benefit   County Ground

NORTHAMPTON TOWN 1   SHEFFIELD UNITED 1

Northampton: Wood; Marston, Southam; Yeomans, Collins, Upton; English, Ramscar, O'Donnell, Anderson, Fowler.

Sheffield United: Hodgkinson, Caldwell, Ridge; Shaw, Tones, Ranson, Ringstead, Haylon, Cross, Brook, McNab.

Stanley Matthews was to have been a guest but he was injured, ran the line instead.

28. April . 1954   Division 3 South   County Ground (Swindon)   5,150

SWINDON TOWN 0   NORTHAMPTON TOWN 0

Swindon: Burton; Page, Milton; Cross, Batchelor, Johnston; Bull, Onslow, Johnston, Lambert, Sampson.

Northampton: Wood; Marston, Southam; Hughes, Collins, Upton; English, Ramscar, O'Donnell, Anderson, Fowler.

Cobblers first 0-0 draw since October.

1. May, 1954   Division 3 South   Portman Road   22,133

IPSWICH TOWN 2   NORTHAMPTON TOWN 1

IPSWICH: Parr; Acres, Feeney; Myles, Rees, Parker, Jones, Callaghan, Phillips, Cross, McLuckie.   **Scorers:** Philips, o.g.

Northampton: Wood; Marston, Southam; Yeoman, Collins, Upton; English, Ramscar, O' Donnell, Jones, Fowler.   **Scorer:** o.g.

Ipswich win the Championship. Cobblers give a game to Ray Yeoman and Bernard Jones.

1954 - 1955

21. August 1954	Division 3 South	Somerset Park	12,709

NEWPORT COUNTY 0   NORTHAMPTON TOWN 1

Newport: Hughes; Lever, Hayward; Hollyman, Wilcox, Newall; McGhee, Lucas, Saward, Graham, Wharton.
Northampton: Wood; Marston, Southam; Hughes, Collins, McLain, English, Hazeldine, Oakley, Ramscar, Fowler.   **Scorer:** English
Cobblers first game under new manager Dave Smith. Hazeldine and Oakley make debuts.

26. August 1954	Division 3 South	County Ground	11,735

NORTHAMPTON TOWN 1   CRYSTAL PALACE 1

Northampton: Wood; Marston, Southam; Hughes, Collins, McLain; English, Hazeldine, Oakley, Ramscar, Fowler.   **Scorer:** English.
Crystal Palace: Bailey; Choules, McDonald; Woods, Briggs, Moss; Grieve , Thomas, Adinall, Tilston, Devonshire.   **Scorer:** Grieve
Ray Bailey the Palace keeper, is the father of Gary Bailey, later of Manchester United.

28. August 1954	Division 3 South	County Ground	9,764

NORTHAMPTON TOWN 2   EXETER CITY 0

Northampton: Wood; Marston, Southam; Hughes, Collins, McLain, English, Hazeldine, Oakley, Ramscar, Fowler.   **Scorers:** Fowler, Oakley.
Exeter: Kelly; Walton, Doyle; Dunne, Davey, Mitchell; Priestley, Anderson, Ellaway, Mackay, McClelland.
John Anderson , the Exeter inside forward, is an ex Cobblers player.

1. September 1954	Division 3 South	Selhurst Park	11,624

CRYSTAL PALACE 3   NORTHAMPTON TOWN 1

Crystal Palace: Bailey; Choules, McDonald;Woods, Briggs, Andrews; Grieve, Thomas, Addinall, Tilston, Devonshire.   **Scorers:** McDonald, Thomas, Addinall.
Northampton: Wood; Marston, Southam; Hughes, Collins, McLain; English, Hazeldine, Oakley, Ramscar, Fowler.   **Scorer:** English
Freddie Ramscar's last game for the Cobblers before joining Millwall.

4. September 1954	Division 3 South	Layer Road	7,468

COLCHESTER UNITED 4   NORTHAMPTON TOWN   1

Colchester: Kirk; Harrison, Lewis; McCourt, Stewart, Hunt: Birch, Dale, Plant, McKim, Grice.   **Scorer:** Plant 3, Birch.
Northampton: Webber; Marston, Southam; Yeoman, Collins, Hughes; Mills, Hazeldine, English, Jones, Fowler.   **Scorer:** Hazeldine
Webber and Mills make their debuts, Yeoman and Jones are recalled

9. September 1954	Division 3 South	County Ground	8,106

NORTHAMPTON TOWN 0   MILLWALL   1

Northampton: Webber, Marston, Patterson; Yeoman, Collins, Hughes; Mills, Hazeldine, English, Jones, Fowler.
Millwall: Finlayson; Fisher, Heydon; Hurley, Saward, Johnson; Reeve, Summers, Ramscar, Jardine, Prior.   **Scorer:** Prior.
Freddie Ramscar, still living in Northampton, lays on the winning goal.

11. September 1954	Division 3 South	County Ground	9,560

NORTHAMPTON TOWN 1   NORWICH CITY 1

Northampton: Wood; Marston, Patterson; Yeoman, Collins, Hughes; English, Hazeldine, Oakley, Jones, Fowler.   **Scorer:** Oakley.
Norwich: Nethercott; Morgan, Lewis; McCrochan, Foulkes, Pickwick; Gavin, Hansell, Johnston, Brennan, McMillan.   **Scorer:** Lewis.
Wood and Oakley return, Cobblers go 17th.

13. September 1954.   Division 3 South   The Den   9,558
MILLWALL 1   NORTHAMPTON TOWN 0
Millwall: Finlayson; Jardine, Ainslow; Heydon, Hurley, Saward; Johnson, Reeves,
Summers, Ramscar, Prior.   **Scorer:** Ramscar.
Northampton: Wood; Marston, Patterson; Yeoman, Collins, Hughes; English,
Hazeldine, Oakley, Jones, Fowler.
Freddie Ramscar travelled down with the Cobblers, scored the winner, then returned.

18. September 1954   Division 3 South   Southend Stadium 10,519
SOUTHEND UNITED 4   NORTHAMPTON TOWN 1
Southend: Threadgold; Pavitt, Anderson A; Duthie, Howe, Burns; Smith, Anderson W,
Hollis, Baron, Bainbridge.   **Scorers:** Hollis 2, Bainbridge 2.
Northampton: Wood; Marston. Patterson; Yeoman, Collins, Hughes; English,
Hazeldine, McLain, Jones, Fowler.   **Scorer:** McLain.
Tommy McLain returns to the first team as Centre forward, Cobblers drop to 21st

21. September 1954   Division 3 South   Vicarage Road   10,692
WATFORD 1   NORTHAMPTON TOWN 1
Watford: Bennett; Bewley, Cooke; Kelly, Shipwright, Mitchell; Cooke, Catleugh, Brown,
Bowie, Adams.   **Scorer:** Brown
Northampton: Wood; Marston, Southam; Yeoman, Collins, Hughes; English,
Hazeldine, McLain, Jones, Fowler.   **Scorer:** McLain.
Seventh consecutive game without a win.

25. September 1954   Division 3 South   County Ground   8,235
NORTHAMPTON TOWN 2   ALDERSHOT 1
Northampton: Wood; Marston, Southam; Yeoman, Collins, Hughes; English,
Hazeldine, McLain, Jones, Fowler.   **Scorers:** Hazeldine, Jones.
Aldershot: Brown; Jefferson A, Jefferson S: Alison, Reddie, Sirrell, Gayner, Cheney,
McCulloch, Lacey, Flint.   **Scorer:** Lacey.
Ex Cobbler Adam McCulloch is in the Aldershot side.

30. September 1954   Division 3 South   County Ground   4,128
NORTHAMPTON TOWN 0   WATFORD 1
Northampton: Wood; Southam, Patterson; Yeoman, Croy, Hughes; Staroscik,
Hazeldine, McLain, Jones, Fowler.
Watford: Bennett; Bewley, Smith; Keley, Shipwright, Mitchell; Cooke, Bowie, Brown,
Catleugh, Paton.   **Scorer:** Bowie (p).
Collins injured, Marston and English dropped; Croy, Southam and Staroscik
replacements

 2. October 1954   Division 3 South   County Ground (Swindon)   8,899
SWINDON TOWN 0   NORTHAMPTON TOWN 1
Swindon: Burton; Hilton, Cross; Hudson, Johnston, Hunter; Brennan, McClelland,
Own, Sampson, Bull.
Northampton: Wood; Southam, Patterson; Yeoman, Croy, Hughes; Starocsik,
Hazeldine, McLean, Jones, Fowler.   **Scorer:** Jones.
Shock win for the Cobblers. Ron Patterson injured, Tommy star player.

 9. October 1954   Division 3 South   County Ground   7,827
NORTHAMPTON TOWN 4   GILLINGHAM 1
Northampton: Wood; Southam, Patterson; Yeoman, Croy, Hughes; Starocsik,
Hazeldine, McLain, Jones, Fowler.   **Scorers:** Hazeldine 2, McLain, Fowler.
Gillingham: Rigg; Marks, West; Boswell, Ayre, Forrester; Scarth, Evans, Sowden,
Morgan, Millar.   **Scorer:** Morgan.
Only one defeat in the last five games.

| 16. October. 1954 | Division 3 South | Elm Park | 9,864. |

READING 0   NORTHAMPTON TOWN 1
Reading: Jones; Hall, Mansell; Davis, Reeves, McLaren; Simpson, Hinshelwood, Uphill, Campbell, Wheeler.
Northampton: Wood; Southam, Patterson; Yeoman, Croy, Hughes; Starocsik, Hazeldine, McLain, Jones, Fowler.   **Scorer:** Starocsik.
Cobblers go 12th. Now won as many away games, as all last season.

| 23. October 1954 | Division 3 South | County Ground | 8,468 |

NORTHAMPTON TOWN 3   SHREWSBURY TOWN 1
Northampton: Wood; Southam, Patterson; Smith, Croy, Hughes; Starocsik, Hazeldine, McLain, Jones, Fowler.   **Scorers:** Starocsik 2, Jones.
Shrewsbury: Crossly; Bannister, Parr; Candlin, Atkins, Maloney; Price, O'Donnell, Dodd, Weigh, McCue.   **Scorer:** Weigh
Ex-Cobblers O'Donnell and Candlin in the Shrewsbury side.

| 29. October. 1954 | Division 3 South | The Dell | 16,039 |

SOUTHAMPTON 4   NORTHAMPTON TOWN 0
Southampton: Kiernan; Turner, Traynor; McLoughlin, Wilkins, Simpson; Flood, Mulgrew, Day, Walker, Hoskins.   **Scorers:** Walker 2, Day, Hoskins.
Northampton: Wood; Southam, Patterson; Smith, Croy, Hughes;Starocsik, Hazeldine, McLain, Jones, Fowler.
Tommy missed a penalty, but was still star player. Tommy Mulgrew ex-Cobbler.

| 6. November 1954 | Division 3 South | County Ground | 11,608 |

NORTHAMPTON TOWN 2   BRISTOL CITY 0
Northampton: Wood; Southam, Patterson; Smith, Croy, Hughes; Starocsik, Hazeldine, McLain, Jones, Fowler.   **Scorer:** Staroscik 2(1 p)
Bristol City: Cook; Guy, Bailey; Regan, Peacock, White; Rogers, Atyeo, Rodgers, Burden, Boxley.
A good victory against the league leaders. Starocsik now the club penalty taker.

| 13. November 1954 | Division 3 South | Plainmoor | 7,246 |

TORQUAY UNITED 5   NORTHAMPTON TOWN 2
Torquay: Jeffries; Towers, Smith H: Lewis, McGuiness, Norman; Bond, Collins, Dobbie, Mills, Smith J.   **Scorers:** Dobbie 2, Mills 2, Smith J.
Northampton: Wood; Southam, Patterson; Smith, Croy, Hughes; Starocsik, Hazeldine, McLain, Jones, Fowler.   **Scorers:** McLain, Smith
Gwyn Hughes injured, rest of defence had a poor game.

| 20. November 1954 | F.A. Cup (Round 1) | County Ground | 14,667 |

NORTHAMPTON TOWN 0   COVENTRY CITY 1
Northampton: Wood; Southam, Patterson; Smith, Croy, Hughes; Starocsik, Hazeldine, McLain, Jones, Fowler;
Coventry: Matthews; Jones, Kirk; Harvey, McDonnell, Simpson; Nutt, Hill, Dutton, Capel, Johnson.   **Scorers:** Kirk
Kirk scored with an 80 yard clearance, Alf Wood went out to collect the ball, but slipped.

| 27. November 1954 | Division 3 South | Griffin Park | 10,029 |

BRENTFORD 1   NORTHAMPTON TOWN 3
Brentford: Feehan; Horne, Latimer; Coote, Dargie, Robinson; Heath, Rainford, Stobbart, Turner, Dare.   **Scorer:** o g.
Northampton: Webber; Southam, Patterson; Yeoman, Croy, Hughes; Starocsik, English, McLain, Jones, Fowler.   **Scorers:** English 2, McLain.
Webber, Yeoman and English recalled. Sonny Feehan is the ex-Cobblers keeper.

4. December. 1954   Division 3 South   County Ground   11,008
NORTHAMPTON TOWN 1   COVENTRY CITY 0
Northampton: Webber; Collins, Patterson; Yeoman, Croy, Hughes; Starocsik, English, McLain, Jones, Fowler.   **Scorer:** Starocsik (p)
Coventry: Matthews; Jones, Kirk; Howes, McDonnell, Simpson; Nutt, Hill, Lee, Capel, Jones.
Ben Collins returns at full back. Cobblers get revenge for their F.A. Cup defeat.

11. December 1954   Division 3 South   County Ground   6,609
NORTHAMPTON TOWN 1   SWINDON TOWN 0
Northampton: Webber; Collins, Patterson; Yeoman, Croy, Hughes; Starocsik, English, McLain, Jones, Fowler.   **Scorer:** Starocsik.
Swindon: Burton; Hunt, Page; Cross, Hudson, Williamson; Gibson, McClelland, Owen, Sampson, Beards.
First double of the season for the Cobblers.

18. December 1954   Division 3 South   County Ground   6,947
NORTHAMPTON TOWN 2   NEWPORT COUNTY 2
Northampton: Webber; Collins, Patterson; Yeoman, Croy, Hughes; Starocsik, English, Oakley, Hazeldine, Fowler.   **Scorer:** Starocsik, English
Newport: Hughes; Staple, Lewis; Hollyman, Wilcox, Thomas ; Shergold, Lucas, Johnston, Harris, Wharton.   **Scorers:** Lucas, Harris.
Ken Oakley and Don Hazeldine return to the side.

25 December 1954   Division 3 South   Loftus road   8,718
QUEENS PARK RANGERS 1   NORTHAMPTON TOWN 0
Q.P.R.: Brown; Wood, Ingham; Nicholson, Rutter, Angell; Fidler, Cameron, Clark, Smith, Shepherd.   **Scorer:** Clark
Northampton: Webber; Collins, Patterson; Yeoman, Croy, Hughes; Starocsik, English, Oakley, McLain, Fowler.
Tommy McLain returns to the side, Cobblers now go 9th.

27. December 1954   Division 3 South   County Ground   12,623
NORTHAMPTON TOWN 1   QUEENS PARK RANGERS 3
Northampton: Webber; Collins, Patterson; Yeoman, Croy, Hughes; Starocsik, English, Oakley, Jones, Fowler.   **Scorer:** o.g.
Q.P.R: Brown; Rutter, Ingham; Nicholas, Powell, Angell; Fidler, Cameron, Clark, Smith, Shepherd.   **Scorers:** Clark 2, Angell.
Webber replaced Wood in goal, but had a poor game.

1. January 1955   Division 3 South   St. James Park   7,040
EXETER CITY 3   NORTHAMPTON TOWN 1
Exeter: Kelly; Walton, Douglas; Setters, Harvey, Mitchell; Thomas, Mackay, John, Ellaway, McClelland.   **Scorers:** Mackay, John, McClelland
Northampton: Webber, Collins, Patterson; Yeoman, Croy, Hughes; English, Hazeldine, Adams, Jones. Fowler.   **Scorer:** o.g.
Hazeldine and Adams were recalled.

8. January 1955   Division 3 South   County Ground   8,864
NORTHAMPTON TOWN 2   LEYTON ORIENT 2
Northampton: Webber; Collins, Patterson; Hughes, Croy, McLain; English, Yeoman, Adams, Jones, Fowler.   **Scorers:** Yeoman, Adams
Leyton Orient: Welton; Lee, Charlton; Blizzard, Aldous, McKnight; Groves, Facey, Rees, Morgan, Hartburn.   **Scorers:** Groves, Rees.
Orient's scorer, Vic Groves is the uncle of Perry Groves, later to play for Arsenal.

22. January 1955   Division 3 South   Carrow Road   11,159
NORWICH CITY 3   NORTHAMPTON TOWN 2
Norwich: Nethercott; Holmes, Lewis; McCrochan, Foulkes, Ashman; Gordon, Brennan, Kearns, Chung, Regan.   **Scorers:** Kearns 2, Gordon.
Northampton: Webber; Marston, Patterson; Hughes, Collins, McLain; English, Yeoman, Adams, Jones, Fowler.   **Scorer:** English 2
Maurice Marston returns, Ben Collins to centre half, Ray Yeoman limps off injured.

29. January 1955   Dvision 3 South   Brisbane Road   17,969
LEYTON ORIENT 2   NORTHAMPTON TOWN 1
Leyton Orient: Welton; Lee, Charlton; Blizzard, Aldous, McMahon; Groves, Facey, Rees, Morgan, Hartburn.   Scorers; Groves, Facey.
Northampton: Wood; Marston, Patterson; Smith J, Collins, McLain; English, Smith E, Adams, Jones, Fowler.   **Scorer:** Jones.
Don Adams and Jack English carried off, Ron Patterson attacked by fan, E. Smith debut

5. February 1955   Division 3 South   County Ground   7,709
NORTHAMPTON TOWN 6   SOUTHEND UNITED 2
Northampton: Wood; Marston, Patterson; Hughes, Collins, McLain; Mills, Smith E, Oakley, Jones, Fowler.   **Scorers:** Smith 2, Oakley, 2, Jones 2
Southend: Threadgold; Pavitt, Anderson; Burns, Howe, Lawler, Sibley, Anderson, Holis, Baron, Lockhart.   **Scorers;** Burns, Hollis
Gwyn Hughes, Ken Oakley and Roly Mills replace the injured players.

12. February 1955   Division 3 South   Recreation Ground   5,237
ALDERSHOT 3   NORTHAMPTON TOWN 4
Aldershot: Brown; Monk, Banks; Alison, Billington, Sirrell; Gaynor, Cheney, Lacey, Ball, Flint.   **Scorers:** Gaynor, Lacey 2
Northampton: Wood; Marston, Patterson; Hughes, Collins, McLain; Mills, Smith E, Oakley, Jones, Fowler.   **Scorers:** Jones 3, Smith
Jones scores his first ever hat trick for the Cobblers.

26. February 1955   Division 3 South   Priestfield   8,523
GILLINGHAM 2   NORTHAMPTON TOWN 2
Gillingham: Rigg; Marks, West; Boswell, Niblett, Rigg; Scarth, Evans, Sowden, Morgan, Millar.   **Scorers:** Marks (p), Morgan
Northampton: Wood; Southam, Patterson; Hughes, Collins, McLain; Mills, Smith E, Oakley, Jones, Fowler.   **Scorer:** Jones 2 (1 p)
Both sides convert a penalty. Southam returns to the Cobblers side,

5. March. 1955   Division 3 South   County Ground   7,191
NORTHAMPTON TOWN 2   READING 6
Northampton: Webber: Southam, Patterson; Hughes, Collins, McLain; Mills, Yeoman, Oakley, Jones, Fowler.   **Scorer:** Oakley 2
Reading: Jones; Penfold, Mansell; Davis, Davies, McLaren; Campbell, Hinshelwood, Uphill, Anderton, Quinlan.   **Scorers:** Uphill 3, Anderton 2, Hinshelwood
Alf Wood and Eddie Smith injured, Webber and Yeoman returned.

12. March 1955   Division 3 South   Gay Meadow   7,778
SHREWSBURY TOWN4   NORTHAMPTON TOWN 0
Shrewsbury: McBride; Bannister, Parr; Wallace, Maloney, Candlin; Price, O'Donnell, Welsh, Russell, McCue..   **Scorers:** O'Donnell, Weigh, Russell, McCue
Northampton: Webber; Collins, Patterson; Hughes, Croy, McLain; Mills, Starocsik, Adams, Jones, Fowler.
Maurice Candlin and Willie O'Donnell ex-Cobblers. Now conceded 10 goals in 2 games.

19. March 1955   Division 3 South   County Ground   6,855

NORTHAMPTON TOWN 2   SOUTHAMPTON 1

Northampton: Wood; Marston, Patterson, Hughes, Collins, McLain; Mills, Smith E, Adams, Jones, Fowler.   **Scorers:** Fowler, o.g.

Southampton: Kiernan; Ellerton, Traynor; McLaughlin, Wilkins, Simpson; Foulkes, Mulgrew, Day, Walker, Hoskins.   **Scorer:** Mulgrew

Tommy Mulgrew is ex-Cobbler. Alf Wood, Maurice Marston and Eddie Smith all return .

26. March 1955   Division 3 South   Ashton Gate   20,955

BRISTOL CITY 5   NORTHAMPTON TOWN 1

Bristol City: Anderson; Guy, Thresher; White, Peacock, Williams; Milton, Atyeo, Rogers, Burden, Boxley.   **Scorers:** Rogers 2, Milton, Atyeo, Boxley.

Northampton: Wood; Marston, Patterson; Hughes, Collins, McLain; Mills, Smith E, Adams, Jones, Fowler.   **Scorer:** Patterson

Bristol City are top of the division, Cobblers drop to 12th.

2. April 1955   Division 3 South   County Ground   5,361

NORTHAMPTON TOWN 1   TORQUAY UNITED 0

Northampton: Wood; Marston, Patterson; Smith, Hughes, McLain; English, Smith E, Adams, Hazeldine, Fowler.   **Scorer:** Adams

Torquay: Jeffries; Towers, Anderton; Lewis, Webber, Smith; Dougan, Collins, Sandys, Mills, Thomas.

The Club's victory is overshadowed by the death of Club President A. J. Darnell.

4. April 1955   Division 3 South   Fellows Park   5,159

WALSALL 6   NORTHAMPTON TOWN 1

Walsall: Chilvers; Gutteridge, Vinall; Feraday, McPherson, Tarrant; Webb, Dorman, Richards, Lowe, Morris.   **Scorers:** Dorman 3, Richards, o.g. 2

Northampton: Wood; Marston, Patterson; Smith J, Huffer, McLain; English, Yeoman, Adams, Smith E, Fowler.   **Scorer:** English

Both the Cobblers full backs, Ron Patterson and Maurice Marston score own goals.

9. April 1955   Division 3 South   Goldstone Ground 13,120

BRIGHTON & HOVE ALBION 2   NORTHAMPTON TOWN 1

Brighton: Gill; Tennant, Langley; Gilbert, Whitfield, Wilson; Gordon, Munday, Moore, Foreman, Howard.   **Scorers:** Munday, Moore.

Northampton: Wood; Southam, Patterson; Smith J, Croy, McLain; Starocsik, Smith E, Adams, Jones, Fowler.   **Scorer:** Starocsik

Manager Dave Smith makes four changes .

11. April 1955   Division 3 South   Dean Court   8,759

BOURNEMOUTH & BOSCOMBE ATHLETIC 0   NORTHAMPTON TOWN 1

Bournemouth: Godwin; Cunningham, Drummond; Rushworth, Crossland, Brown; Murray, Siddall, Hobbs, Newsham, Harrison.

Northampton: Wood; Southam, Marston; Yeoman, Croy, Smith J: English, Newman, Adams, Danks, Fowler.   **Scorer:** Newman

Ron Newman and Derek Danks made their debuts. Newman scored from a Danks pass.

12. April 1955   Division 3 South   County Ground   6,618

NORTHAMPTON TOWN 5   BOURNEMOUTH & BOSCOMBE ATHLETIC 0

Northampton: Wood; Marston, Patterson; Smith J, Croy, McLain; Staroscik, Smith E, Dawson, Jones, Fowler.   **Scorers:** Jones 4, Starocsik

Bournemouth: Godwin; Cunningham, Drummond; Rushworth, Crossland, Brown; Murray, Fidler, Hobbs, Newsham, Harrison;

Newman and Danks are both dropped, Bill Dawson makes his debut.

16. April 1955   Division 3 South   County Ground   6,980

NORTHAMPTON TOWN 1   BRENTFORD 2
Northampton: Wood; Marston, Patterson; Smith J, Hughes, McLain; Starocsik, Smith
E, Dawson, Jones, Fowler.   **Scorer:** Dawson.
Brentford: Newton; Basham, Horne; Bristow, Hart, Coote; Stobbart, Taylor, Dudley,
Towers, Robertson.   **Scorer:** Taylor, Towers.
No sooner than Bernard Jones discovers his scoring boots, he is called up for the Army.

---

18. April 1955   Division 3 South   County Ground   3,198

NORTHAMPTON TOWN 6   COLCHESTER UNITED 1
Northampton: Wood; Marston, Patterson; Smith J, Hughes, McLain; Starocsik,
Newman, Dawson, Smith E, Fowler.   **Scorers:** Dawson 3, Starocsik, Smith E, o.g.
Colchester: Kirk; Harrison, Lewis;Everton, Harris , Dale; Grice, Leonard, McCurley,
McKim, Wright..   **Scorer:** McKim
Twelve goals scored in the last three home games, Dawson nets his first hat trick.

---

21. April 1955   Maunsell Cup (Semi Final)   London Road

PETERBOROUGH UNITED 1   NORTHAMPTON TOWN 0
Peterborough: Lowery. Moody, Stafford G: Taft, McCabe, Stafford E: Campbell,
Davey, Kelley, Martin, Hair.   **Scorer:** unknown
Northampton: Wood; Southam, Marston; Yeoman, Croy, McLain; Staroscik, Smith E,
Adams, Danks, Fowler.
Peterborough's 14th home game, without defeat.

---

23. April 1955   Division 3 South   Highfield Road   11,631

COVENTRY CITY 0   NORTHAMPTON TOWN 0
Coventry: Matthews; Timmins, Austin; Jamieson, Kirk, Simpson; Moore, Hill ,
Hawkings, Capel, Johnson.
Northampton: Wood; Marston, Patterson; Smith J, Hughes, Mclain; Staroscik, Smith E,
Dawson, Jones, Fowler.
The Cobblers last 0-0 draw was exactly 12 months previous, v Swindon Town.

---

27. April 1955   Division 3 South   County Ground   4,349

NORTHAMPTON TOWN 1   BRIGHTON & HOVE ALBION 0
Northampton: Wood; Marston, Patterson; Smith J, Hughes, McLain; Starocsik,
English, Dawson, Smith E, Fowler.   **Scorer:** o.g.
Brighton: Gill; Tennant, Langley; McNeil, Whitfield, Wilson; Gilbert , Murphy,
Harburn, Leadbetter, Howard.
The Cobblers rise to mid table after three games without defeat.

---

30. April 1955   Division 3 South   County Ground   6,842

NORTHAMPTON TOWN 1   WALSALL 1
Northampton: Wood; Marston, Patterson; Smith J, Hughes, McLain; Starocsik,
English, Dawson, Smith E, Fowler.   **Scorer:** Dawson
Walsall: Chilvers; Gutteridge, Vinall; Ferriday, McPherson, Tarrant; Morris, Dorman,
Richards, Myerscough, Love.   **Scorer:** Dorman.
Cobblers finish 13th.

1955- 1956

| 20. August 1955 | Division 3 South | Selhurst Park | 13,841 |

CRYSTAL PALACE 2   NORTHAMPTON TOWN 3
Crystal Palace: Bailey; Edwards, Greenwood; Moss, Saunders, Anderson; Berry, Belcher, Deakin, Tilson, Gunning.   **Scorers:** Deakin, Tilson
Northampton: Pickering; Marston,. Patterson; Yeoman, Collins, Smith; English, Smith E, Dawson, Jones, Fowler.   **Scorers:** English, Dawson
Peter Pickering, only new face in the Cobblers side. played in over 90 degrees.

| 24. August 1955 | Division 3 South | County Ground (Swindon) | 8,642 |

SWINDON TOWN 0   NORTHAMPTON TOWN 1
Swindon: Burton; Hunt, Hilton; McShane, Hudson, Williams; Riseborough, Sampson, Owen, Edwards, Edds.
Northampton: Pickering; Marston, Patterson; Yeoman, Collins, Smith J: English, Newman, Dawson, Smith E., Fowler.   **Scorer:** English
Bernard Jones was to have played, but could not get leave, replaced by Ron Newman.

| 27. August 1955 | Division 3 South | County Ground | 10,694 |

NORTHAMPTON TOWN 3   BRIGHTON & HOVE ALBION 0
Northampton: Pickering; Marston, Patterson; Yeoman, Collins, Smith J: English, Newman, Dawson, Smith E, Fowler.   **Scorers:** Yeoman, English, Fowler.
Brighton: Gill, Tennant, Langley, Gilberg, Whitfield, Wilson, Gordon, Munday, Bissett, Foreman, Howard.
Cobblers go joint top of Division 3 South.

| 1. September 1955 | Division 3 South | County Ground | 11,102 |

NORTHAMPTON TOWN 2   SWINDON TOWN 1
Northampton: Pickering; Marston, Patterson; Yeoman, Collins, Smith J: English, Newman, Dawson, Smith E, Fowler.   **Scorers:** Fowler, Smith E (p)
Swindon: Burton; Hunt, Hilton; McShane, Hudson, Williams; Riseborough, Gibson, Owen, Edwards, Sampson.   **Scorer:** Edwards
Swindon equalised with the last kick of the game, not allowed as it was after the whistle

| 3. September 1955 | Division 3 South | The Dell | 12,373 |

SOUTHAMPTON 2   NORTHAMPTON TOWN 3
Southampton: Kiernan; Oakley, Gunter; McLaughlan, Wilkins, Elliott; Brown, Mulgrew, Day, Walker, Hoskins.   **Scorer:** Day 2
Northampton: Pickering; Marston, Patterson; Yeoman, Collins, Smith J: English, Newman, Dawson, Smith E, Fowler.   **Scorer:** English, Newman, Smith E.
Mixed fortunes for Saints full back Gunter, married a.m. defeated p.m.

| 8. September 1955 | Division 3 South | County Ground | 12,534 |

NORTHAMPTON TOWN 3   ALDERSHOT 2
Northampton: Pickering; Marston, Patterson; Yeoman, Collins, Smith J: English, Newman, Dawson, Smith E, Fowler.   **Scorers:** English, Dawson, Smith E.
Aldershot: Platt; Monk, Gilchrist; Alison, Billington, Lacey; Gaynor J, Cheney, Gaynor L, Menzies, Ball.   **Scorer:** Cheney 2
Cobblers have not suffered a defeat for ten games.

| 10. September 1955 | Division 3 South | County Ground | 13,144 |

NORTHAMPTON TOWN 1   SHREWSBURY TOWN 0
Northampton: Pickering; Marston, Patterson; Yeoman, Wallace, Smith J: English, Newman, Dawson, Smith E. Fowler.   **Scorer:** Fowler
Shrewsbury: McBride; Bannister, Parr; Wallace, Maloney, Simpson; Price, O'Donnell, Weigh, Russell, Tyrer.
Injury to Ben Collins gives Jim Wallace a debut, Tommy scores his 3rd goal of the season

14. September 1955   Division 3 South   Recreation Ground   5,811
ALDERSHOT 2   NORTHAMPTON TOWN 0
Aldershot: Platt; Monk, Gilchrist; Alison, Billington, Lacey; Gaynor J, Cheney, Gaynor
L, Menzies, Ball.   **Scorers:** Gaynor L. Ball
Northampton: Pickering; Marston, Patterson; Yeoman, Collins, Smith J; English,
Newman, Draper, Smith E, Fowler.
Debut for Richard Draper. Peter Pickering saves TWO penalties, still top by two points.

17. September 1955   Division 3 South   Portman Road   17,629
IPSWICH TOWN 1   NORTHAMPTON TOWN 0
Ipswich: McMillan; Acres, Malcolm; Myles, Rees, Elsworthy; Reed, Grant, Garvey,
Parker, Mcluckie.   **Scorers:** o.g.
Northampton: Pickering; Marston, Patterson; Yeoman, Hughes, Smith J: Newman,
Smith E, Draper, Jones, Fowler.
Ben Collins and Gwyn Hughes are both injured. Parker of Ipswich plays his 450th game.

19 September 1955   Division 3 South   County Ground   8,735
NORTHAMPTON TOWN 5   QUEENS PARK RANGERS 2
Northampton: Pickering; Marston, Patterson; Yeoman, Hughes, Smith J: Mills,
Newman, Draper, Smith E, Fowler.   **Scorers:** Newman 2, Smith J, Fowler, Draper
Q.P.R.: Brown; Wood, Ingham; Petchley, Powell, Angell; McKay, Smith, Clark, Cameron,
Shepherd.   **Scorer:** Smith 2
Still top of the division, but by just one point.

24. September 1955   Division 3 South   County Ground   14,247
NORTHAMPTON TOWN 3   WALSALL 1
Northampton: Pickering; Marston, Patterson; Yeoman, Hughes, SmithJ: Mills,
Newman, Draper, Smith E, Fowler.   **Scorers:** Smith E. 2, Mills.
Walsall: Chilvers; Gutteridge, Hoddington; Dyas, Vinall, Brook; Morris, Dorman,
Richards, Love. McClaren.   **Scorer:** McLaren
Jack Love, player manager of Walsall, played against the Cobblers for Llanelly in 1953.

29. September 1955   Division 3 South   Somerset Park   8,076
NEWPORT COUNTY 0   NORTHAMPTON TOWN 1
Newport: Weare; Lever, Hollyman; Thomas, Wilcox, Docherty; Hughes, Shepherd,
Johnston, Harris, Beech.
Northampton: Pickering; Marston, Patterson; Yeomans, Collins, Smith J: Mills,
Newman, Draper, Smith E, Fowler.   **Scorer:** Newman
Ron Newman's family travelled from Pontypridd , Johnston missed a penalty.

1 October 1955   Division 3 South   Plainmoor   9,686
TORQUAY UNITED 3   NORTHAMPTON TOWN 1
Torquay: Kirk; Smith J, Smith H: Lewis, Norman, Lloyd; Shaw, Collins, Dobbie, Mills,
Collins T.   **Scorers:** Shaw 2, Dobbie.
Northampton: Pickering; Marston, Patterson; Yeoman, Collins, Smith J: Mills,
Newman, Draper, Smith E, Fowler.   **Scorer:** Draper.
There were four Smith's, three Collins and two Mills on the field.

8. October 1955   Division 3 South   County Ground   20,370
NORTHAMPTON TOWN 2   COVENTRY CITY 1
Northampton: Pickering; Marston, Patterson; Yeoman,Collins, Smith J: Mills,
Newman, Draper, Smith E, Fowler.   **Scorer:** Draper 2
Coventry: Matthews; Wassall, Patrick; Austin, Kirk, Simpson; Moore, Sambrook,
Hawkings, Hill R, Hill J.   **Scorer:** Hawkings
Biggest crowd at the County Ground since the F.A. cup tie v Bournemouth in 1950

15 October 1955   Division 3 South   Roots Hall   17,009
SOUTHEND UNITED 2   NORTHAMPTON TOWN 0
Southend: Brewster; Williamson, May; Duthie, Howie, Lawther; Lockhart, McCrory,
Hollis, Whyte, McvGuigan.   **Scorers:** Whyte, Hollis
Northampton: Pickering; Marston, Patterson; Yeoman, Collins, Smith J:Mills,
Newman, Draper, Smith E, Fowler.
Marston, Patterson and Draper of Cobblers, and McCrory of Southend all booked.

22. October 1955   Division 3 South   County Ground   10,804
NORTHAMPTON TOWN 3   EXETER CITY 0
Northampton: Pickering, Marston, Patterson; Yeoman, Collins, Smith J: Mills, Smith
E, Draper, Jones, Fowler.   **Scorers:** Yeoman, Smith E, Draper.
Exeter: Hunter; Walton, Mitchell; Davey, Harvey, Murphy; Simpson, Worthington,
Burke, John, Buckle.
Ex-Cobbler, Eddie Murphy is the Exeter captain.

29. October 1955   Division 3 South   Brisbane Road   24,030
LEYTON ORIENT 1   NORTHAMPTON TOWN 1
Leyton Orient: Welton; Lee, Charlton; McMahon, Aldous, McKnight; Facey, Woosnam,
Groves, Heckman, Hartburn.   **Scorer:** Hartburn.
Northampton: Pickering; Marston, Patterson; Yeoman, Collins, Smith J: Mills, Smith
E, Draper, Jones, Fowler.   **Scorer:** Draper
Cobblers first away point for three games.

 5. November 1955   Division 3 South   County Ground   14,091
NORTHAMPTON TOWN 0   COLCHESTER UNITED 2
Northampton: Pickering; Marston, Patterson; Yeoman, Collins, Smith J: Mills, Smith
E, Draper, Jones, Fowler.
Colchester: Ames; Harrison, Fisher; Fenton, Stewart, Dale; Grice, McLeod, McCurley,
Plant, Wright.   **Scorer:** Grice 2
Cobblers first home defeat of the season. referee,Alf Bond, the one armed referee.

12. November 1955   Division 3 South   Carrow Road   21,845
NORWICH CITY 4   NORTHAMPTON TOWN 1
Norwich: Oxford; McCrochan, Morgan; Chung, Foulkes, Ashman; Gavin, Gordon, Hunt,
Brennan, Coxon.   **Scorers:** Hunt 2, Gavin, Coxon
Northampton: Pickering, Marston, Patterson; Yeoman, Collins, Smith J: Mills,English,
Draper, Smith E, Fowler.   **Scorer:** Fowler
Eddie Smith misses a penalty.

19. November 1955   F.A. Cup (Round1)   County Ground   12,878
NORTHAMPTON TOWN 4   MILLWALL 1
Northampton: Pickering; Marston, Patterson; Yeoman, Collins, Smith J: English,
Jones, Draper, Smith E, Fowler.   **Scorer:** English 3, o.g.
Millwall: Finlayson; Jardine, Ainslow; Short, Hurley, Rawson; Hazlett, Mackay, Pacey,
McAllister, Summers.   **Scorer:** Hurley.
Charlie Hurley, later to be an Eire International, scored for both sides.

26. November 1955   Division 3 South   Priestfield Stadium   8,429
GILLINGHAM 0   NORTHAMPTON TOWN 2
Gillingham: Rigg; Parry, West; Buswell, Niblett, Riggs; Crosson, Baxter, Fondin,
Morgan, Millar.
Northampton: Pickering: Marston, Patterson; Yeoman, Collins, Smith J: English, Smith
E,Draper, Jones, Fowler.   **Scorers:** Draper, Fowler.
The Cobblers fifth win of the season.

3. December 1955   Division 3 South   County Ground   10,759
NORTHAMPTON TOWN 4   MILLWALL 0
Northampton: Pickering; Marston, Patterson; Smith J, Collins, Yeoman; English, Smith
E, Draper, Jones, Fowler.   **Scorers:** English 2, Draper, Jones
Millwall: Finlayson; Jardine, Anslow; Sommerby, Henderson, Rawson; Johnson, Smith
E, Summers, Pacey, Prior.
Draper suffered head injuries and left the field. Second time scored 4 against Millwall in
two weeks.

10. December 1955   Division 3 South   County Ground   15,534
NORTHAMPTON TOWN 4   HASTINGS 1
Northampton: Pickering; Marston, Patterson; Yeoman, Collins, Smith J: English, Smith
E, Draper, Jones, Fowler.   **Scorers:** Draper 2, Smith E. 1, English 1
Hastings: Ball; Crapper, Thompson; Peacock, Boor, Chadwick; Taylor, Burgess, Asher,
Bull, Girling.   **Scorers:** Asher.
Hastings are managed by ex-Cobbler, Jack Tresadern.

17. December 1956   Division 3 South   County Ground   9,302
NORTHAMPTON TOWN 1   CRYSTAL PALACE 1
Northampton: Pickering; Marston, Patterson; Yeoman, Hughes, Smith J: English,
Newman, Draper, Smith E, Fowler.   **Scorer:** English
Crystal Palace: Bailey; Choulds, Greenwood; Moss, Saunders, Andrews; Berry, Cooper,
Deakin, Pierce, Gunney.   **Scorer:** Gunney.
Ben Collins injured, Bernard Jones, dropped at his own request.

24 December 1955   Division 3 South   Goldstone Ground   11,004
BRIGHTON & HOVE ALBION 4   NORTHAMPTON TOWN 0
Brighton: Gill; Bissett, Langley; Tennant, Whitfield, Wilson; Gordon, Munday, Harburn,
Foreman, Howard.   **Scorers:** Gordon, Wilson, Munday, Harburn
Northampton: Pickering; Marston, Patterson; Yeoman, Collins, Smith J: English,
Newman, Draper, Smith E, Fowler.
After this defeat the Cobblers lose top spot.

26. December 1955   Division 3 South   Vicarage Road   7,041
WATFORD 2   NORTHAMPTON TOWN 2
Watford: King; Bateman C, Atkinson; Catleugh, Bateman e, Mitchell; Cook, Bowie,
Marden, Graham, Adams.   **Scorer:** Graham 2
Northampton: Pickering; Marston, Patterson; Yeoman, Collins, Smith J: English, Smith
E.,Draper, Adams, Fowler.   **Scorers:** English, Adams
Ben Collins was booked. There was 16 places between the two sides.

27. December 1955   Division 3 South   County Ground   13,778
NORTHAMPTON TOWN 1   WATFORD 3
Northampton: Pickering; Marston, Patterson; Yeoman, Collins, Smith J: English, Smith
E, Draper, Adams, Fowler.   **Scorer:** English
Watford: King; Bateman C. Atkinson; Catleugh, Bateman E. Mitchell; Cook, Hernon,
Marden, Graham, Meadows.   **Scorers:** Cook, Hernon, Graham
Shock result for the Cobblers. Don Adams carried off injured.

31. December 1955   Division 3 South   County Ground   11,035
NORTHAMPTON TOWN 3   SOUTHAMPTON 1
Northampton: Pickering; Marston, Patterson; Yeoman, Hughes, Smith J: English,
Smith E, Draper, Jones, Fowler.   **Scorers:** Smith E, English, Draper.
Southampton: Kiernan; Wilkins, Gunter; McCoughlan, Page, Elliott; Flood, Walker,
Day, Mulgrew, Hoskins.   **Scorer:** Day.
Don Adams and Ben Collins injured, replaced by Gwyn Hughes and Bernard Jones.

7. January 1956   F.A. Cup (Round 3)   County Ground   14,087

NORTHAMPTON TOWN 1   BLACKBURN ROVERS 2

Northampton: Pickering; Marston, Patterson; Yeoman, Hughes, Smith J: English, Smith E, Draper, Jones, Fowler.   **Scorer:** English

Blackburn: Elvy; Clinton, Eckersley; Clayton R, Kelly, Clayton K: Douglas, Crossan, Briggs, Smith W, Vernon.   **Scorer:** Briggs 2

Played in thick fog, changed straight round at half time. W. Smith is the ex-Cobbler.

14. January 1956   Division 3 South   Gay Meadow   7,974

SHREWSBURY TOWN 1   NORTHAMPTON TOWN 1

Shrewsbury: Crossley; Bannister, Parr; Wallace, Maloney, Simpson; Loughnane, Arnott, Tyrer, O'Donnell, McCue.   **Scorer:** McCue

Northampton: Pickering; Marston, Patterson; Yeoman, Collins, McLain; English, Dawson, Draper, Smith E, Fowler.   **Scorer:** Fowler

Manager Smith rings the changes, Ben Collins, Tommy McLain and Bill Dawson return

21. January 1956   Division 3 South   County Ground   13,103

NORTHAMPTON TOWN 0   IPSWICH TOWN 5

Northampton: Pickering; Marston, Patterson; Yeoman, Collins, Smith J: English, Mills, Draper, Smith E.,Fowler.

Ipswich: McMillan, Acres, Malcolm; Baker, Rees, Elsworthy; Reed, Grant, Garney, Parker, Leadbetter.   **Scorers:** Garney 3, Reed, Parker

Jack Smith and Roly Mills return to the side. Jack English misses a penalty.

28. January 1956   Division 3 South   Elm Park   6,807

READING 4   NORTHAMPTON TOWN 1

Reading: Jones; McLaren, Campbell; Evans, Davie, Leach; Hinshelwood, Alexander, Kirkup, Wheeler, Dixon.   **Scorers:**Alexander, Kirkup, Wheeler, Dixon

Northampton: Pickering; Marston, Patterson; Yeoman, Collins, Hughes; English, Mills, Draper, Smith J, Fowler.   **Scorer:** Mills

Gwyn Hughes retuns at left half, Jack Smith replaces his namesake in the forwards

11. February 1956   Division 3 South   County Ground   5,656

NORTHAMPTON TOWN 2   TORQUAY UNITED 0

Northampton: Pickering; Collins, Marston; Yeoman, Hughes, Smith J: English, Mills, Draper, Smith E. Fowler.   **Scorers:** Draper, Smith E.

Torquay: Kirk; Smith J, Anderton; Lewis, Norman, James; Shaw, Collins R, Dobbie, Mills, Collins D.

The Cobblers side is reshuffled again, Eddie Smith returns, Ron Patterson is dropped.

18.February 1956   Division 3 South   Highfield Road   19,366

COVENTRY CITY 0   NORTHAMPTON TOWN 1

Coventry: Matthews; Austen, Timmins; Jamieson, Kirk, Simpson; Johnson, Uphill, McPherson, Hill P. Sambrook.

Northampton: Pickering; Collins, Marston; Yeoman, Hughes, Smith J: English, Mills, Draper, Smith E. Fowler.   **Scorer:** English.

First time the Cobblers strung two consecutive victories together since November.

25. February 1956   Division 3 South   County Ground   9,535

NORTHAMPTON TOWN 1   SOUTHEND UNITED 1

Northampton: Pickering; Collins, Marston; Yeoman, Hughes, Smith J: English, Mills, Draper, Smith E, Fowler.   **Scorer:** English

Southend: Threadgold; Williamson, Howe; Duthie, Stirling, Lawler; Lockhart, McCrory, Hollis, Baron, McGuigan.   **Scorer:** Baron

The Cobblers are now 7th.

3. March 1956   Division 3 South   St. James Park   6,996

EXETER CITY 3   NORTHAMPTON TOWN 1

Exeter: Hunter; Doyle, Mitchell; John,Harvey, Porteous; Simpson, Houghton, Sword, Willis, Rees.   **Scorers:** Mitchell (p), Sword, Willis.

Northampton: Pickering; Collins, Marston; Yeoman, Huighes, Smith J: English, Mills, Adams, Smith E, Fowler.   **Scorer:** o.g.

Don Adams, Jack Smith, Peter Pickering and Tommy Fowler all picked up injuries.

10. March 1956   Division 3 South   County Ground   13,544

NORTHAMPTON TOWN 0   LEYTON ORIENT 1

Northampton: Pickering; Marston, Patterson; Yeoman, Collins, Smith J: English, Mills, Draper, Smith E, Fowler.

Leyton Orient: Welton; Lee, Earl; Blizzard, Aldous, McKnight; White, Facey, Johnston, Heckman, Hartburn.   **Scorer:** Facey

In view of the previous clashes between the two sides, top referee Arthur Ellis took charge.

17. March 1956   Division 3 South   Layer Road   8,333

COLCHESTER UNITED 2   NORTHAMPTON TOWN 0

Colchester: Ames; Harrison, Fisher; Fenton, Stuart, Dale; Grice, McLeod, McCurley, Plant, Wright.   **Scorers:** Wright, McCurley

Northampton: Pickering; Collins, Marston; Yeoman, Gale, Smith J: English, Williams, Dutton, Smith E. Fowler.

Roly Williams and Colin Gale from Cardiff, Charlie Dutton from Coventry all debutants

24. March 1956   Division 3 South   County Ground   9,387

NORTHAMPTON TOWN 1   NORWICH CITY 1

Northampton: Pickering; Collins, Marston; Yeoman, Gale, Smith J: English, Smith E, Dutton, Leek, Fowler.   **Scorer:** Marston

Norwich: Oxford; McCrochan, Lockwood; Foulkes, Ashman; Gavin, Brennan, Hunt, Woan, Coxon   **Scorer:;** Coxon.

Cobblers 5th 1-1 draw of the season

31. March 1956   Division 3 South   Dean Court   9,010

BOURNEMOUTH & BOSCOMBE ATHLETIC 0   NORTHAMPTON TOWN 0

Bournemouth: Godwin; Cunningham, Drummond; Clayton, Crosland, Brown, Allen, Siddall, Norris, Newsham, Harrison.

Northampton: Pickering, Collins, Patterson; Yeoman, Gale, Smith J: English, Mills, Dutton, Leek, Fowler.

Mills and Patterson return, Godwin makes his 150th appearance for the Cherries.

2. April 1956   Division 3 South   Griffin Park   9,527

BRENTFORD 2   NORTHAMPTON TOWN 1

Brentford: Cakebread; Lowden, Tickbridge; Bristow, Robinson , Coote˙ Heath, Goundry, Taylor, Towers, Roberts.   **Scorer:** Towers 2 (1 p)

Northampton: Pickering; Collins, Paterson; Yeoman, Gale, Smith J: Mills, Dutton, Draper, Smith E, Fowler.   **Scorer:** Dutton;

Ray Yeomans gives away the penalty that wins the game for the 'Bees'.

3. April 1956   Division 3 South   County Ground   8,248

NORTHAMPTON TOWN 1   BRENTFORD 0

Northampton: Pickering; Collins, Patterson; Yeoman, Gale, Smith J: English, Smith E, Dutton, Leek, Fowler.   **Scorer:** Smith J.

Brentford: Cakebread; Lowden, Tickbridge; Bristow, Robinson, Coote; Hector, Rainford, Francis, Towers, Goundry.

Although played only 24 hours later, Cobblers made 3 changes, Brentford 4.

12. April 1956   Division 3 South   County Ground   6,553

NORTHAMPTON TOWN 0   GILLINGHAM 2

Northampton: Pickering; Collins, Patterson; Yeoman, Gale, Smith J: English, Smith E, Dutton, Leek, Fowler.

Gillingham: Kingshott; Parry, West; Boswell, Nekrens, Rigg; Crossan, Morgan, Hawkins, Hughes, Baxter   **Scorers:** Morgan, Hawkins.

Larry Baxter, is the ex-Cobblers player. Colin Gale scored but the goal was ruled offside

12. April 1956   Division 3 South   County Ground   4,179

NORTHAMPTON TOWN 2   BOURNEMOUTH & BOSCOMBE ATHLETIC 1

Northampton: Pickering; Collins, Marston; Yeoman, Gale, Smith J: Mills, Williams, Dutton, Draper, Fowler.   **Scorer:** Draper 2

Bournemouth: Godwin; Cunningham, Keithley; Rushworthy, Crosland, Brown; Wilkinson, Siddall, Norris, Newsham, Allen.   **Scorer:** Newsham

The Cobblers made 4 changes.

14. April 1956   Division 3 South   The Den.   3,682

MILLWALL 4   NORTHAMPTON TOWN 1

Millwall: Brewer; Jardine, Anslow; Veitch, Brand, Rawson; Hazlett, Smith, Summers, Tyrell, Prior.   **Scorers:** Tyrell, Summers, Prior

Northampton: Pickering, Collins, Marston, Yeoman, Gale, Smith J: Mills, Williams, Dutton, Draper, Fowler.   **Scorer:** Dutton.

This defeat drops the Cobblers down to 9th.

16. April 1956   Division 3 South   Fellows Park   11,934

WALSALL 2   NORTHAMPTON TOWN 0

Walsall: Davie; Haddington, Vinall; Dorman , McPherson, Crook; Morris, Hodgkisson, Walsh, Love, Taylor.   **Scorer:** McPherson 2 (2 p)

Northampton: Pickering; Collins, Marston; Yeoman, Gale, Smith J: Mills, Williams, Dutton, McLain, Fowler.

Vinall was carried off with a broken leg, Dutton was also injured during the game.

21. April 1956   Division 3 South   County Ground   5,612

NORTHAMPTON TOWN 1   READING 2

Northampton:: Pickering; Collins, Marston; Yeoman, Gale, Smith J: English, Williams, Draper, Leek, Fowler.   **Scorer:** Leek.

Reading: Jones; McLaren, Reeves; Sufford, Spiers, Leech; Wheeler, Green, Kirkup, Dixon, Quinlan.   **Scorers:** Quinlan, Dixon.

Third consecutive defeat for the Cobblers.

26, April 1956   Division 3 South   County Ground   3,536

NORTHAMPTON TOWN 5   NEWPORT COUNTY 0

Northampton: Pickering; Marston, Patterson; Yeoman.Gale, Smith J: Mills, Williams, Draper, Leek, Fowler.   **Scorers:** Draper 3, Leek 2.

Newport County: Weare, Staples, Hayward; Tenant, Wilcox, Docherty; Hudson, Shergold, Burgess, Harris, Brown.

Cobblers biggest win, for over a year.

28. April. 1956   Division 3 South   Loftus Road   7,157

QUEENS PARK RANGERS 3   NORTHAMPTON TOWN   2

Q.P.R. Springett; Rhodes, Ingham; Petchley, Rutter, Dean; Kerrins, Smith, Clark, Cameron, Angell.   **Scorers:** Clark 2. Smith.

Northampton: Pickering; Coleman, Marston; Yeoman, Gale, Patterson; Mills, Williams, Draper, Leek, Fowler.   **Scorers:** Leek, Mills.

Geoff Coleman makes his debut. Cobblers finish in 11th position.

1956 - 1957

---

18. August 1956   Division 3 South   Somerset Park   11,371

NEWPORT COUNTY 3   NORTHAMPTON TOWN 10

Newport County: Weare; Hollyman, Sherwood; Thomas, Wilcox, Docherty; Hudson, Sheppard, Terry, Harris, Brown.   **Scorers:** Terry 2, Harris.

Northampton: Pickering; Marston, Collins; Yeomans, Gale, Smith J: Morrow, Williams, Draper, Leek, Fowler.

Ron Patterson dropped out before kick off, Ben Collins replace him, and was injured.

---

23. August 1956   Division 3 South   County Ground   8,914

NORTHAMPTON TOWN 3   READING 0

Northampton: Pickering, Marston, Coleman; Smith J, Gale, Yeoman; Morrow, Williams, Draper, Leek, Fowler.   **Scorers:** Smith (p), Leek, o.g.

Reading: Jones, Reeves, Campbell; Penford, Davies, Leach; Wheeler, Whitehouse, Kirkup, Cronin, Dixon.

Geoff Coleman is in for the injured Ben Collins, Ken Leek has a 4th goal ruled offside.

---

25. August. 1956   Division 3 South   County Ground   9,269

NORTHAMPTON TOWN 1   COLCHESTER UNITED 0

Northampton: Pickering; Coleman, Marston; Yeoman, Gale, Smith J.; Morrow, Williams, Draper, Leek, Fowler.   **Scorer:** Draper.

Colchester: Ames; Fisher, Fowler; Hill B, Milligan, Dale; Hill R. Smith, McCurley, Plant, Wright.

Eddie Smith is the ex-Cobblers player.

---

29. August 1956   Division 3 South   Elm Park   11,698

READING 1   NORTHAMPTON TOWN 1

Reading: Jones, McLaren, Reeves; Penford, Davies, Leech; Campbell, Whitehouse, Kirkup, Cronin, Wheeler.   **Scorer:** o.g.

Northampton: Pickering; Coleman, Marston; Yeoman, Gale, Smith J: Morrow, Woan, Dutton, Leek, Fowler.   **Scorer:** Woan

Alan Woan scores on his Cobblers debut. Geoff Coleman was booked.

---

1. September 1956   Division 3 South   Carrow Road   15,246

NORWICH CITY 2   NORTHAMPTON TOWN 1

Norwich: Oxford; McChrohan; Lockwood; McNeil, Billington, Englesfield; Bacon, Gordon, Hunt, Gavin, Stenner.   **Scorers:** Gordon, Gavin.

Northampton: Pickering, Coleman, Marston; Yeoman, Gale, Smith J: Morrow, Woan, Draper, Leek, Fowler.   **Scorer:** Draper

Peter Gordon is Northampton born, and played Town League football.

---

6. September 1956   Division 3 South   County Ground   7,591

NORTHAMPTON TOWN 3   QUEENS PARK RANGERS 0

Northampton: Pickering; Coleman, Marston; Yeoman, Gale, Smith J: Morrow, Woan, Draper, Leek, Fowler.   **Scorers:** Woan, Leek, Smith (p)

Q.P.R.: Springett; Wood, Ingham; Pechley, Rutter, Andrews, Hellawell, Longbottom, Quigley, Locke, Angell

Cobblers have not only won all their home games, but have not conceded a goal.

8. September 1956   Division 3 South   County Ground   15,291
NORTHAMPTON TOWN 4   COVENTRY CITY 0
Northampton: Pickering; Coleman, Marston; Yeoman, Gale, Smith J: Morrow, Mills, Draper, Woan, Fowler.   **Scorers:** Morrow 2, Draper 2
Coventry: Matthews; Austin, Curtis; Regan, Kirk, Simpson; Newman, Uphill, McPherson, Churns, Sambrooke.
Ron Newman is the ex-Cobblers player.

10. September 1956   Division 3 South   Loftus Road   10,785
QUEENS PARK RANGERS 1   NORTHAMPTON TOWN 0
Q.P.R. Springett; Woods, Ingham; Petchley, Rutter, Andrews; Hellawell, Longbottom, Quigley, Locke, Angell.   **Scorer:** Longbottom.
Northampton: Pickering; Coleman, Marston; Yeoman, Gale, Smith J: Morrow, Mills, Draper, Woan, Fowler.
The Cobblers players strongly disputed the goal as they felt Pickering was impeded.

15. September 1956   Division 3 South   The Dell   16,018
SOUTHAMPTON 2   NORTHAMPTON TOWN 0
Southampton: Christie; Wilkins, Traynor; McLaughlin, Parker, Elliott; Flood, Greeves, Shields, Mulgrew, Walker.   **Scorer:** Walker, Mulgrew.
Northampton: Pickering: Coleman, Marston; Yeoman, Gale, Smith J: Morrow, Woan, Draper, Leek, Fowler.
Tommy made his 200th consecutive league appearance, and was made captain.

17. September 1956   Division 3 South   County Ground   7,736
NORTHAMPTON TOWN 2   PLYMOUTH ARGYLE 0
Northampton: Pickering; Coleman, Marston; Yeoman, Gale, Smith J: English, Mills, Draper, Woan, Fowler.   **Scorers:** Mills, English.
Plymouth: Brown; Robertson, Jones; Williams, Lanman, Tilley; Davies, Kearns, Mitchell, Rowley, Twissell.
Jack English and Roly Mills are reinstated and both score.

22. September 1956   Division 3 South   County Ground   9,421
NORTHAMPTON TOWN 1   EXETER CITY 1
Northampton: Pickering; Coleman, Marston; Yeoman, Gale, Smith J: English, Mills, Draper, Woan, Fowler   **Scorer:** Draper.
Exeter: Hunter; Doyle, Ferrier; Mitchell, Harvey, Porteous; Beer, John, Currie, Willis, Rees.   **Scorer:** John.
Graham Rees made his debut for Exeter.

24. September 1956   Division 3 South   Home Park   13, 27
PLYMOUTH ARGYLE 4   NORTHAMPTON TOWN 3
Plymouth: Dyer; Robertson, Jones; Wiliams, Langman, Tiley; Twissell, Douglas, Rowley, Kearns, Arundel.   **Scorers:** Douglas 2, Twisell, Kearns.
Northampton: Pickering; Marston, Patterson; Yeoman, Gale, Smith J: English, Draper, Mills, Woan, Fowler.   **Scorers:** English, Mills, Woan.
Ron Patterson returned for Coleman .

29. September 1956   Division 3 South   Selhurst Park   13,904
CRYSTAL PALACE 1   NORTHAMPTON TOWN 1
Crystal Palace: Potter; Edwards, Greenwood; Belcher, Choules, Long; Harrison, Berry, Deakin, Cooper, Norris.   **Scorer:** Berry
Northampton: Pickering; Coleman, Marston, Collins, Smith J: English, Woan, Mills, Williams, Fowler.   **Scorer:** Woan.
Colin Gale out with 'flu. Geoff Coleman and Roly Williams are both recalled.

6. October 1956   Division 3 South   Griffin Park   10,733
BRENTFORD 2   NORTHAMPTON TOWN 1
Brentford: Cakebread; Horne, Roe; Robinson, Coote, Newcombe; Taylor, Francis,
Tickbridge, Goundry, Morgan.   **Scorer:** Francis, og
Northampton: Pickering; Coleman, Marston; Yeomans, Collins, Smith J: English,
Woan, Draper, Williams, Fowler.   **Scorer:** English
Roly Mills pulls out with a foot injury, Richard Draper returns.

13. October, 1956   Division 3 South   County Ground   8,825
NORTHAMPTON TOWN 4   ALDERSHOT 2
Northampton: Pickering; Coleman, Marston; Yeoman, Gale, Smith J: English, Woan,
Mills, Williams, Fowler.   **Scorers:** Smith, English, Mills, Fowler.
Aldershot: Jackman,Giilchrist, Mann; Alison, Richardson, Lacey; Gaynor, Tyrer,
Costello, Menzies, Flint.   **Scorers:** Flint, Lacey.
Colin Gale and Roly Mills return.

20. October 1956   Division 3 South   Vicarage Road   9,906
WATFORD 2   NORTHAMPTON TOWN 1
Watford: Gooch; Shipwright, Harropp; Catleugh, Bateman, Mitchell; Walker, Meadows,
Cook, Graham, Allen.   **Scorers:** Catleugh, Graham
Northampton: Pickering; Coleman, Marston; Canning, Gale, Smith J: English, Woan,
Mills, Williams Fowler.   **Scorer:** English.
Larry Canning makes his Cobblers debut, Geoff Coleman limps off during the game.

27. October 1956   Divison 3 South   County Ground   8,951
NORTHAMPTON TOWN 1   SHREWSBURY TOWN 1
Northampton: Elvy; Coleman, Marston; Canning, Gale, Smith J:English, Woan,
Draper, Williams Fowler.   **Scorer:** Woan
Shrewsbury: Curran; Bannister, Skeetch; Wallace, Maloney, Simpson; Price,
O'Donnell, Rodgers, Rusell, Whittaker.   **Scorer:** O'Donnell
Reg Elvy makes his debut in goal for the Cobblers. Willie O'Donnell, ex-Cobbler scores.

3 November 1956   Division 3 South   Fellows Park   9,842
WALSALL 2   NORTHAMPTON TOWN 2
Walsall: Davies; Hadlington, Perkins; Dorman, McPherson, Rawlings; Morris, Leverton,
Taylor D, Moore, Taylor B.   **Scorers:** Taylor D, Taylor B.
Northampton: Elvy; Marston, Patterson; Yeoman, Gale, Smith J; English, Leek, Asher,
Woan, Fowler.   **Scorers:** English, Leek.
All change. Sid Asher makes his debut, Patterson, Yeoman and Leek all return.

5. November 1956   Friendly   York Street Stadium
BOSTON UNITED 2   NORTHAMPTON TOWN 6
Boston: Line up and scorers not available
Northampton: line ups not available Scorers; English 3, Woan 2, Fowler.
Played on a Monday afternoon.

10. November 1956   Division 3 South   County Ground   9,655
NORTHAMPTON TOWN 2   IPSWICH TOWN 1
Northampton: Elvy; Marston, Patterson; Yeoman, Gale, Smith J: Morrow, English,
Asher, Leek, Fowler.   **Scorers:** Leek, Fowler.
Ipswich: Bailey; Acres, Malcolm; Myles, Rees, Elsworthy; Reed, Millward, Garvey,
Phillips, Leadbetter.   **Scorer:** Myles.
Hugh Morrow returns, Jack English moves inside.

17. November 1956   F.A. Cup (Round1)   The Dell   16,757
SOUTHAMPTON 2   NORTHAMPTON TOWN 0
Southampton: Christie; Wilkins, Traynor; McLaughlin, Parker, Elliott; Day, Reeves,
Shields, Mulgrew, Hoskins.   **Scorers:** Reeves, Mulgrew,
Northampton: Elvy; Marston, Patterson; Yeoman, Gale, Smith J: English, Woan,
Asher, Leek, Fowler.
The Cobblers keep up their tradition of going out at the first round every other season.

22. November 1956   Division 3 South   County Ground   8,524
NORTHAMPTON TOWN 3   TORQUAY UNITED 0
Northampton: Elvy; Marston, Patterson; Yeoman, Gale, Smith J: Morrow, Asher,
Draper, Leek,Fowler.   **Scorers:** Leek 2, Fowler.
Torquay: Wakenham; Smith, Langstreth; Lewis, Norman, Jones; Shaw, Collins R,
Calland, Mills, Colins A.
Both the Cobblers goalkeepers were injured, as Elvy was the fitter of the two, he played

1. December 1956   Division 3 South   The Den   10,940
MILLWALL 1   NORTHAMPTON TOWN 0
Millwall: Lloyd; Jardine, Anslow; Veitch, Brand, Rawson; Hazlett, Shepherd, Pacey,
Hill, Pulley.   **Scorer:** Pacey
Northampton: Elvy; Marston, Patterson; Yeoman, Gale, Smith J: Morrow, Mills,Asher,
Leek, Fowler.
Bob Dennison was in the stands, believed to be watching Ray Yeoman.

8. December 1956   Friendly   County Ground   3,813
NORTHAMPTON TOWN 1   ROCHDALE 2
Northampton: Elvy: Marston, Patterson; Yeoman, Gale, Smith J: Morrow, Mills, Asher,
Leek, Fowler.   **Scorer:** Leek
Rochdale: Jones; Ferguson, Parr; Grant, McCullough, McGuigan; Lyons, Wainwright,
Green, McLaren, Molloy.   **Scorers:** Lyons, McLaren.
Both teams were out of the F.A. Cup, so they arranged this friendly.

15. December 1956   Division 3 South   County Ground   6,289
NORTHAMPTON TOWN 0   NEWPORT COUNTY 3
Northampton: Elvy; Marston, Patterson; Yeoman, Gale, Smith J: Morrow, Woan,
Asher, Leek, Fowler.
Newport: Weare; Lever, Sherwood; Thomas, Wilcox, Docherty; Hudson, Sheppeard,
Terry, Harris, Brown.   **Scorers:** Hudson, Harris, Brown.
The Cobblers biggest home defeat for nearly a year

22. December 1956   Division 3 South   Layer Road   5,890
COLCHESTER UNITED 5   NORTHAMPTON TOWN 1
Colchester: Ames; Fisher, Fowler; Fenton, Milligan, Dale; Williams, McLeod, Smith,
Plant, Wright.   **Scorers:** McLeod 2, Wright 2, Smith
Northampton: Elvy; Marston, Patterson; Yeoman, Gale, Smith J: Morrow, English,
Leek, Woan, Fowler.   **Scorer:** Leek
Now the biggest defeat for a year.

25. December 1956   Division 3 South   County Ground   5,165
NORTHAMPTON TOWN 2   SOUTHEND UNITED 2
Northampton: Pickering; Coleman, Patterson; Yeoman, Gale, Smith J: Morrow, Mills,
Leek, English, Fowler.   **Scorer:** Mills 2
Southend: Threadgold; Williamson, Anderson; Duthie, Stirling, Lawler; Barker,
McGrory, Hollis, Thompson, McGuigan.   **Scorers:** Barker, McGrory.
Played on a frozen pitch. Jack English played as Tommy's partner at inside left.

26. December 1956   Division 3 South   Roots Hall   8,696

SOUTHEND UNITED 0   NORTHAMPTON TOWN 1
Southend: Threadgold; Wiliamson, Anderson; Duthie, Stirling, Lawler; Barker,
McGrory, Hollis, Thompson, McGuigan.
Northampton: Pickering; Marston, Patterson; Yeoman, Gale, Smith J: English, Asher,
Mills, Leek, Fowler.   **Scorer:** Smith
The Cobblers make two changes, Southend field the same team.

29. December 1956   Division 3 South   County Ground   7,603

NORTHAMPTON TOWN 1   NORWICH CITY 1
Northampton: Pickering; Marston, Patterson; Yeoman, Gale, Smith J: Morrow, Asher,
Mills, Leek, Fowler   **Scorer:** Asher
Norwich: Nethercott; McCrohan, Wilson; Bannister, McNeil, Ashman; Bacon, Gavin,
Bly, Hunt, Cole.   **Scorer:** Hunt
Jack Smith misses a penalty. The Cobblers forward line is changed again.

 5. January 1957   Division 3 South   County Ground   6,601

NORTHAMPTON TOWN 4   GILLINGHAM 1
Northampton: Pickering; Marston, Patterson; Yeoman, Gale, Smith; Morrow, Mills,
Asher, Leek, Fowler.   **Scorers:** Asher 2, Morrow, Fowler
Gillingham: Chiswick; Parry, West; Rigg, Boswell, Greenhaulgh, Crosson, Taylor,
Morgan, Baxter, Lucas,   **Scorer:** Taylor.

12. January 1957   Division 3 South   Highfield Road   15,371

COVENTRY CITY 3   NORTHAMPTON TOWN 1
Coventry: Bentley; Timmins, Curtis; Regan, Kirk, Simpson; Rogers, Moore, Sambrook
,Hill, Boxley.   **Scorers:** Sambrook 2, Boxley.
Northampton: Pickering; Marston, Patterson; Yeoman, Gale, Smith J: Morrow, Mills,
Asher, Leek, Fowler.   **Scorers:** Leek.
Yeoman and Simpson sent off. Smith, Leek and Timmins all carried off.

19. January 1957   Division 3 South   County Ground   8,923

NORTHAMPTON TOWN 2   SOUTHAMPTON 1
Northampton: Pickering; Marston, Patterson; Yeoman, Gale, Poole; Morrow, Mills,
Asher, Leek, Fowler.   **Scorers:** Asher, Fowler
Southampton: Christie; Wilkins, Traynor; McLaughlin , Parker, Elliott; Flood, Reeves,
Roper, Mulgrew, Page.   **Scorer:** Reeves
Ken Poole made his debut in place of the injured Jack Smith.

26. January 1957   Division 3 South   Priestfield Stadium   5,724

GILLINGHAM 1   NORTHAMPTON TOWN 2
Gillingham: Chiswick; Monks, West; Greenhaulgh, Boswell, Rigg; Crosson, Taylor,
Morgan, Lucas, Baxter.   **Scorer:** Taylor
Northampton: Pickering; Marston, Patterson; Yeoman, Gale, Poole; Morrow, Mills,
Asher, Leek, Fowler   **Scorer:** Asher 2.
Roly Williams has been loaned out to Bath, and Charlie Dutton joins Leamington.

1. February. 1957   Division 3 South   St. James Park   5,931

EXETER CITY 0   NORTHAMPTON TOWN   0
Exeter: Hunter; Mitchell, Ferrier; Lockenby, Harvey, Packer; Thomas, Divers, Currie,
John, Rees.
Northampton: Pickering; Marston, Patterson; Yeoman, Gale, Poole; Morrow, Mills,
Asher, Leek, Fowler.
Ken Poole was carried off. Cobblers first 0-0 draw for nearly two years.

9. February 1957   Division 3 South   County Ground   8,651

NORTHAMPTON TOWN 1   CRYSTAL PALACE 0

Northampton: Pickering; Marston, Patterson; Yeoman, Gale, Leek; Morrow, Mills, Asher, Woan, Fowler.   **Scorer:** Woan

Crystal Palace: Rouse; Edwards, Noakes; Belcher, Choules, Long; Harrison, Berry, Deakin, Pierce, Gunny.

Ken Leek moves to wing half, Alan Woan returns and scores only goal of the game.

---

16. February 1957   Division 3 South   County Ground   9,306

NORTHAMPTON TOWN 5   BRENTFORD   1

Northampton: Pickering; Marston, Patterson; Yeoman, Gale, Leek; Morrow, Mills, Asher, Woan, Fowler.   **Scorers:** Asher 2, Woan 2, og

Brentford: Feehan; Bragg, Russell; Morgan, Drage, Coote; Parsons, Peplow, Francis, Taylor, Gournay.   **Scorer:** Francis

Sonny Feehan is the ex-Cobblers player.

---

2. March 1957   Division 3 South   County Ground   9,309

NORTHAMPTON TOWN 1   WATFORD 2

Northampton: Pickering; Marston, Patterson; Yeomans, Gale, Leek; Morrow, Mills, Asher, Woan, Fowler.   **Scorer:** Asher

Watford: Gooch; Shipwright, Harropp; Catleugh, Brown, Mitchell; Cook, Meadows, Anderson, Wilson, Walker.   **Scorers:** Cook, Anderson.

The attendance was just three more than that of two weeks ago

---

9. March 1957   Division 3 South   Goldstone Ground   11,922

BRIGHTON AND HOVE ALBION 5   NORTHAMPTON TOWN 0

Brighton: Gill; Tennant, Jennings; Burtenshaw, Whifield, Wilson; Gordon, Munday, Hartburn, Foreman, Neale.   **Scorers:** Munday 2, Hartburn 2, Foreman

Northampton: Pickering, Marston, Patterson; Yeomans, Poole, Leek; Morrow, Mills, Asher, Woan, Fowler.

Colin Gale dropped out through injury, Ken Poole struggled at centre half.

---

23. March 1957   Division 3 South   Portman Road   17,143

IPSWICH TOWN 0   NORTHAMPTON TOWN 1

Ipswich: Bailey; Carberry, Malcolm; Myles, Rees, Elsworthy; Reed, Millward, Grant, Phillips, Leadbetter.

Northampton: Pickering; Marston, Patterson; Yeomans, Gale, Smith J: English Mills, Asher, Woan, Fowler   **Scorer:** Asher

Tommy returns to the first team after being dropped for the first time since April 1952.

---

30. March 1957   Division 3 South   County Ground   7,549

NORTHAMPTON TOWN 2 BOURNEMOUTH & BOSCOMBE ATHLETIC 2

Northampton: Pickering; Marston, Patterson; Yeoman, Gale, Smith J: English, Mills, Asher, Woan, Fowler.   **Scorers:** Mills, Woan.

Bournemouth: Godwin, Lyons, Woollard, Clayton, Hughes, Brown; Loughnane, Bedford, Arnott, Newsham, Cutlins.   **Scorer:** Arnott 2

Arnold Woollard is the ex-Cobblers player.

---

6. April 1957   Division 3 South   Plainmoor   7,612

TORQUAY UNITED 2   NORTHAMPTON TOWN 0

Torquay: Gill; Smith J, Smith H: Lewis, Norman, Clarke; Shaw, Smith J, Mills, Collins S, Collins T.   **Scorer:** Collins S. 2

Northampton: Elvy; Collins, Patterson; Yeomans, Gale, Smith J: English, Mills, Asher, Woan, Fowler.

Reg Elvy and Ben Collins replace the injured Peter Pickering and Maurice Marston.

8. April 1957   Benefit for Patterson/Fowler   County Ground   2,000
NORTHAMPTON TOWN 2   PARTICK THISTLE 0
NORTHAMPTON: Elvy; Collins, Patterson; Yeoman, Gale, Smith J: Morrow, Mills, Asher, Leek, Fowler.   **Scorers:** unknown
PARTICK: line up not available.
Tommy and Ron received the maximum £200.

10. April 1957   Division 3 South   Recreation Ground 2,677
ALDERSHOT 4   NORTHAMPTON TOWN 0
Aldershot: Amos; Jefferson, Jackson; Lacey, Price, Welton; Gaynor, Flint, Henry, Richardson, Tyrer.   **Scorer:** Welton, Gaynor, Henry, o.g.
Northampton: Elvy; Collins, Patterson; Yeoman, Gale, Smith J: Morrow, Mills, Asher, Leek, Fowler.
Adam McCulloch attending the game, prior to sailing out to Australia.

13. April 1957   Division 3 South   County Ground   5,465
NORTHAMPTON TOWN 2   MILLWALL 1
Northampton: Elvy; Collins, Patterson; Yeoman, Gale, Smith J: Morrow, Mills, Draper, Woan, Fowler.   **Scorers:** Woan, Mills.
Millwall: Lloyd; Jardine, Smith; Craig, Hurley, Rawson; Haylet, Shepherd, Anslow, Tyrell, Pulley   **Scorer:** Anslow
Richard Draper is recalled in place of Sid Asher.

20. April 1957   Division 3 South   Gay Meadow   7,214
SHREWSBURY TOWN 2   NORTHAMPTON TOWN 0
Shrewsbury: Crossley, Bannister, Skeetch; Wallace, Maloney, Simpson; Kerr, O'Donnell, Weigh, Russell, Whittaker.   **Scorers:** Whittaker (p), Weigh.
Northampton: Elvy; Collins, Patterson; Yeoman,Gale, Leek; Morrow,, Mills, Draper, Woan, Fowler.
Ken Leek replaced Jack Smith at half back.

22. April 1957   Division 3 South   County Ground (Swindon)   7,523
SWINDON TOWN 4   NORTHAMPTON TOWN 0
Swindon: Burton; Hunt, Earl; Cross, Hudson, Fountain,; Riseborough, Micklewright, O'Mahoney, Edwards, Darcy.   **Scorers:** Micklewright 2, O'Mahoney, Edwards
Northampton: Elvy; Collins, Patterson; Smith J, Gale, Leek; Morrow, Mills, Draper, Woan, Fowler.
Ray Yeoman's injury allows Jack Smith back in to the side.

23. April 1957   Division 3 South   County Ground   4,950
NORTHAMPTON TOWN 2   SWINDON TOWN 0
Northampton: Elvy; Marston, Patterson; Smith J,Gale, Leek; English, Miller, Mills, Tebbutt, Fowler.   **Scorers:** English, Miller
Swindon: Burton; Hunt, Earl; Cross, Hudson, Fountain; Risborough, Micklewright, O'Mahoney, Edwards, Darcy.
The Cobblers make five changes including debuts for Roger Miller and Bobby Tebbutt.

27. April 1957   Division 3 South   Dean Court   8,392
BOURNEMOUTH & BOSCOMBE ATHLETIC 4   NORTHAMPTON TOWN 1
Bournemouth: Heath; Lyons, Woollard; Brown, Hughes, Melville; Loughrane, Ellaway, Arnott, Newsham, Cutler.   **Scorers:** Newsham 3, Loughrane
Northampton: Elvy; Marston, Patterson; Smith J, Gale, Leek; English, Miller, Mills, Tebbutt, Fowler.   **Scorer:** English
Ex-Cobbler Arnold Woollard is in the Bournemouth side.

30. April. 1957   Division 3 South   County Ground   4,463
NORTHAMPTON TOWN 1   BRIGHTON & HOVE ALBION 0
Northampton: Pickering; Claypole, Patterson; Smith J, Gale, Leek; English, Mills,
Bright, Woan, Fowler.   **Scorer:** Fowler
Brighton: Gill; Thomas, Jennings; Burtenshaw, Whitfield, Wilson; Gordon, Munday,
Humphries, Foreman, Howard .
Tony Claypole and Gerry Bright are given their debuts.

1957 - 1958

31. August 1957.   Division 3 South   County Ground   12,037
NORTHAMPTON TOWN 4   COVENTRY CITY 0
Northampton: Pickering; Robinson T, Patterson; Yeoman, Gale, Smith; Robinson M,
Woan, Hawkins, Leek, Fowler.   **Scorers:** Robinson M. 2 (2p), Woan, o.g.
Coventry: Ashcroft; Patrick, Timmins; Jamieson, Kirk, Austin; Pounder, Hill,
McPherson, Rogers, Boxley.
Tommy is recalled after missing the first two games of the season.

4. September 1957   Division 3 South   Recreation Ground   4,188
ALDERSHOT 0   NORTHAMPTON TOWN 0
Aldershot: Amos; Jefferson, Jackson; Rainey, Henry, Welton; Gaynor, Matthews,
Weigh, Waters, Tyrer.
Northampton: Pickering; Robinson T, Corbett; Yeomans, Gale, Smith ; Robinson M,
Woan, Hawkins, Leek, Fowler.
Bob Corbett makes his debut. A member of the crowd ran the line, official failed to arrive.

7. September 1957   Division 3 South   Gay Meadow   9,542
SHREWSBURY TOWN 3   NORTHAMPTON TOWN 1
Shrewsbury: Crossley; Bannister, Hobson; Wallace, Maloney, Simpson; Owen, Jones,
McAlinden, Russell, Whittaker.   **Scorers:** Jones 2, Owen
Northampton: Pickering; Robinson T, Corbett; Yeoman, Gale, Smith ; Robinson M,
Woan, Hawkins, Leek, Fowler.   **Scorer:** Woan
Bernard Jones, the ex-Cobbler, scores twice against his old club.

10. September 1957   Division 3 South   Griffin Park   10,697
BRENTFORD 7   NORTHAMPTON 1
Brentford: Cakebread; Wilson, Russell; Bristow, Dargie, Coote; Parsons, Ranford,
Francis, Towers, Newcombe.   **Scorers:** Ranford 2, Francis 2, Towers 2, Parsons
Northampton: Pickering; Robinson T; Corbett; Yeoman, Gale, Smith; Robinson M,
Woan. Hawkings, Leek, Fowler.   **Scorer:** Woan.
Maurice Robinson leaves the field with a dislocated shoulder. 1-1 after seven minutes

14. September 1957   Division 3 South   County Ground   6,986
NORTHAMPTON TOWN 1   READING 2
Northampton: Elvy; Corbett, Patterson; Yeoman, Gale, Smith; Mills, Woan, Hawkings,
Leek, Fowler.   **Scorer:** Leek
Reading: Jones; Lawrence, Reeves; Anderton, Spiers, Evans. Cumming, Campbell,
Dixon, Webb, Wheeler.   **Scorers:** Dixon, Wheeler
Tommy gets star rating. Reg Elvy, Ron Patterson and Roly Mills get a recall.

145

16. September 1957   Division 3 South   County Ground   4,528

NORTHAMPTON TOWN 3   BRENTFORD 1
Northampton: Elvy; Robinson T, Patterson; Yeoman, Gale, Smith; English, Woan, Bright, Leek, Fowler.   **Scorers:** English 2, Leek.
Brentford: Cakebread; Wilson, Russell; Bristow, Darge, Coote; Parsons, Rainford, Francis, Towers, Newcombe.   **Scorer:** Francis
Jack English and Terry Robinson return to the Cobblers side. Russell is carried off

21. September 1957   Division 3 South   County Ground (Swindon)   9,967

SWINDON TOWN 5   NORTHAMPTON TOWN 1
Swindon Burton; Neal, Lee; Clayton, Hudson, McDonald; Skull, Richards, Micklewright, Edwards, Davey   **Scorers:** Richards 2. Edwards 2. Skull.
Northampton: Elvy; Robinson T. Patterson; Yeoman, Gale, Mills; English, Woan, Bright, Leek, Fowler.   **Scorer:** Leek.
The Cobblers could not adapt to the very greasy pitch.

26. September 1957   Division 3 South   County Ground   3,454

NORTHAMPTON TOWN 4   COLCHESTER UNITED 1
Northampton: Elvy; Corbett, Patterson; Yeoman, Gale, Smith; Hawkings, Leek, Mills,Woan, Fowler.   **Scorers:** Corbett(p), Hawkings, Leek, Mills
Colchester: Ames; Fisher, Fowler; Parker, Milligan, Fenton; Blake, Plant , MCurley, McNeil, Wright.   **Scorer:** Plant
Lowest home gate since April 1955, against . . . .Colchester !

28. September 1957   Division 3 South   Vicarage Road   11,579

WATFORD 0   NORTHAMPTON TOWN 2
Watford: Curran; Shipwright, Bell; Catleugh, Brown, Barber; Walker, Cook, Anderson, Chung, Collins.
Northampton: Elvy; Corbett, Patterson; Yeoman, Gale, Smith; Hawkings, Leek, Mills, Woan, Fowler.   **Scorers:** Hawkings, Woan.
The Cobblers first away win in 10 outings.

30. September, 1957   Division 3 South   Layer Road   4, 391

COLCHESTER UNITED 1   NORTHAMPTON TOWN 0
Colchester: Ames; Fisher, Fowler; Hill, Dobson, Fenton; Williams, Plant, McCurley, Wright, Hutt.   **Scorer:** Wright
Northampton: Elvy; Corbett, Patterson; Yeoman, Gale, Smith; Hawkings, Woan, Mills, Leek, Fowler.
Ron Patterson, Ray Yeoman and the 'U's player manager Benny Fenton, were all booked.

5. October 1957   Division 3 South   County Ground   7,594

NORTHAMPTON TOWN 1   CRYSTAL PALACE 2
Northampton: Elvy; Robinson T, Patterson; Yeoman, Gale, Smith; Hawkings, Woan, Mills, Leek, Fowler.   **Scorer:** Patterson.
Crystal Palace: Rouse; Edwards, Greenwood; Belcher, Proudlove , Long; Harrison, Berry, Deakin, Cooper, Byrne.   **Scorer:** Cooper 2.
Johnny Byrne the Palace outside left would later play for England, while in Division 3.

9. October 1957   Division 3 South   Carrow Road   22,852

NORWICH CITY 2   NORTHAMPTON TOWN 2
Norwich: Oxford; Wilson J: Ashman; McRoahan, Butler, Wilson R: Gordon, Crowe, Hunt, Brennan, Gavin.   **Scorer:** Gavin 2
Northampton: Elvy; Collins, Patterson; Yeoman, Gale, Smith; Hawkings, Woan, Mills, Leek, Fowler.   **Scorer:** Leek 2
Collins returns as full back, Ron Patterson is booked.

9. November 1957   Division 3 South   County Ground   7,088

NORTHAMPTON TOWN 2   BRIGHTON AND HOVE ALBION 4
Northampton: Elvy; Collins, Patterson; Yeoman, Gale, Smith; English, Tebbutt, Hawkings, Leek, Fowler.   **Scorer:** Hawkings, Leek.
Brighton: Gill; Tennant, Jennings; Burtenshaw, Brown, Wilson; Gordon, Munday, Hartburn, Sexton, Howard.   **Scorer:** Hartburn 2, Munday, Sexton.
Tommy returns after being out for a month, only to be dropped again!

30. November 1957   Division 3 South   St. James Park   7.933

EXETER CITY 0   NORTHAMPTON TOWN 1
Exeter: Bell; John, Mitchell; Butterworth, Harvey, Waterman, Robinson; Nicholls, Atkinson, Rees, Dale.
Northampton: Pickering; Collins, Patterson; Yeoman, Gale, Mills; English, Woan, Hawkings, Leek, Fowler   **Scorer:** Leek
During the match a message was relayed to Jack English, that his son John was born.

7. December 1957   F.A. Cup (Round 2)   County Ground   12,691

NORTHAMPTON TOWN 4   BOURNEMOUTH & BOSCOMBE ATHLETIC 1
Northampton: Pickering; Collins, Patterson; Yeomans, Gale, Mills; English, Woan, Hawkings, Leek, Fowler.   **Scorers:** Woan, Leek, 2 o.g.
Bournemouth: Godwin; Lyons, Woollard; Melville, Hughes, Brown; Loughrane, Dowsett, Bedford, Norris, Cutler.   **Scorer:** Dowsett.
Both Norris and Hughes put in their own net.

14. December 1957   Division 3 South   The Den   6,761

MILLWALL 0   NORTHAMPTON TOWN 0
Millwall: Lloyd; Brady, Smith; Veich, Brand, Dawson; Shepherd, Summersby, Morrison, Heckman, Pulley.
Northampton: Elvy; Collins, Patterson, Yeoman, Gale, Mills; English, Woan, Hawkings, Leek, Fowler.
After a run of five straight defeats in the league, the Cobblers start to pick up form.

21. December 1957   Division 3 South   County Ground   7,058

NORTHAMPTON TOWN 3   WALSALL 0
Northampton: Elvy; Collins, Patterson; Yeoman, Gale, Mills; English, Tebbutt, Hawkings, Leek, Fowler.   **Scorers:** Tebbutt 2 Hawkings
Walsall: Chilvers, Haddington, Cultridge; Jarman, Jones, Rawlings, Stewart, Hodgkinson, Brownlie, Richards, Taylor.
Bobby Tebbutt opens his account for the club with a brace of goals.

26. December 1957   Division 3 South   County Ground   11,125

NORTHAMPTON TOWN 0   NORWICH CITY 1
Northampton: Elvy; Collins, Patterson; Yeoman, Gale, Mills; English, Tebbutt, Hawkings, Leek, Fowler.
Norwich: Nethercott; McCrohan, Ashman; Wilcox, Birtles, Crowe; Snowden, Moran, Hunt, Brennan, Gavin.   **Scorer:** Hunt.
The Cobblers have now lost more games at home, in the league, than they have won.

28. December 1957   Division 3 South   Highfield Road   20,375

COVENTRY CITY 1   NORTHAMPTON TOWN 1
Coventry: Spratt; Shepherd, Austin; Harvey, Kirk, Johnson; Smith, Hill, Rogers, Straw, Boxley.   **Scorer:** Hill
Northampton: Elvy; Collins, Patterson; Yeoman, Gale, Mills; English, Tebbutt, Hawkings, Leek, Fowler.   **Scorer:** Leek
Alan Woan drops out with blood poisoning.

4. January 1958   F.A.Cup (Round 3)   County Ground   21,344
NORTHAMPTON TOWN 3   ARSENAL 1
Northampton: Elvy; Collins, Patterson; Yeoman, Gale, Mills; English, Tebbutt, Hawkings, Leek, Fowler.   **Scorer:** Tebbutt, Hawkings, Leek.
Arsenal: Kelsey; Wills, Evans; Holton, Dodgin, Bowen; Clapton, Herd, Groves, Bloomfield, Nutt.   **Scorer:** Clapton
Northampton Town's biggest post war giant killing act.

11. January 1958   Division 3 South   County Ground   8,391
NORTHAMPTON TOWN 2   SHREWSBURY TOWN 0
Northampton: Elvy; Collins, Patterson; Yeomans, Gale, Mills, English, Tebbutt, Hawkings, Leek, Fowler.   **Scorers:** Leek, Hawkings.
Shrewsbury Town: Crossley, Bannister, Hobson; Wallace, Maloney, Walters; Price, McAlindon, Smith, Jones, Edgley.
Despite Alan Woan returning to full fitness, Bobby Tebbutt keeps his place,

18. January 1958   Division 3 South   Elm Park   10,846
READING 5   NORTHAMPTON TOWN 2
Reading: Jones; McLaren, Reeves; Anderton, Davies, Evans; Harrison, Webb, Dixon, Walker, Wheeler.   **Scorers:** Webb 4, Dixon.
Northampton: Elvy; Collins. Patterson; Yeoman, Gale, Mills; English, Tebbut, Hawkings, Leek, Fowler.   **Scorers:** Tebbutt, Hawkings.
Despite the heavy defeat, Tommy is one of the few players who won praise.

25. January, 1958   F. A. Cup (Round 4)   Anfield   56,939
LIVERPOOL 3   NORTHAMPTON TOWN 1
Liverpool: Younger; Molyneux, Moran; Wheeler, White, Twentyman, Macnamara, Rowley, Liddle, Bimpson, A'Court.   **Scorers:** Liddle, Bimpson, o.g.
Northampton: Elvy; Collins, Patterson; Yeoman, Gale, Mills; English, Tebbutt, Hawkings, Leek, Fowler.   **Scorer:** Hawkings.
Played on a glue pot of a pitch. Ben Collins score an own goal, the only time in his career

1. February 1958   Division 3 South   County Ground   9,845
NORTHAMPTON TOWN 3   SWINDON TOWN 0
Northampton: Elvy; Collins, Patterson; Yeoman, Gale, Mills; English, Tebbutt, Hawkings, Leek, Fowler.   **Scorer:** Hawkings, Leek, Fowler.
Swindon: Buxton; Neal, Bingley; Owen, Hudson, Thompson; Moore, Richards, Micklewright, Edwards, Darcy.
Bobby Tebbutt hit the upright, Ken Leek had two cleared off the line.

8. February 1958   Division 3 South   County Ground   8,400
NORTHAMPTON TOWN 2   WATFORD 3
Northampton: Elvy; Collins, Patterson; Yeoman, Gale, Mills; English, Tebbutt, Hawkings, Leek, Fowler.   **Scorer:** Leek 2
Watford: Curran; Bell, Harrop; McNeice, Meadows, Catleugh; Howfield, McMillan, Anderson, Chung, Walker.   **Scorers:** Walker 2, Chung.
Manager Dave Smith missed the match due to his father's death.

15. February 1958   Division 3 South   Selhurst Park   16,245
CRYSTAL PALACE 1   NORTHAMPTON TOWN 3
Crystal Palace: Rouse; Edwards, Greenwood; Long, Choules, Sanders; Harrison, Cooper, Berry, Pierce, Collins.   **Scorer:** Long
Northampton: Elvy; Collins, Patterson; Yeoman, Gale, Mills; Tebbutt, Woan, Hawkings, Leek, Fowler.   **Scorer:** Hawkings 2, Tebbutt.
Colin Gale was concussed and Alan Woan pulled a muscle.

148

22. February 1958   Division 3 South   Home Park   16,667
PLYMOUTH ARGYLE 3   NORTHAMPTON TOWN 0
Plymouth: Barnsley; Roberts, Fulton; Williams, Wyatt, Barrett; Anderson, Carter,
Baker, Kearney, Penk.   **Scorers:** Williams, Carter, Baker.
Northampton: Elvy; Collins, Patterson; Yeoman, Gale, Mills; Tebbutt, Woan, Hawkins,
Leek, Fowler.
Alan Woan leaves the field injured for the second successive game.

1. March 1958   Division 3 South   County Ground   8,711
NORTHAMPTON TOWN   3   PORT VALE 2
Northampton: Elvy; Collins, Patterson; Smith, Gale, Mills; English, Tebbutt,
Hawkings, O'Neill, Fowler.   **Scorers:** Hawkins 2, O'Neill
Port Vale: Jones; Donaldson, Raines; Poole, Hayward, Sproson; Askey, Kinsey,
Wilkinson, Steele, Cunliffe.   **Scorer:** Steele 2
Jack English, Joe O'Neill and Jack Smith all return to the first team.

8. March 1958   Division 3 South   Somerset Park   7,011
NEWPORT COUNTY 0   NORTHAMPTON TOWN 1
Newport: Hughes; Hollyman, Sherwood; Tennant, Wilcox, Docherty; Dixon, McSeventy,
Harris, Graham, Brown.
Northampton: Elvy; Collins. Patterson; Smith, Gale, Mills; English, O'Neil, Hawkings,
Leek, Fowler.   **Scorer:** Hawkings
Ken Leek returns for Bobby Tebbutt, Ray Yeoman to represent Div, 3 South .

15. March 1958   Division 3 South   County Ground   9,374
NORTHAMPTON TOWN 1   SOUTHAMPTON 3
Northampton: Elvy; Collins, Patterson; Yeoman, Gale, Mills; Tebbutt, O'Neil,
Hawkings, Leek, Fowler.   **Scorer:** Patterson (p)
Southampton: Christie; Wilkinson, Traynor; Birch , Page, McLaughlin; Flood, Roper,
Reeves, Mulgrew, Hoskins.   **Scorers:** Rogers, Reeves, Hoskins
Tommy Mulgrew is the Ex-Cobbler. Bobby Tebbutt and Ray Yeoman return.

22. March 1958   Divsion 3 South   Loftus Road   7,531
QUEENS PARK RANGERS 1   NORTHAMPTON TOWN 0
Q.P.R.: Drinkwater; Woods, Ingham; Petchley, Rutter, Angell; Dawson, Longbottom,
Cameron, Lock, Tomkyn.   **Scorer:** Longbottom
Northampton: Elvy; Collins. Patterson; Yeoman, Gale, Mills; Tebbutt, Woan,
Hawkings, Leek, Fowler.
Alan Woan returned in place of Joe O'Neill, who instantly slapped in a tranfer request.

27 March 1958   Division 3 South   County Ground   2,412
NORTHAMPTON TOWN 3   GILLINGHAM 1
Northampton: Elvy, Collins, Patterson; Yeoman, Gale, Mills; English, Tebbutt,
Hawkings, Woan, Fowler.   **Scorers:** English, Woan, Fowler.
Gillingham: Simpson; Parry, Hanavey; Proverbs, Nekroos, Riggs; Payne, Taylor,
Fletcher, Laing, Lucas.   **Scorer:** Riggs.
Simpson was carried off injured, lowest post war crowd at Northampton for a league game.

29. March 1958   Division 3 South   County Ground   6, 392
NORTHAMPTON TOWN 7   MILLWALL 2
Northampton: Elvy; Claypole, Patterson; Yeoman, Gale, Mills; English, Tebbutt,
Hawkings, Woan, Fowler.   **Scorers:** Woan 3, Hawkings 2, Tebbutt, English
Millwall: Lloyd; Brady, Smith; Veitch, Brand, Ranson; Shepherd, Summersby, Pacey,
Heckman, Pulley.   **Scorers:** Heckman, Shepherd.
Ken Leek has now moved to Leicester City. Tommy never scored but was the best forward.

4. April 1958   Division 3 South   Dean Court   15,196
BOURNEMOUTH & BOSCOMBE ATHLETIC 1   NORTHAMPTON TOWN 1
Bournemouth: Godwin; Thomas, Woollard, Brown, Burgess, Rule, Hampson, Bedford, Arnott, Dowsett, Cutler.   **Scorer:** Arnott
Northampton: Elvy; Claypole, Patterson; Yeoman, Gale, Mills; English, Tebbutt, Hawkings, Woan, Fowler.   **Scorer:** Yeoman
Second half of the match broadcast on the radio.

5. April 1958   Division 3 South   Goldstone Ground   20,066
BRIGHTON & HOVE ALBION 1   NORTHAMPTON TOWN 4
Brighton: Gill; Tenant, Ellis; Bates, Whitfield, Wilson; Gordon, Sexton, Harburn, Foreman, Howard.   **Scorer:** Sexton.
Northampton: Elvy; Claypole, Patterson; Yeoman, Gale, Smith; Mills, Tebbutt, Hawkings, Woan, Fowler.   **Scorers:** Woan 2, Patterson(p), Mills.
More watched the game at Brighton than in the total of the last three Cobblers home games.

8. April 1958   Division 3 South   County Ground   9,858
NORTHAMPTON TOWN 4   BOURNEMOUTH & BOSCOMBE ATHLETIC 0
Northampton: Elvy; Claypole, Patterson; Yeoman, Gale, Smith; Mills, Tebbutt, Hawkings, Woan, Fowler.   **Scorer:** Tebbutt, Hawkings, Woan, Patterson (p)
Bournemouth: Godwin; Thomas, Woollard; Brown, Burgess, Rule; Hampson, Gibb, Arnott, Dowsett, Cutler.
Cobblers make it five consecutive games without defeat in an effort to stay up.

12. April 1958   Division 3 South   County Ground   9,465
NORTHAMPTON TOWN 9   EXETER CITY 0
Northampton: Elvy; Claypole, Patterson; Yeoman, Gale, Smith; Mills, Tebbutt, Hawkings, Woan, Fowler.   **Scorers:** Tebbutt 3, Woan 3, Mills 2, Hawkings
Exeter: Hunter; Foley, MacDonald; Mitchell, Oliver, Harvey; Stiffle, Hill, Calland, Rees, Dale.
Every time a shot was aimed at the Exeter goal it seemed to go in, Cobblers biggest win.

16. April 1958   Division 3 South   Plainmoor   6,598
TORQUAY UNITED 1   NORTHAMPTON TOWN 0
Torquay: Wakeman; Bettary, Smith; Lewis, Northcott G, Johnson; Cox, Northcott T, Baxter, Mills, Pym.   **Scorer:** Pym.
Northampton: Elvy; Claypole, Patterson; Yeoman, Gale, Smith; Mills, Tebbutt, Hawkings, Woan, Fowler.
Larry Baxter is the ex-Cobblers player.

19. April 1958   Division 3 South   Priestfield   5,721
GILLINGHAM 1   NORTHAMPTON TOWN 2
Gillingham: Simpson; Parry, Hannaway; Laing, Buswell, Riggs; Taylor, Hutton, Saunders, Morgan, Clarke.   **Scorer:** Taylor
Northampton: Elvy; Claypole, Patterson; Yeoman, Gale, Smith; Mills, Tebbutt, Hawkings, Woan, Fowler.   **Scorers:** Hawkings, Woan.
The Cobblers do the double over Gillingham

24, April 1958   Division 3 South   County Ground   10,123
NORTHAMPTON TOWN 1   TORQUAY UNITED 0
Northampton: Elvy; Claypole, Patterson; Yeoman, Gale, Smith; Mills, Tebbutt, Hawkings, Woan, Fowler.   **Scorer:** Woan.
Torquay: Wakeman; Bettany, Smith; Lewis, Nortcott G, Collins, Cox, Northcott T, Baxter, Mills Pym.
The referee disallows a Torquay equaliser. Despite this win, it's Div. 4 next season.

26. April 1958   Division 3 South   County Ground   11,975
NORTHAMPTON TOWN 1   SOUTHEND UNITED 3
Northampton: Elvy; Claypole, Patterson; Yeoman, Gale, Smith; Mills, Tebbutt, Hawkings, Woan, Fowler.   **Scorer:** Hawkings.
Southend: Threadgold; Williamson, Anderson; Duthie, Stirling, Smith; Crossan, McCrory, Price, Baron, McGuigan.   **Scorers**; McGrory 2, McGuigan 1
Southend are safe, they stay in Division Three.

29. April 1958   Benefit Mills/Leek   County Ground   3,446
NORTHAMPTON TOWN 7   ALL STAR X1 5
Northampton: Elvy; Collins, Claypole; Yeoman, Gale, Smith; Mills, Tebbutt, Hawkings, Woan, Fowler.   **Scorers:** unknown
All Star X1: Sullivan (Arsenal); Wills (Arsenal),O'Neill (Cobblers); Scoular (Newcastle), Charles M (Swansea), Revie (Manchester City); Allchurch L (Swansea), Jones C (Swansea), Tapscott (Arsenal), Allchurch I.(Swansea), Mitchell (Newcastle).
Injury prevented Ken Leek from playing in his own testimonial.

2. May. 1958   Division 3 South   Roots Hall   9,391
SOUTHEND UNITED 6   NORTHAMPTON TOWN 3
Southend: Ronson; Williams, Anderson; Morrison, Stirling, Smith; Crossan, McGrory, Price, Baron, McGuigan.   **Scorers:** McGrory 3, Price 2, Smith
Northampton: Elvy; Collins, Claypole; Smith, Gale, Mills; English, Tebbutt, Hawkings, Woan, Fowler.   **Scorers:** Tebbutt, Hawkings,Woan.
The last ever Division 3 South match.

1958 - 1959

23, August 1958 Division 4   Vale Park   15,018
PORT VALE 1   NORTHAMPTON TOWN 4
Port Vale: Jones; Donaldson, Pritchard; Poole, Leake, Sproson, Jackson, Kinsey, Wilkinson, Steele, Cunliffe.   **Scorer:** Wilkinson
Northampton: Elvy; Bannister, Patterson; Yeoman, Gale, O'Neil; Mills, Kirkup, Hawkings, Woan, Fowler.   **Scorers:** Woan 2, Hawkings, Kirkup.
Alan Woan scores the very first goal ever scored in Division 4.

28. August 1958   Division 4   County Ground   11,916
NORTHAMPTON TOWN 3   CREWE ALEXANDRA 0
Northampton: Brewer; Bannister, Patterson; Yeoman, Gale, O'Neill; Mills, Kirkup, Hawkings, Woan, Fowler.   **Scorer:** Kirkup, Hawkings, Woan.
Crewe: Lowery;McDonnell, Millar; Campbell, Barnes, Ward; McNamara, Monk, Llewellyn, Pearson, Daley.
Bert Llewellyn, later to be a Cobblers player, was booked.

30. August. 1958   Divison 4   County Ground   11,288
NORTHAMPTON TOWN 3   CRYSTAL PALACE 0
Northampton: Brewer; Banister, Patterson; Yeoman, Gale, O'Neill; Mills, Kirkup, Hawkings, Woan, Fowler.   **Scorers:** Woan, Fowler, Kirkup.
Crystal Palace: Rouse; Edwards, Noakes; Truett, Choules, Long; Harrison, McNicholl, Deakin, Byrne, Collins.
Cobblers go top of the division.

2. September   1958   Division 4   Gresty Road   7,016
CREWE ALEXANDRA 1   NORTHAMPTON TOWN 2
Crewe: Lowery; McDonnell, Millar; Campbell, Cheadle, Jones; McNamara, Llewellyn, Riley, Pearson, Daley.   **Scorer:** McNamara (p)
Northampton: Brewer; Bannister, Patterson; Yeoman, Gale, O'Neill; Mills, Kirkup, Hawkings, Woan, Fowler.   **Scorer:** Woan 2
Tony Brewer concedes his first goal for the Cobblers, and then it's from a penalty.

6. September 1958   Division 4   Sealand Road   9,723
CHESTER 2   NORTHAMPTON TOWN 3
Chester: Griffiths; Gill, Souter; Hunt, Saunders, Mason; Foulkes, Webster, Jepson, Bullock, Richards.   **Scorer:** Bullock 2
Northampton: Brewer; Bannister, Patterson; Yeoman, Gale, O'Neill; Mills, Kirkup, Hawkings, Woan, Fowler.   **Scorers:** Woan, Fowler, Mills.
Two bottles were thrown onto the pitch during the match.

9. September 1958   Division 4   Brunton Park   11,283
CARLISLE UNITED 2   NORTHAMPTON TOWN 1
Carlisle: Thompson; Brown, Troops; Bradley, Doran, Thompson; Mooney, Broadis, Ackerman, Tulloch, McKenna.   **Scorer:** McKenna 2
Northampton: Brewer; Bannister, Patterson; Yeoman, Gale, O'Neil; Mills, Kirkup, Hawkings, Woan, Fowler   **Scorer:** Woan
Cobblers first defeat in the Fourth division, Colin Gale left the field injured.

13. September 1958   Division 4   County Ground   11,106
NORTHAMPTON TOWN 2   WATFORD 1
Northampton: Brewer; Bannister, Patterson; Yeoman, Gale, O'Neil; Mills, Kirkup, Hawkings, Woan, Fowler.   **Scorers:** Mills, Hawkings
Watford: Collins; Bell, Harrop; Catleugh, McNeice, Meadows; Gavin, Gordon, Chung, Howfield, Devine.   **Scorer:** Chung.
Watford goalscorer, Sammy Chung would later become manager of Wolves.

20. September. 1958.   Division 4   Victoria Ground   7,463
HARTLEPOOL UNITED 3   NORTHAMPTON TOWN 0
Hartlepool: Oakley; Waugh, Gibbon; Anderson, Moore, Johnson; Mitchell, Clark, Langland, Thompson, Luke.   **Scorers:** Thompson 2, Luke.
Northampton: Brewer, Bannister, Patterson; Yeoman, Gale, O'Neill; Mills, Kirkup, Hawkings, Tebbutt, Fowler.
Bobby Tebbutt replaced the injured Alan Woan,

25. September 1958   Division 4   County Ground   6,487
NORTHAMPTON TOWN 1   WORKINGTON 1
Northampton: Brewer; Bannister, Patterson; Yeoman, Gale, O'Neill; Hawkings, Baron, Norris, Woan, Fowler.   **Scorer:** Baron.
Workington: Newlands, Brown, Thompson; Tennant, Aitken, Finlay; Hinchcliffe, Gordon, Dodd, Hoey, Colbridge.   **Scorer:** Hinchcliffe.
Kevin Barron and Ollie Norris make their debuts. Norris and Brewer go off injured.

27. September 1958   Division 4   County Ground   10,999
NORTHAMPTON TOWN 3   SOUTHPORT 1
Northampton: Elvy; Bannister, Patterson; Yeoman, Gale, O'Neill; Mills, Baron, Hawkings, Woan, Fowler   **Scorers:** Woan 2 (1 p), Fowler
Southport: Richardson; Lawless, Rankin; Kinloch, Darvell, Morgans; McDermott, Schofield, Smith, Baker, Lee.   **Scorer:** Schofield.
Reg Elvy and Roly Mills replace the injured Brewer and Norris.

1. October 1958   Division 4   Borough Park   6,613

WORKINGTON 3   NORTHAMPTON TOWN 3

Workington: Newlands; Brown, Thompson; Tennant, Aitkin, Finlay; Hinchcliffe, Alexander, Gordon, Robson, Colbridge.   **Scorers:** Colbridge 2, o.g.

Northampton: Elvy; Bannister, Patterson; Yeoman, Gale, O'Neill; Mills, Baron, Kirkup, Woan, Fowler.   **Scorers:** Mills, Woan, Fowler.

Brian Kirkup replaces Barry Hawkings, Reg Elvy saved a penalty.

---

4. October 1958   Division 4   Plainmoor   5,399

TORQUAY UNITED 4   NORTHAMPTON TOWN 2

Torquay: Gill; Bettray, Smith; Lewis, Northcott, Johnson; Brown, Bond, Northcott, Baxter, Pym.   **Scorers:** Pym 3, Bond

Northampton: Elvy; Bannister, Patterson; Yeoman, Gale, O'Neil; Mills, Baron, Norris, Woan, Fowler.   **Scorers:** Baron, Norris

Ollie Norris returns, in place of Kirkup.

---

9. October 1958   Division 4   County Ground   5.826

NORTHAMPTON TOWN 1   YORK CITY 0

Northampton: Elvy; Bannister, Patterson; Yeoman, Gale, O'Neill; Mills, Baron, Norris,Woan, Fowler.   **Scorer:** Baron.

York: Forgan, Wardle, Howe; Patterson, Jackson, Spence; Hughes, Wilkinson, Wragg, Addison, Greensmith.   **Scorers:** Wragg, Addison.

Cobblers first home defeat in Division 4. Colin Addison later manager of Derby and Hereford

---

11. October 1958   Division 4   County Ground   10,077

NORTHAMPTON TOWN 1   EXETER CITY 1

Northampton: Elvy; Bannister, Patterson; Yeoman, Collins, Mills; Hawkings, Baron, Norris, Woan, Fowler.   **Scorer:** Woan

Exeter: Hunter; Foley, McDonald; Harvey, Oliver, Mitchell; Stittle, Rees, Calland, Nicholls, Dale.   **Scorer:** Nicholls

Ben Collins and Barry Hawkings replace Colin Gale and Joe O'Neil.

---

18. October 1958   Division 4   Highfield Road   22,305

COVENTRY CITY 2   NORTHAMPTON TOWN 0

Coventry: Wood; Kirk, Harvey; Nicholas, Curtis, Kearns; Hill, Straw, Rogers, Ryan, Satchwell.   **Scorer:** Straw 2

Northampton: Elvy; Bannister, Patterson; Yeoman, Collins, Mills; Hawkings, Baron, Norris, Woan, Fowler.

Ex-Cobbler Alf Wood is keeping goal for Coventry, during the Club's goalkeeping crisis.

---

25. October 1958   Division 4   County Ground   9,897

NORTHAMPTON TOWN 3   SHREWSBURY TOWN 3

Northampton: Elvy; Bannister, Claypole; Yeoman, Gale, Mills; English, Tebbutt, Hawkings, Woan, Fowler.   **Scorers:** Tebbutt 2, Woan.

Shrewsbury: Crossley; Hobson, Skeetch; Wallace, Maloney, Walters; Jones, Russell, Edgley, Rowley, Whittaker   **Scorers:** Jones 2, Whittaker.

Wholesale changes in the side, Barron, Norris, Collins are dropped, Patterson injured.

---

1. November 1958   Division 4   Feethams   5,579

DARLINGTON 2   NORTHAMPTON TOWN 2

Darlington: Tinsley; Leeder, Furphy; Bulch, Watson, Bell; Fletcher, McGrath, Carr, Milner, Morton.   **Scorers:** Carr, Milner.

Northampton: Elvy; Claypole, Patterson; Yeoman, Gale, Mills; English, Tebbutt, Hawkings, Woan, Fowler.   **Scorers:** Hawkings, Fowler

Bob Dennison, Middlesbrough manager, signed Ray Yeoman straight after the match.

8. November 1958   Division 4   County Ground   11,858

NORTHAMPTON TOWN 3   WALSALL 2
Northampton: Elvy; Claypole, Patterson; Smith, Gale, Mills; Woan, Tebbutt,
Hawkings, Baron, Fowler   **Scorers:** Tebbutt, Woan, o.g.
Walsall: Savage; Haddington, Guttridge; Billingham, Jones, Rawlings; Askey,
Hodgkisson, Brownlee, Richardson, Taylor.   **Scorers:** Hodgkisson, Brownlee.
Smith replaced Yeoman, Tebbutt was injured dring the game.

15. November 1958   F.A. Cup (Round 1)   County Ground   12,934

NORTHAMPTON TOWN 2   WYCOMBE WANDERERS 0
Northampton: Elvy; Claypole, Patterson; Smith, Gale, Mills; Woan, Kirkup, Hawkings,
Baron, Fowler   **Scorers:** Kirkup, Fowler.
Wycombe Syrett; Lawson, Moring; Truett, Fisher, Fryer; Rockwell, Trott, Bates,
Edwards, Tomlin.
The match was played in a thick swirling fog.

22. November 1958   Division 4   County Ground   7,598

NORTHAMPTON TOWN 1   ALDERSHOT 0
Northampton: Elvy, Claypole, Patterson; Smith, Gale, Mills; Tebbutt, Woan, Kirkup,
Baron, Fowler.   **Scorer:** Kirkup.
Aldershot: Marshall; Henry, Jackson; McMahon, Howe, Pearson; Walters, Munday,
Pacey, Lacey, Tyrer.
Bobby Tebbutt returns at Barry Hawkings expense.

29. November 1958   Division 4   Redheugh   2,870

GATESHEAD 4   NORTHAMPTON TOWN 1
Gateshead: Patterson; Ashe, Batty; Appleton, Trewick, Alexander; Robinson, Smith
Ken(1), Baldridge, Smith Ken (2), Kirtley.   **Scorers:** Baldridge 2, Smik Ken (1), Robinson
Northampton: Elvy; Bannister, Patterson; O'Neill, Gale, Mills; Tebbutt, Norris, Kirkup,
Baron, Fowler.   **Scorer:** Kirkup.
Tony Claypole, Jack Smith and Alan Woan were all out injured.

6. December 1958   F.A. Cup (Round 2)   Sandy Lane   10,203

TOOTING & MITCHAM 2   NORTHAMPTON TOWN 1
Tooting: Pearson; Harlow, Edwards; Holden, Bennett, Murphy; Grainger, Viney, Hasty,
Shade, Flanagan.   **Scorers:** Viney, Hasty
Northampton: Elvy; Bannister, Patterson; Norris, Collins, Mills; English, Tebbutt,
Kirkup, Baron, Fowler.   **Scorer:** Kirkup
F.A. Cup upset! Bannister is injured during the game, Mills goes full back, Baron half back.

13. December 1958   Division 4   Holker Street   4,209

BARROW 2   NORTHAMPTON TOWN 2
Barrow: Knowles; Jackson,Cahill; Proctor, Wilson, Keen; Torrance, Roberts, Robertson,
Purdon, Murray.   **Scorers:** Robertson, Purdon.
Northampton: Elvy; Coleman, Patterson; Norris, Collins, Mills; Hawkings, Tebbutt,
Kirkup, Baron, Fowler.   **Scorers:** Tebbutt, Mills.
The Cobblers first ever visit to Holker street.

20. December 1958   Division 4   County Ground   6,907

NORTHAMPTON TOWN 2   PORT VALE 4
Northampton: Elvy; Claypole, Patterson; Norris, Collins,Mills; Hawkings, Tebbutt,
Kirkup, Baron, Fowler.   **Scorer:** Fowler 2 (1 p)
Port Vale: Hancocks; Raine, Pritchard; Kinsey, Leake, Miles; Jackson, Steele, Poole,
Barnett, Cunliffe.   **Scorers:** Poole 2, Benett, Kinsey.
Tommy was given the penalty taker's job again, and converted his first effort.

26, December 1958   Division 4   Priestfield   6,947

GILLINGHAM 4   NORTHAMPTON TOWN 1
Gillingham: Simpson; Provervbs, Hunt; Hannaway, Parry, Laing; Bacon, Edgar, Terry, Patrick, Pulley.   **Scorer:** Terry 2, Bacon, Edgar
Northampton: Elvy; Claypole, Patterson; Mills, Collins, O'Neil; Olah, Woan, Kirkup, Baron, Fowler.   **Scorers:** Mills.
Bela Olah makes his debut, Kevin Barron is the new team captain.

27. December 1958   Division 4   County Ground   9,538

NORTHAMPTON TOWN 4   GILLINGHAM 2
Northampton: Brewer; Claypole, Patterson; Mills, Collins, O'Neil; Baron, Woan, Kirkup, Norris, Fowler.   **Scorers:** Fowler 3   Woan
Gillingham: Simpson; Hannary, Hunt; Smith, Parry, Laing; Bacon, Edgar, Terry, Patrick, Pulley.   **Scorer:** Smith, o.g.
Tommy hits the second hat trick og his career, 10 years after his first.

3. January 1959   Division 4   Selhurst Park   17,162

CRYSTAL PALACE 1   NORTHAMPTON 1
Crystal Palace: Rouse; Edwards, Noakes; McNichol, Choules, Long, Priestley, Summersley, Deakin, Byrne, Collins.   **Scorer:** Priestley
Northampton: Brewer; Claypole, Patterson; Mills, Collins, Smith; Baron, Woan, Hawkings, Norris, Fowler.   **Scorer:** Hawkings
Barry Hawkings and Jack Smith come back into the side,

10 January 1959   Division 4   The Den   11,388

MILLWALL 3   NORTHAMPTON TOWN 0
Millwall: Davies; Redmond, Brady; Humphries, Harper, Ranson: Broadfoot, Bumstead, Moyse, Heckman, Crowshaw.   **Scorers:** Broadfoot, Brady(p), og
Northampton: Brewer; Claypole, Patterson; Mills, Collins, Smith; Baron, Woan, Hawkings, Norris, Fowler.
Jack Smith scores an own goal. Joe Broadfoot later became a club record signing.

24. January 1959   Division 4   County Ground   7,168

NORTHAMPTON TOWN 2   OLDHAM ATHLETIC 1
Northampton: Brewer; Claypole, Patterson; Mills, Collins, Smith; Baron, Hawkings, Woan, Norris, Fowler.   **Scorers:** Woan, Claypole
Oldham: Reece; Beswick, Taylor; Hobson, Murphy, Chaytor; Bazley, Robinson, Stringfellow, Marsh, Phoenix.   **Scorer:** Phoenix
Story of the two full backs, Tony Claypole scores, Ron Patterson goes off injured.

31. January 1959   Division 4   Vicarage Road   6,200

WATFORD 3   NORTHAMPTON TOWN 1
Watford: Smith; Bell, Harrop: Catleugh, Chung, Meadows; Gavin, Gordon, Holton, Howfield, Bunce.   **Scorers:** Holton 2, Meadows.
Northampton: Brewer; Claypole, Patterson; O'Neil, Collins, Smith; Mills, Woan, Hawkings, Baron, Fowler.   **Scorer::** Woan
Two of the top scorers in the division faced each other, Cliff Holton and Alan Woan

7. February 1959   Division 4   County Ground   6,055

NORTHAMPTON TOWN 2   HARTLEPOOLS UNITED 1
Northampton: Brewer; Bannister, Phillips; Mills, Gale, Smith; Olah, Baron, Norris, Woan, Fowler.   **Scorers:** Baron, Woan.
Hartlepool: Oakley; Cameron, Waugh; Johnson, Moore, Anderson; Denham, Scott, Smith, Clark, Dunn.   **Scorer:** Smith.
Cobblers made six changes. Ralph Phillips made his debut.

14. February 1959   Division 4   Haigh Avenue   3,630
SOUTHPORT 1   NORTHAMPTON TOWN 2
Southport: Richardson; Dodd, Rankin; Kinloch, Parkinson, Grant; McDermott,
Fielding, Darvell, Barker, Woodhouse.   **Scorer:** Woodhouse
Northampton: Brewer; Bannister, Phillips; Mills, Gale, Smith; Baron, Tebbutt, Norris,
Woan, Fowler.   **Scorer:** Woan 2.
Bobby Tebutt returned to the side, Woodhead made his Southport debut.

21. February 1959   Division 4   County Ground   6,329
NORTHAMPTON TOWN 1   TORQUAY UNITED 1
Northampton: Brewer; Bannister, Claypole; Mills, Gale, Smith; Baron, Tebbutt, Kirkup,
Woan, Fowler.   **Scorer:** Woan.
Torquay: Gill; Smith J, Smith H: Clarke, Northcott G, Hancock; Brown, Bond, Northcott
T, Mils, Pym.   **Scorer:** o.g.
Jim Bannister put through his own goal.

28. February 1959   Division 4   St. James. Park   9,870
EXETER CITY 3   NORTHAMPTON TOWN 4
Exeter: Hunter; Foley, MacDonald; Mitchell, Oliver, Thompson; Stiffle, Rees, Calland,
Nicholls, Dale.   **Scorers:**; Calland 2, Mitchell (p).
Northampton: Brewer; Bannister, Claypole; Mills, Gale, Smith; English, Baron, Leck,
Woan, Fowler   **Scorers:** Leck, Woan, English, Fowler.
Derek Leck made his debut for the Cobblers. Kevin Baron asks for a transfer.

7. March 1959   Division 4   County Ground   14,365
NORTHAMPTON TOWN 4   COVENTRY CITY 0
Northampton: Brewer; Bannister, Claypole; Mills, Gale, Smith; English, Baron, Leck,
Woan, Fowler.   **Scorers:** Leck 2, Woan, Fowler.
Coventry: Lightening; Kirk, Harvey; Kearns, Curtis, Farmer; Satchell, Straw, Stewart,
Ryan, Daley.
Five consecutive games without defeat moves the Cobblers closer to the top four.

14. March. 1959   Division 4   Gay Meadow   7, 227
SHREWSBURY TOWN 4   NORTHAMPTON TOWN 0
Shrewsbury: Crossley, Hobson, Skeetch; Wallace, Maloney, Walters; Tucker, Jones,
Edgley, Rowley, Whittaker.   **Scorers:** Rowley 3, Whittaker
Northampton: Brewer, Bannister, Claypole; Mills, Gale, Smith; English, Baron, Leck,
Woan, Fowler.
The Shrews player-manager Arthur Rowley scores his second hat trick in a month.

21. March 1959   Division 4   County Ground   6,399
NORTHAMPTON TOWN 1   DARLINGTON 3
Northampton: Brewer; Bannister, Claypole; O'Neil, Gale, Smith; English, Baron, Leck,
Woan, Fowler.   **Scorer:** Woan
Darlington: Turner, Furphy, Henderson; Butch, Spencer, Bell; Foster, McGrath, Carr,
Milner, Lancaster.   **Scorers:** Lancaster, Carr, McGrath
Darlington full back Ken Furphy later managed Watford.

27. March 1959   Division 4   Park Avenue   5,988
BRADFORD 1   NORTHAMPTON TOWN 2
Bradford: Routledge; Dean, Lawton; Brims, Williams, Dick; Kendall, Atkinson,
Buchanan, Harvey, Byron.   **Scorer:** Williams (p)
Northampton: Brewer; Claypole, Patterson; Mills, Gale, Smith; English, O'Neil, Leck,
Woan, Fowler.   **Scorers:** O'Neil, Woan.
The two clubs had met in the F.A. Cup and Southern League, but first time in the League.

28. March 1959   Division 4   Fellows Park   5,991

WALSALL 2   NORTHAMPTON TOWN 1

Walsall: Savage, Haddington, Gutteridge; Billingham, McPherson, Rawlings: Davies, Faulkner, Richards, Hodgkison, Taylor.   **Scorer:** Richards 2

Northampton: Brewer; Claypole, Patterson; Mills, Gale, Phillips; English, O'Neil, Tebbutt, Woan, Fowler.   **Scorer:** English.

Ralph Phillips returns at wing half. Bobby Tebbutt replaces Derek Leck.

31. March 1959   Division 4   County Ground   7,544

NORTHAMPTON TOWN 4   BRADFORD 1

Northampton: Brewer; Claypole, Patterson; Mills,Gale, Smith; English, O'Neil, Leck, Woan, Fowler.   **Scorers:** Fowler, Woan, Leck, English

Bradford: Routledge,; Dean, Lawton: Brine, Williams, Dick; Atkinson, Buchanan, Allan,, Harvey, Byron.   **Scorer:** Buchanan

The press report that Claypole is being watched by Arsenal and Woan by Leicester

4. April 1959   Division 4   County Ground   7,284

NORTHAMPTON TOWN 0   MILLWALL 1

Northampton: Brewer; Claypole, Patterson; Mills, Gale, Smith; English, O'Neil, Leck, Woan, Fowler.

Millwall: Davies; Redmond, Toraday; Harper, Straw, Vasser; Broadfoot, Bumstead, Moyse, Ackerman, Heckman.   **Scorer:** Ackerman.

Tommy picked up an injury that would keep him out for the next game.

11. April. 1959   Division 4   Recreation Ground   2,567

ALDERSHOT 1   NORTHAMPTON TOWN 3

Aldershot: Brodie; Henry, Jackson; Gough, Hough. Pearson; Wathe, Stepney, Lacey, Tyrer, Parnell.   **Scorer:** Tyrer

Northampton: Brewer; Claypole, Patterson; Phillips, Gale, Smith; Miller, Mills, Leck, Woan, Fowler.   **Scorers:** Leck, Woan, Phillips.

Chic Brodie in the 'shots' goal, would later join the Cobblers.

13. April 1959   Division 4   County Ground   3,865

NORTHAMPTON TOWN 4   CHESTER 0

Northampton: Brewer; Claypole, Patterson; Phillips, Gale, Smith; Miller, Mills, Leck, Woan, Fowler.   **Scorers:** Woan 3, Fowler

Chester: Howells; Hughes, Gill; Souter, Spruce, Mason; Wiliams, Whitlock, Davis, Bullock, Richards.

Alan Woan scores his 28th, 29th and 30th league goal, only 6 away from club record

18. April 1959   Division 4   County Ground   5,799

NORTHAMPTON TOWN 1   GATESHEAD 0

Northampton: Brewer; Claypole, Patterson; Phillips, Gale, Smith; Loasby, Mills, Leck, Woan, Fowler.   **Scorer:** Mills.

Gateshead: Williamson; Dawson, Batty; Aitken, Trewick, Moffitt; Hogg, Smith Ken (2), Baldridge, Kirtley, Johnson.

Despite the win, promotion is out of the Cobblers reach.

20. April 1959   Division 4   Bootham Crescent   9,123

YORK CITY 2   NORTHAMPTON TOWN 1

York: Forgan; Ramsay, Howe; Patterson, Boyes, Moffatt; Hughes, Wilkinson, Farmer, Twigg, Powell.   **Scorer:** Wilkinson 2

Northampton: Brewer; Claypole, Patterson; Phillips, Gale, Smith; Kirkup, Mills, Leck, Woan, Fowler.   **Scorer:** Woan

Brian Kirkup gets a game at outside right in place of Alan Loasby.

25. April 1959   Division 4   Boundary Park   2,671

OLDHAM ATHLETIC 2   NORTHAMPTON TOWN 1

Oldham: Reece; Beswick, West; Spurdle, Taylor, Chayton; Bazley, Robinson, Mallon, Stringfellow, Hall.   **Scorer:** Robinson, Mallon (p)

Northampton: Brewer; Claypole, Patterson; Phillips, Gale, Smith. English, Tebbutt, Leck, Woan, Fowler.   **Scorer:** Fowler (p)

Tommy converts a penalty. Tony Brewer, both concedes and saves one.

30. April 1959   Division 4   County Ground   4,324

NORTHAMPTON TOWN 2   BARROW 0

Northampton: Brewer; Claypole, Patterson; Phillips, Gale, Smith; English, Tebbutt, Leck, Woan, Fowler.   **Scorers:** English, Woan.

Barrow: Knowle;Wilson, Jackson; Clarke, Marsden, McNab;Torrance, Gray, Durden, Keen, Kemp.

Last game of the season. The Cobblers finish 8th, seven points from promotion.

1959 - 1960

22. August 1959   Division 4   St. James Park   9,678

EXETER CITY 1   NORTHAMPTON TOWN 1

Exeter: Lobbett; Foley, Whitnall; Mitchell, Oliver, Thompson; Stiffle, Rees, Calland, Micklewright, Dale.   **Scorer:** Micklewright

Northampton: Brewer; Claypole, Patterson; Mills, Fotheringham, Bowen, Griffin, Ward, Leck, Woan, Fowler.   **Scorer:** Leck

First game under new manager Dave Bowen. Three players make their debuts.

27. August 1959   Division 4   County Ground   12,974

NORTHAMPTON TOWN 3   TORQUAY UNITED 0

Northampton: Brewer; Claypole, Patterson; Mills, Fotheringham, Bowen, Griffin, Tebbutt, Leck, Kirkup, Fowler.   **Scorers:** Leck 2, Tebbutt.

Torquay: Gill; Smith, Penford; Bettany, Northcott G, Rawson; Baxter, Cox, Anderson, Northcott T, Arundal.

Jim Fotheringham injured during the game. Larry Baxter is the ex-Cobbler.

29. August 1959   Division 4   Belle Vue   7,033

DONCASTER ROVERS 3   NORTHAMPTON TOWN 2

Doncaster: Nimmo; Makepiece, Gavin; Kilkenny, Mordue, Walker; Leighton, Fearnley, Chappell, Broadbent, Sharp.   **Scorers:** Fearnley 2, Chappell.

Northampton: Brewer; Claypole, Patterson; Mills, Gale, Smith; Griffin, Kirkup, Leck, Woan, Fowler.   **Scorers:** Leck, Woan.

Colin Gale, Alan Woan and Jim Smith all return , replacing the injured players.

2. September 1959   Division 4   Plainmoor   7,447

TORQUAY UNITED 5   NORTHAMPTON TOWN 3

Torquay: Gill; Smith, Penford; Bettaby, Northcott G, Rawson; Baxter, Bond, Northcott T, Mills, Pym.   **Scorers:** Northcott T. 2, Bond 2, Baxter.

Northampton: Brewer; Claypole, Haskins; Mills, Gale, Smith; Griffin, Kirkup, Leck, Woan Fowler.   **Scorers:** Kirkup 2, Leck.

Tommy set up all three Cobblers goals. Tony Haskins made his debut.

5. September 1959   Division 4   County Ground   11,298
NORTHAMPTON TOWN 0   WORKINGTON 0
Northampton: Brewer: Claypole, Patterson; Mills, Fotheringham, Bowen; Griffin, Kirkup, Leck, Woan, Fowler.
Workington: Newlands; Wilson, Rollo; Burkinshaw, Tennant, Finley; Jones, Morrison, Brownlee, Booth, Kirkup.
Dave Bowen, Ron Patterson and Jim Fotheringham, all returned to the defence.

10. September 1959   Division 4   County Ground   9 622
NORTHAMPTON TOWN 2   GILLINGHAM 1
Northampton: Brewer; Phillips, Patterson; Mills, Fotheringham, Bowen; Griffin, Kirkup, Leck, Woan, Fowler.   **Scorers:** Mills, Woan.
Gillingham: Simpson; Parry, Hunt; Smith, Hughes, Hannaway; Payne, Moore, Terry, Albury, Brown.   **Scorer:** Terry.
Pat Terry would later join the Cobblers. Referee was Jack Taylor, later a world cup official

12. September 1959   Division 4   Spotland   5,686
ROCHDALE 2   NORTHAMPTON TOWN 2
Rochdale: Jones; Edwards, Powell; Thompson, Milburn, Busby; Barnes, Cairns, Cooper, Spencer, Collins.   **Scorers:** Thompson, Milburn.
Northampton: Brewer; Phillips, Patterson; Mills, Fotheringham, Bowen; Griffin, Tebbutt, Leck, Kirkup, Fowler.   **Scorer:** Leck 2
Bobby Tebbutt comes in for Alan Woan who was injured.

16. September 1959   Division 4   Priestfield Stadium   5,970
GILLINGHAM 2   NORTHAMPTON TOWN 1
Gillingham: Simpson; Parry, Hunt; Smith, Hughes, Proverbs; Payne, Albury, Terry, Payton, Brown.   **Scorers:** Albury, Terry.
Northland: Brewer; Phillips, Patterson; Mills, Fotheringham, Bowen; Griffin, Kirkup, Leck, Woan, Fowler.   **Scorer:** Woan
Alan Woan, returned, scored the Cobblers goal, then replaced the injured Tony Brewer.

19. September 1959   Division 4   County Ground   9,426
NORTHAMPTON TOWN 2   GATESHEAD 0
Northampton: Isaac; Phillips, Patterson; Mills, Fotheringham, Bowen; Griffin, Kirkup, Leck, Woan, Fowler.   **Scorer:** Leck 2
Gateshead: Williamson; Hedley, Moffatt; Hobson, Lackenby, Aitken; Baldridge, Lumley, Smith, Murray, Hogg.
Peter Isaac makes his debut in goal. Best team performance of the season.

21. September 1959   Division 4   County Ground   8,675
NORTHAMPTON TOWN 0   MILLWALL 3
Northampton: Isaac; Phillips, Patterson; Mills, Fotheringham, Smith; Griffin, Kirkup, Leck, Woan, Fowler.
Millwall: Davies; Jackson, Brady; Harper, Brand, Howells; Broadfoot, Wilson, Ackerman, Pierce, Smith.   **Scorers:** Broadfoot, Wilson, Ackerman
Tommy missed a penalty. Peter Isaac saved one. Colin Gales asks for a move.

26. September 1959   Division 4   Feethams   7,199
DARLINGTON 3   NORTHAMPTON TOWN 2
Darlington: Turner; Dunn, Henderson; Furphy, Spencer, Poole; Carr, Downie, Darbyshire, Milner, Redfern.   **Scorers:** Carr, Milner, Redfern.
Northampton: Isaac; Phillips, Patterson; Mills, Fotheringham, Smith; English, Tebbutt, Leck, Woan, Fowler.   **Scorer:** English 2
Ron Patterson was carried off injured.

159

28. September 1959   Division 4   The Den   18,950
MILLWALL 2   NORTHAMPTON TOWN 1
Millwall: Davies; Jackson, Brady; Harper, Brand, Howells; Broadfoot, Wilson, Moyse,
Pierce, Crowshaw.   **Scorer:** Pierce 2.
Northampton: Isaac; Phillips, Haskins; Mills, Gale, Bowen; English, Tebbutt, Leck,
Woan, Fowler   **Scorer:** English
At 1-1, someone in crowd blew a whistle, players left field, returned and Millwall scored.

3. October 1959   Division 4   County Ground   8,316
NORTHAMPTON TOWN 2   ALDERSHOT 0
Northampton: Isaac; Phillips, Haskins; Mills, Gale, Smith; English, Tebbutt, Leck,
Woan, Fowler.   **Scorers:** Leck, Woan.
Aldershot: Brodie; Bannister, Jackson; Mibnday, Shipwright, Griffiths; Norris, Stepney,
Henry, Tyrer, Parrott.
Jack Bannister, late of the Cobblers is in the Aldershot team.

10. October 1959   Division 4   Boundary Park   5,419
OLDHAM ATHLETIC 0   NORTHAMPTON TOWN 1
Oldham: Ferguson; Beswick, West; Richardson, Ferguson C, Jarvis; Spurdle, Scott,
Bourne, Stringfellow, Phoenix.
Northampton: Isaac; Phillips, Haskins; Mills, Gale, Smith; English, Tebbutt, Leck,
Woan, Fowler.   **Scorer:** o.g.
The Latics centre half Charlie Ferguson put through his own goal.

17. October 1959   Division 4   County Ground   8,789
NORTHAMPTON TOWN 2   CARLISLE UNITED 2
Northampton: Isaac; Phillips, Haskins; Mills, Gale, Smith; English, Tebbutt, Leck,
Woan, Fowler.   **Scorers:** Woan, Fowler (p)
Carlisle: Thompson, G: Brown, Fletcher; McMilan, Doran, Bradley; Mooney,Walker,
McGill, Thompson, Murray.   **Scorers:** Murray, Walker.
Tommy converts a penalty.

24.October 1959   Division 4   Meadow Lane   14,867
NOTTS COUNTY 2   NORTHAMPTON TOWN 1
Notts County: Smith; Butler, Beeby; Noon, Loxley, Carver; Roby. Horobin, Newsham,
Forrest, Withers.   **Scorers:** Newsham, Withers
Northampton: Brewer; Phillips, Haskins; Smith, Gale, Bowen; Mills, Olah, Leck.
Woan, Fowler.   **Scorer:** Woan
Alan Woan had a goal disallowed.

31, October 1959   Division 4   County Ground   13,041
NORTHAMPTON TOWN 0   WALSALL 1
Northampton: Brewer; Phillips, Haskins; Smith, Gale, Bowen; English, Olah, Deakin,
Mills, Fowler.
Walsall: Christie; Haddington, Sharples, Billingham, McPherson, Rawling; Davies,
Hodkisson, Richards, Faulkner, Taylor.   **Scorer:** Faulkner.
Mike Deakin makes his debut, having joined fromCrystal Palace in exchange for Woan.

7. November 1959   Division 4   Victoria Ground   1,953
HARTLEPOOL UNITED 1   NORTHAMPTON TOWN 4
Hartlepool: Oakley; Anderson, Waugh; Burlison, Atkinson, Johnson; McKenna,
Scott, Smith, Clark, Dunn.   **Scorer:** Smith
Northampton: Brewer; Phillips, Patterson; Mills, Fotheringham, Bowen; Griffin, Kane,
Deakin, Leck, Fowler   **Scorers:** Deakin 2, Kane, Leck.
Peter Kane makes his debut. Smallest crowd of the season for a Cobblers game.

14. November 1959   F.A. Cup (Round1)   Plaimoor   5,661
TORQUAY UNITED 7   NORTHAMPTON TOWN 1
Torquay: Gill, Rentford, Donns; Bettany, Northcott G, Rawson; Baxter, Cox, Northcott T, Bond, Pym.   **Scorers:** Bond 3, Pym 3, Northcott T
Northampton: Brewer; Phillips, Patterson; Mills, Fotheringham, Bowen; Griffin, Kane. Leck, Deakin, Fowler.   **Scorer:** Deakin
All three scorers in the Torquay side, were Torquay born.

21. November 1959   Division 4   Sealand Road   7,283
CHESTER 1   NORTHAMPTON TOWN 1
Chester: Howells; Hughes, Gill; Hunt, Spruce, Clempson; Cooper, Foulkes, Kelly, Pimlott, Richards.   **Scorer:** Pimlott
Northampton: Isaac; Phillips, Patterson; Smith, Gale, Bowen; Griffin, Kane, Leck, Deakin, Fowler.   **Scorer:** Deakin.
Peter Isaac, Jack Smith and Colin Gale are all recalled to the defence .

28. November 1959   Division 4   County Ground   8,121
NORTHAMPTON TOWN 0   CRYSTAL PALACE 2
Northampton: Brewer;Phillips, Patterson; Smith, Gale, Bowen, Olah, Kane, Leck, Deakin, Fowler.
Crystal Palace: Rouse; Long, Noakes; Summersley, Evans, McNichol; Roche, Easton, Sexton, Byrne, Colfar.   **Scorers:** Roche, Byrne.
Tommy picked up an injury that would rule him out for the next few weeks.

28. December 1959   Division 4   County Ground   8,369
NORTHAMPTON TOWN 1   WATFORD 2
Northampton: Brewer; Phillips, Patterson; Cooke, Gale, Mills; Tebbutt, Leck, Kane, Ward, Fowler.   **Scorer:** Tebbutt
Watford: Linton; Bell, Nicholson; Catleugh, McNeice, Chung; Benny, Holton, Uphill, Hartle, Bunce.   **Scorer:** Uphill 2
Tommy returns together with Ralph Phillips, Bobby Tebbutt and Derek Leck.

2, January 1960   Division 4   County Ground   6,253
NORTHAMPTON TOWN 3   DONCASTER ROVERS 1
Northampton: Brewer; Phillips, Patterson; Cooke, Gale, Bowen; Griffin, Tebbutt, Mills, Kane, Fowler.   **Scorers:** Tebbutt, Mills, Fowler
Doncaster: Nimmo; Makepiece, White; Marshall, Lunn, Kilkenny; Sharp, Broadbent, Fernie, Walker, Meredith.   **Scorer:** Walker.
Match played in very muddy conditions, despite the win the Cobblers are 18th,

9. January 1960   Friendly   County Ground
NORTHAMPTON TOWN 2   SHREWSBURY TOWN 1
Northampton: Brewer; Phillips, Patterson; Cooke, Fotheringham, Carson; Wright, Tebbutt, Mills, Kane, Fowler;   **Scorer:** Wright, Tebbutt
Shrewsbury: Humphreys; Hobson, Skeetch; Wallace, Poutney, Harley; Ireland, Eagley, Whittaker, Starkey, Cornfield.   **Scorer:** Hobson
Alex Carson and Mickey Wright make their debuts.

16. January 1960   Division 4   Borough Park   3,788
WORKINGTON 5   NORTHAMPTON TOWN 1
Workington: Newlands; Wilson, Rollo; Hinchcliffe, Tennant, Burkinshaw; Jones, Morrison, Hartburn, Booth, Kirkup.   **Scorer:** Hartburn 2, Morrison, Booth, Kirkup
Northampton: Brewer; Phillips, Patterson, Cook, Gale, Bowen; Griffin, Tebbutt, Mills, Wright, Fowler.   **Scorer:** Bowen.
The Cobblers biggest league defeat for nearly a year

23. January 1960   Division 4   County Ground   5,355

NORTHAMPTON TOWN 3   ROCHDALE 1
Northampton: Brewer; Phillips, Patterson; Cooke, Gale, Bowen; Olah, Kane,
Mills, Deakin, Fowler.   **Scorers:** Olah, Kane, Deakin.
Rochdale: Heys; Thompson, Edwards; Bodell, Aspden, Busby; Spencer, Cooper,
Milburn, Anderson, Barnes.   **Scorer:** Milburn.
John Anderson is the ex-Cobblers player.

6. February 1960   Division 4   Redheugh Park   3,164

GATESHEAD 1   NORTHAMPTON TOWN 3
Gateshead: Williamson; Dawson, Moffitt; Hobson, Lackenby, Aitken; Wimshurst,
Lumley, Wilson, Armstrong, Steele.   **Scorer:** Wilson
Northampton: Brewer; Phillips, Patterson; Cooke, Gale, Bowen; Olah, Kane, Mills,
Deakin, Fowler.   **Scorers:** Kane 2 Mills

13. February 1960   Division 4   County Ground   3,477

NORTHAMPTON TOWN 3   DARLINGTON 1
Northampton: Brewer; Phillips, Patterson; Cooke, Gale, Bowen; Olah, Kane, Deakin,
Vickers, Fowler   **Scorers:** Olah 2, Kane
Darlington: Tingley; Leeder, Henderson; Poole, Spencer, Furphy; Morton, Milner,
Smith, Baxter, Redfern.   **Scorer:** Baxter.
Peter Vickers makes his debut, Tony Brewer saves a penalty.

20. February 1960   Division 4   Recreation Ground   4,197

ALDERSHOT 3   NORTHAMPTON TOWN 0
Aldershot: Brodie; Bannister, Devereux; Munday, Henry, Tyrer; Middleton, Stepney,
Kirkup, Howfield, Lawlor.   **Scorers:** Howfield 2, Kirkup.
Northampton: Brewer; Phillips, Patterson; Cooke, Fotheringham, Bowen; Olah, Kane,
Deakin, Vickers, Fowler,
Brian Kirkup joins Jim Bannister at Aldershot.

22. February 1960   Friendly   County Ground

NORTHAMPTON TOWN 2   BRITISH OLYMPIC X1 2
Northampton: Brewer; Phillips, Patterson; Cooke, Gale, Mills; Olah, Kane, Deakin,
Tebbutt, Fowler.   **Scorers:** Tebbutt, Kane
Olympic X1: line up not available
Cobblers coach Jack Jennings is also the coach to the Olympic side.

27. February 1960   Division 4   County Ground   6,746

NORTHAMPTON TOWN 8   OLDHAM ATHLETIC 1
Northampton: Brewer; Phillips, Patterson; Cooke, Gale, Mills; Olah, Kane, Deakin,
Tebbutt, Fowler.   **Scorers:** Tebbutt 3, Deakin 2, Kane 2, og.
Oldham: Ferguson J: McGill, West; Spurdle, Ferguson C, Richardson; O'Loughlin, Scott,
Stringfellow, Birch, Phoenix..   **Scorer:** Stringfellow.
Cobblers still in 18th position; Bela Olah missed a penalty,

1. March 1960   Division 4   Vicarage Road   13,024

WATFORD 3   NORTHAMPTON TOWN 1
Watford: Linton; Bell, Nicholas; Catleugh, McNeice, Chung; Benning, Holton, Uphill,
Hartle, Gordon..   **Scorers:** Uphill 2, Holton (p).
Northampton: Brewer; Phillips, Patterson, Cooke, Gale, Mills, Olah, Kane, Deakin,
Tebbutt, Fowler.   **Scorer:** Kane,
Watford do the double over the Cobblers this season.

| 5. March 1960 | Division 4 | Brunton Park | 3,503 |

CARLISLE UNITED 0   NORTHAMPTON TOWN 2
Carlisle: Thompson; Troops, Terris; Bradley, Doran, Thompson; Brayton, Walker,
McGill, Robson, Bevin.
Northampton: Brewer; Philips, Patterson; Cooke, Gale, Mills; Olah, Kane, Deakin,
Tebbutt, Fowler.   **Scorers:** Mills, Deakin
The Club's 'up and down' form continues.

| 12. March 1960 | Division 4 | County Ground | 8,902 |

NORTHAMPTON TOWN 4   NOTTS COUNTY 2
Northampton: Brewer; Phillips, Patterson; Cooke, Gale, Mills; Olah, Kane, Deakin,
Tebbutt, Fowler..   **Scorers:** Deakin 2, Kane, Tebbutt (p)
Notts County: Smith; Butler, Noon; Gibson, Loxley, Sheriden; Roby, Joyce, Newsham,
Forrest, Bircumshaw..   **Scorer:** Bircumshaw 2
Tony Brewer saves a penalty.

| 19. March 1960 | Division 4 | Fellows Park | 9,852 |

WALSALL 1   NORTHAMPTON TOWN 2
Walsall: Christie; Haddington, Guttridge; Dudley, McPherson, Rawlings; Davies,
Faulkner, Richards, Hodgkisson, Taylor..   **Scorer:** Richards
Northampton: Brewer; Phillips, Patterson, Cooke, Gale, Mills; Olah, Kane, Deakin,
Tebbutt, Fowler..   **Scorer:** Deakin 2
Bobby Tebbutt is taken off with a broken leg.

| 26. March 1960 | Division 4 | County Ground | 5,945 |

NORTHAMPTON TOWN 3   HARTLEPOOL UNITED 0
Northampton: Brewer;Phillips, Patterson; Cooke, Gale, Mills; Olah, Kane, Deakin,
Wright, Fowler..   **Scorer:** Wright, Deakin, Kane.
Hartlepool: Wilkinson; Waugh, Peck; Macgregor, Moore, Anderson; Bircumshaw.
Scott, McKenna, Smith, Clark
Five wins in the last six matches lift the Cobblers up the table

| 2. April 1960 | Division 4 | County Ground | 5,901 |

CREWE ALEXANDRA 0   NORTHAMPTON TOWN 1
Crewe: Jones K. Jones D. Campbell; Keeley, Wilmott, Warmhurst; Coleman, Russell,
Riley, Wheatley, Jones M.
Northampton: Brewer; Phillips, Patterson; Cooke, Gale, Mills;Olah, Kane, Deakin,
Leck, Fowler.   **Scorer:** Deakin.
Wheatley was carried off, Cobblers now 14th,

| 6. April 1960 | Division 4 | Park Avenue | 4,916 |

BRADFORD 3   NORTHAMPTON TOWN 0
Bradford: Hough; Walker, Dick; Brims, McCalam, Atkinson; Gibson, Buchanan, Allan,
Reilly, Byron.   **Scorer:** Allen 3
Northampton: Brewer; Phillips, Patterson; Cook, Gale, Mills; Olah, Kane, Deakin,
Ward, Fowler.
Richard Ward is the fourth player to be tried at inside left in as many games.

| 9. April 1960 | Division 4 | County Ground | 7,037 |

NORTHAMPTON TOWN 1   CHESTER 0
Northampton: Brewer; Claypole, Patterson; Cooke, Gale, Mills; Olah, Kane, Deakin,
Ward, Fowler.   **Scorer:** Deakin
Chester: Howells; Hughes, Gill; Hunt, Spruce, Clemson; Foulkes, Stopford, Davies,
Pimlot, Croft.
Cobblers take on Three new directors, Dr, Hollinsworth, Eric Northover & Archie Whatton

---

11. April 1960   Division 4   County Ground   5,710

NORTHAMPTON TOWN 6   BARROW 0

Northampton: Brewer; Claypole, Patterson; Cooke, Gale, Mills; Olah, Kane, Deakin, Leck, Fowler.   **Scorers:** Deakin 4, Kane 2

Barrow: Heyes; Staniforth, Robinson; Clarke, Marsden, Cahill; Kerr, Barlow, Robertson, McCheproe, Kemp.

Mike Deakin had already scored four goals against Barrow while playing for Palace.

---

15. April 1960   Division 4   Haigh Avenue   3,612

SOUTHPORT 0   NORTHAMPTON TOWN 4

Southport: Barnard; Ashe, Rankin; Rutherford, Darvell, Grant; Harrison, Moss, Fielding, Blain, Norcross.

Northampton: Brewer; Claypole, Patterson; Cooke, Gale, Mills; Olah, Kane, Deakin, Leck, Fowler   **Scorers:** Kane 3, Olah.

Now Nine Victories in last Eight games for the Cobblers.

---

23. April 1960   Division 4   County Ground   8,667

NORTHAMPTON TOWN 3   BRADFORD 1

Northampton: Brewer; Claypole, Patterson; Cooke, Gale, Mills; Olah, Kane, Deakin, Leck, Fowler.   **Scorers:** Fowler 2, Deakin

Bradford: Hough; Walker, Lawton; Brims, McCalam, Dick; McHard, Buchanan, Allen, Reilly, Byron.   **Scorer:** Reilly

Tommy returns from Injury and nets a brace of goals, Mike Deakin scored after 10 seconds.

---

25. April 1960   Division 4   Holker Street   5,400

BARROW 0   NORTHAMPTON TOWN 1

Barrow: Heyes; Stamford, Cahill; Clark, Robinson, McGlennon; Reid, Bannan, Robertson, Murdoch, Kemp.

Northampton: Brewer' Claypole, Patterson; Cooke, Gale, Mills; Olah, Kane, Deakin, Leck, Fowler.   **Scorer:** Leck

The Cobblers outside chance of a promotion spot is dependent on the reaults of others.

---

28. April 1960   Division 4   County Ground   10,847

NORTHAMPTON TOWN 0   CREWE ALEXANDRA 0

Northampton: Brewer; Claypole, Patterson; Mills, Gale, Bowen; Olah, Kane, Deakin, Leck, Fowler.

Crewe: Jones K: Jones R, Campbell; Keery, Wilmott, Warhurst, Coleman, Riley, Llewellyn, Russell , Jones. H.

First home game the Cobblers have failed to score in, since November.

1960 - 1961

---

20. August 1960   Division 4   Boundary Park   8,929

OLDHAM ATHLETIC 1   NORTHAMPTON TOWN 2

Oldham: Rollo; Beswick, West; Spurdle, Ferguson, Jarvis; Phoenix, Frizzell, McCurley, Stringfellow, O'Loughlin.   **Scorer:** Stringfellow

Northampton: Brewer; Claypole, Patterson; Cooke, Gale, Mills; Tucker, Laird, Deakin, Wright, Fowler.   **Scorer:** Deakin 2

David Laird is the only new face in the Cobblers team

| 24. August 1960 | Division 4 | Borough Park | 3,439 |

WORKINGTON 3   NORTHAMPTON TOWN 0
Workington: Wright; Brown, Copeland; Hinchcliffe, Tennant, Burkinshaw; Aitken, Harburn, Brownlee, Dixon, Kirkup.   **Scorers:** Dixon, Brown, Kirkup
Northampton: Brewer; Claypole, Patterson; Cooke, Gale, Mills; Leck, Laird, Deakin, Wright, Fowler.
Derek Leck returns to the side in place of Ken Tucker.

| 27. August 1960 | Division 4 | County Ground | 8,092 |

NORTHAMPTON TOWN 2   ALDERSHOT 1
Northampton: Brewer; Claypole, Patterson; Cooke, Gale, Mills; Olah, Leck, Deakin, Wright, Fowler.   **Scorers:** Deakin, Leck.
Aldershot: Brodie; Bannister, Jackson; Munday, Shipwright, Tyrer; Taylor, Norris, Matthews, Howfield, Parnell. **Scorer:** Howfield.
Ex-Cobblers manager Dave Smith is now the 'Shots' manager.

| 29. August 1960 | Division 4 | County Ground | 6,835 |

NORTHAMPTON TOWN 3   WORKINGTON 2
Northampton: Brewer; Claypole, Patterson; Cooke, Gale, Mills; Olah, Leck, Deakin, Wright, Fowler.   **Scorers:** Leck 2, Wright.
Workington: Wright; Wilson, Brown; Hinchcliffe, Tennant, Birkinshaw; Aitken, Harburn, Brownlee, Dixon, Kirkup.   **Scorers:** Harburn, Kirkup.
This victory puts the Cobblers in seventh place.

| 3. September 1960 | Division 4 | County Ground | 8,661 |

NORTHAMPTON TOWN 4   STOCKPORT COUNTY 2
Northampton: Brewer; Claypole, Phillips; Cooke, Gale, Mills, Olah, Leck, Deakin, Wright, Fowler.   **Scorers:** Deakin 2, Wright 2.
Stockport: Lea; Ashton, Webb; Bennion, Hodder, Porteous; Wilson, Anderson, Fletcher, Murdoch, Davock.   **Scorers:** Fletcher, Murdoch.
Ralph Phillips replaced Ron Patterson

| 7. September 1960 | Division 4 | Gresty Road | 8,449 |

CREWE ALEXANDRA 0   NORTHAMPTON TOWN 2
Crewe: Ferguson; Tansey, Campbell; Keery, Willmott, Jones D: Morris, Foster, Llewellyn, Wheatley, Jones M.
Northampton: Brewer, Claypole, Phillips; Cooke, Gale, Mills; Olah, Leck, Deakin, Wright, Fowler.   **Scorers:** Leck, Deakin.
A top four place for the Cobblers after this game.

| 10. September 1960 | Division 4 | Park Avenue | 7,616 |

BRADFORD 1   NORTHAMPTON TOWN 3
Bradford: Hough; Walker, Baillie; Atkinson, McCalman, Dick P: Gibson, Buchanan, Dick T, Reilly, Allan.   **Scorer:** Gibson
Northampton: Brewer; Claypole, Phillips, Cooke, Gale, Mills, Olah, Leck, Deakin, Wright, Fowler.   **Scorer:** Mills, Deakin, Wright
Bradford paraded nine Scotsmen in their side.

| 13. September 1960 | Division 4 | County Ground | 9,034 |

NORTHAMPTON TOWN 4   CREWE ALEXANDRA 1
Northampton: Brewer; Claypole, Phillips;Cooke, Gale, Mills; Olah, Leck, Deakin, Wright, Fowler.   **Scorers:** Leck, Deakin, Fowler, og
Crewe: Ferguson; Tansey, aCampbell, Keery, Barnes, Jones D: Coleman, Foster, Morris, Wheatley, Jones M.   **Scorer:**Wheatley.
Tommy opens his account for the season. The side is now almost picking itself.

17. September 1960   Division 4   County Ground   9,575

NORTHAMPTON TOWN 3   GILLINGHAM 1
Northampton: Brewer; Claypole, Phillips; Cooke, Gale, Mills; Olah, Leck, Deakin, Wright, Fowler.   **Scorer:** Wright 2, Olah.
Gillingham: Simpson; Proverb, Hunt; Wilson, Hughes, Cockburn, Bacon, Shepperd, Terry, Farrell, Brown.   **Scorer:** Terry.
Dave Bowen has made it known he would like to sign Pat Terry from Gillingham

19. September 1960   Division 4   County Ground   9,320

NORTHAMPTON TOWN 3   CHESTER 2
Northampton: Brewer; Claypole, Phillips; Cooke, Gale, Mills; Olah, Leck, Deakin, Wright, Fowler   **Scorer:** Fowler, Olah, Leck.
Chester: Brown; Hughes, Gill; Jones, Barrett, Clempson; Cooper, Anderson, Davies, Pimlott, Croft.   **Scorer:** Davies 2
Mike Deakin goes off injured, Bela Olah has a penalty saved.

24. September 1960   Division 4   Holker Street   5,583

BARROW 1   NORTHAMPTON TOWN 0
Barrow: Fullerton; Robinson, Cahill; Clarke, McEvoy, McGlennon; Jones, Roberson, Green, Flemming, Pashley.   **Scorer:** Fleming
Northampton: Brewer; Claypole, Phillips; Cook, Gale, Mills; Olah, Leck, Laird, Wright, Fowler.
Tommy makes his 500th Appearance for the Cobblers.

1. October 1960   Division 4   County Ground   11,558

NORTHAMPTON TOWN 2   MILLWALL 2
Northampton: Brewer; Claypole, Phillips; Cooke, Gale, Mills; Olah, Leck, Brown, Wright, Fowler.   **Scorer:** Brown, Leck.
Millwall: Davies; Jackson, Brady; Anderson, Brand, Howells; Broadfoot, Bumstead, Jones, Burridge, Rickis.   **Scorers:** Jones, Burridge.
Laurie Brown makes his debut and scores. Millwall equalise two minutes from time

3. October 1960   Division 4   Peel Park   4,603

ACCRINGTON STANLEY 3   NORTHAMPTON TOWN 2
Accrington: McInnes; Forrest, Lord; Smith, Stones, Hamilton; Entwhistle, Swindells, Hudson, Ferguson, Devine.   **Scorers:** Smith, Hudson, Swindells
Northampton: Brewer; Claypole, Phillips; Cooke, Gale, Mills; Olah, Leck, Brown, Wright, Fowler.   **Scorer:** Leck, Brown
Tommy's old team mate, Bill Smith is player coach of Accrington.

8. October 1960   Division 4   London Road   22,959

PETERBOROUGH UNITED 3   NORTHAMPTON TOWN 3
Peterborough: Walls; Stafford, Walker; Raynor, Rigby, Bonham; Hails, Emery, Bly, Smith, McNamee.   **Scorer:** McNamee 2, Emery
Northampton: Brewer; Claypole, Phillips; Cooke, Gale, Branston; Olah, Leck Deakin, Wright, Fowler.   **Scorer:** Leck, Fowler, Deakin.
Tommy was injured and went off. Terry Branston's debut. 3-0 up at one stage.

28. January 1961   Division 4   Belle Vue   3,028

DONCASTER ROVERS 0   NORTHAMPTON TOWN 2
Doncaster: Nimmo; Mordue, Curtis; Haig, Lunn, Swallow; Brettall, Fernie, Leighton, Broadbent, Meredith.
Northampton: Coe; Phillips, Claypole Cooke, Gale, Mills; Spelman, Brown, Deakin, Moran, Fowler.   **Scorer:** Brown, Deakin.
Jimmy Moran (Cobblers) and Ray Brettall (Doncaser) both made their debuts.

11. February 1961   Division 4   County Ground   9,255
NORTHAMPTON TOWN 3   BARROW 0
Northampton: Coe; Phillips, Claypole; Branston, Gale, Mills; Spelman, Brown, Deakin, Moran, Fowler.   **Scorer:** Brown 2, Deakin
Barrow: Heys; Warburton, Robinson; McNab, McEvoy, Webster; Armstrong, Robertson, Howard, Pashlewy, Hunter.
Terry Branston returns for the injured Barry Cooke.

18. February 1961   Division 4   The Den   11,707
MILLWALL 3   NORTHAMPTON TOWN 1
Millwall: Walters; Jackson, Brady; Bumstead, Harper, Anderson; Broadfoot, Jones, Brand, Burridge Spears.   **Scorer:** Burridge 2, Jones
Northampton: Coe; Phillips, Claypole; Cook, Gale, Mills;Spelman, Brown, Deakin. Moran, Fowler.   **Scorer:** Cooke
Ralph Brand (Millwall) and Colin Gale (Northampton) both sent off, Gale had 7 stitches.

25. February 1961   Division 4   County Ground   21,000
NORTHAMPTON TOWN 0   PETERBOROUGH UNITED 3
Northampton: Coe; Phillips, Claypole; Cooke, Gale, Mills; Spelman, Brown, Everitt, Moran, Fowler.
Peterborough: Walls; Whittaker, Walker; Raynor, Rigby, Ripley; Hails, Emery, Bly, Smith, McNamee.   **Scorer:** Bly, Smith, McNamee.
Mike Everitt makes his debut at centre forward.

4. March 1961   Division 4   Haigh Avenue   4,693
SOUTHPORT 2   NORTHAMPTON TOWN 0
Southport: Harris; Leeder, Griffiths; Hannowey, Darrell, Rutherford; Jones, Blain, Fielding, Harrison, Blore.   **Scorers:** Jones, Fielding.
Northampton: Coe; Phillips, Claypole; Cook, Gale, Mills; Tucker, Everitt, Brown, Moran, Fowler.
After Three consecutive defeats, wholesale changes are made, Tommy loses his place

1961 - 1962

26. August 1961   Division 3   Boothferry Park   8,027
HULL CITY 1   NORTHAMPTON TOWN 0
Hull: Fisher; Davidson, Garvey; Collison, Feasey, Bulless; Clarke, Price, Chilton, Henderson, Crickmore.   **Scorer:** Chilton
Northampton: Coe; Foley, Claypole; Leck, Branston, Everitt; Dixon, Mills, Terry, Moran, Fowler.
Tommy and Roly Mills are recalled to first team action, Cecil Dixon makes his debut.

29. August 1961   Division 3   County Ground   12,832
NORTHAMPTON TOWN 0   BRISTOL CITY 1
Northampton: Coe; Foley, Claypole; Leck, Branston, Everitt; Dixon, Clapton, Terry, Moran, Fowler,
City: Nicholls; Briggs, Thresher; Etheridge, Connor, Low; Rogers, Williams, Atyeo, Casey, Peters.   **Scorer:** Williams.
Dennis Clapton makes his debut. Pat Terry equalised but the goal was ruled offside.

2. September 1961   Division 3   County Ground   9,573
NORTHAMPTON TOWN 1   PORT VALE 1
Northampton: Coe; Foley, Claypole; Leck, Branston, Mills; Dixon, Everitt, Terry,
Moran, Fowler.   **Scorer:** Terry
Port Vale: Hancock; Whalley, Sproson, Poole, Nicholson, Miles; Jackson, Longbottom,
Llewellyn, Steele, Fidler.   **Scorer:** Llewellyn.
Only the second point for the Cobblers in five games, and their first goal.

6. September 1961   Division 3   Selhurst Park   25,535
CRYSTAL PALACE 1   NORTHAMPTON TOWN 4
Crystal Palace: Rouse, Noakes, Little; Long, Choules, Petchley,, Werge, Summersby,
Byrne, Smillie, Allen.   **Scorer:** Little;
Northampton: Coe; Foley, Claypole; Everitt, Branston, Leck; Dixon, Holton, Terry,
Moran, Fowler.   **Scorers:** Holton 3, Terry
Cliff Holton became the first post war Cobbler to score a hat trick on his debut.

9. September 1961   Division 3   County Ground   11,850
NORTHAMPTON TOWN 2   LINCOLN CITY 2
Northampton: Coe; Foley, Claypole; Everitt, Branston, Leck; Dixon, Holton, Terry,
Edwards, Fowler.   **Scorer:** Dixon 2
Lincoln: Graves; Jackson, Smith; Drysdale, Heward, Linnecur; McClelland, Harbertson,
Calland, Barrett.   **Scorers:** Harbertson, Barrett.
Tommy's last ever game for Northampton Town.

ALDERSHOT
1961 - 1962

28, December 1961   Division 4   Sealand Road   2,775
CHESTER 2   ALDERSHOT 3
Chester: Hardie; Hughes, Evans; Hennin, Gill, Bellett; Fitzgerald, Clarke, Davies,
Edwards, Jones.   **Scorer:** Davies 2
Aldershot: Jones; Eagles, Carey; Stepney, Shipwright, Tyrer; Taylor, Howfield, Norris,
Woan, Fowler.   **Scorers:** Howfield, Norris, Woan.
Aldershot's second win in the last six games. Tommy teams up with Alan Woan again.

13. January 1962   Division 4   Saltergate   2,509
CHESTERFIELD 2   ALDERSHOT 3
Chesterfield: Powell; Clarke, Sears; Poole, Blakey, Witham; Gissing, Lovie, Frost,
Frear, Lunn.   **Scorers:** Lovie, Blakey.
Aldershot: Jones; Eagles, Carey; Stepney, Shipwright, Tyrer; Taylor, Howfield, Norris,
Woan, Fowler.   **Scorers:** Howfield 2, Woan.
The first time Aldershot had two consecutive away wins since February 1957.

20. January 1962   Division 4   Recreation Ground   5,960
ALDERSHOT 4   STOCKPORT COUNTY 1
Aldershot: Jones; Eagles, Carey; Stepney, Shipwright, Tyrer; Taylor, Howfield, Hasty,
Woan, Fowler.   **Scorers:** Taylor 2. Howfield 2
Stockport: Beighton; Ashton, Webb; Murray, Hodder, Ricketts; Bentley, Ward,
Whitelaw, McDonnell, Davock.   **Scorer:** Ward.
George Norris out injured. Aldershot move into the promotion zone.

26. January 1962   Division 4   Recreation Ground   6,897
ALDERSHOT 3   DONCASTER ROVERS 1
Aldershot: Jones, Eagles,Carey; Stepney, Shipwright, Tyrer; Taylor, Howfield,
Norris,Woan, Fowler.   **Scorers:** Norris 2, Woan.
Doncaster: Nimmo; Parry, Staton; Marshall, Malloy, Bratt; Robinson, Anderson,
Youngers, Larkin, Ballagher.   **Scorer:** Anderson.
Fourth consecutive win for the 'Shots' since Tommy joined them.

3. February 1962   Division 4   Boundary Park   15,168
OLDHAM ATHLETIC 2   ALDERSHOT 1
Oldham: Rollo; Brannagan, McCue; Scott, Williams, Jarvis; Phoenix, Johnstone, Lister,
Frizzell, Colquhoun.   **Scorers:** Phoenix, Colquhoun.
Aldershot: Jones; Eagles, Carey; Stepney, Shipwright, Tyrer; Taylor, Howfield, Norris,
Woan, Fowler.   **Scorer:** Howfield.
The bubble burst, it was the biggest crowd Aldershot played in front of this season.

9. February 1962   Division 4   Recreation Ground   6,988
ALDERSHOT 2   ACCRINGTON STANLEY 2
Aldershot: Jones; Eagles, Carey; Stepney, Shipwright, Tyrer; Taylor, Howfield, Norris,
Woan, Fowler.   **Scorers:** Howfield, Woan
Accrington: Smith; Forrester, Walton; Pickup, Wilson, Cuddihey; Bennett, Hamilton,
Milner, Ferguson, Mulvey.   **Scorer:** Milner 2
Accrington resigned from the league a month later, this game was expunged.

17. February 1962   Division 4   Feethams   3,725
DARLINGTON 2   ALDERSHOT 0
Darlington: Peacock; Henderson, Mullholland; Furphy, Greener, Scott; Rayment,
France, Robson, Luke, Martin.   **Scorers:** Furphy, Robson
Aldershot: Jones; Eagles, Carey; Stepney, Shipwright, Tyrer; Taylor, Howfield, Norris,
Woan, Fowler.
George Norris leaves the field with an injury.

24. February 1962   Division 4   Recreation Ground   8,360
ALDERSHOT 0   MILLWALL 2
Aldershot: Jones, Eagles, Carey; Stepney, Shipwright, Tyrer; Taylor, Mathewws,
Howfield, Woan, Fowler.
Millwall: Davies; Gilchrist, Brady T; Obeney, Brady T, Anderson; Broadfoot, Townsend,
Terry, Jones, Mcquade.   **Scorer:** Terry, McQuade
Three months ago Tommy and Pat Terry were team mates at Northampton.

2. March 1962   Division 4   Field Mill   5,356
MANSFIELD TOWN 4   ALDERSHOT 1
Mansfield: Treharne; Toon, Humble; Williams, Phillips, Coates; Morris, Chapman,
Straw, Chapman, Wastaffe.   **Scorers:** Chapman 3, Wagstaff.
Aldershot: Jones: Eagles, Carey; Stepney, Shipwright, Tyrer; Taylor, Howfield, Kirkup,
Woan, Fowler.   **Scorer:** Woan
Another old team mate, Brian Kirkup, reappears in the Aldershot side.

7. March. 1962   Division 4   Gresty Road   4,739
CREWE ALEXANDRA 2   ALDERSHOT 0
Crewe Alexandra: Ferguson; McGill, Leigh; Keerey, Barnes, Tighe; Haydock, Connolly,
Lord, Wheatley, Smith R.   **Scorers:** Haydock, Connolly.
Aldershot: Jones; Eagles, Carey; Stepney, Shipwright, Tyrer; Taylor, Woan, Kirkup,
Howfield, Fowler.
After four consecutive wins, the Club follow it with five consecutive defeats.

9. March   1962   Division 4   Recreation Ground   5,223

ALDERSHOT 3   BARROW 1

Aldershot: Jones, Eagles, Devereaux; Stepney, Shipwright, Tyrer; Taylor, Woan,
Norris, Howfield, Fowler.   **Scorers:** Norris 2, Howfield.
Barrow: Caine, Richardson, Cahill; Hale, Robinson, Clark; Maddison Robertson,Dixon,
Darwin, Kemp.   **Scorer:** Darwin.
George Norris returns from injury with a brace of goals.

14. March 1962   Divison 4   Valley Parade   6,521

BRADFORD CITY 2   ALDERSHOT 1

Bradford City: Downie; Flocton, Storton; Mollatt, Smith M, Harland; Tate, Stowell,
Layne, Devitt, McCole.   **Scorers:** Stowell, Layne.
Aldershot: Jones; Eagles, Devereaux; Smitjh, Shipwright, Tyrer; Taylor, Woan, Norris,
Howfield, Fowler.
Aldershot's fifth consecutive away defeat.

17. March   1962   Division 4   Spotland   3,629

ROCHDALE 1   ALDERSHOT 0

Rochdale: Burgin, Milburn, Winton; Phoenix , Aspden, Thompson; Wragg, Richardson,
Bimpson, Cairns, Whittaker.   **Scorer:** Cairns.
Aldershot: Jones; Eagles, Devereaux; Smith, Shipwright, Tyrer; Taylor, Woan, Norris,
Howfield, Fowler.
Manager Dave Smith wields the axe after this game, Tommy is one of the players dropped

20. April 1962   Division 4   Layer Road   6,399

COLCHESTER UNITED 3   ALDERSHOT 0

Colchester: Ames;,Griffiths, Fowler; Harris, Forbes, Hunt RM: Hill, Hunt RR, King,
Macleod, Wright.   **Scorers:** Harris(p), McLeod, Wright.
Aldershot: Jones; Thomas, Devereaux; Carey, Shipwright, Tyrer; Howfield, Stepney,
Norris, Woan, Fowler.
Tommy returned to cover for the injured Alan Burton

1962 - 1963

8 December   1962   Division 4   Edgley Park   1,966

STOCKPORT COUNTY 3   ALDERSHOT 0

Stockport: Beighton; Murray, Porteous; Wylie, Hodder, Ricketts, Cutler, Ward, Bently,
McDonnell, Davock.   **Scorers:** Ward, Bentley, McDonnell
Aldershot: Jones; Thomas, Carey; Mulgrew, Henry, Tyrer; Priscott, Woan, Hasty,
Stepney, Fowler.
Tommy's last ever league game. Over 20 years after his first for Everton.

SUBSCRIBERS

ADDIS, Ian, KETTERING
ANSTRUTHERS, Abraham, LONDON
ARNETT, Les, RAUNDS
ATTREED, Claire, ST, JAMES
BAILEY, Ian, BEDFORD
BAKER, Richmond, HARDINGSTONE
BANDY, Terry, PARKLANDS
BECKINGHAM, Mavis & Harry, BIRKDALE,
BELL, Chris & Keith, SOUTHAMPTON
BOLTON, Beryl, SPRING PARK
BRIDGEMENT, F., RUSHDEN
CLARKE, John, BRIAR HILL
CLARKE, Roger, DUSTON
COCKERILL, Nick, DUSTON
COLES, J. H., KETTERING
COLES, Stephen, BLISWORTH
COLLYER, ABINGTON
COOKSON, Rebekah, CHAPEL BRAMPTON
COOKSON, Susan & Laurie, CHAPEL BRAMPTON
COOPER, Christian, DUSTON
COOPER, Ian, SHARNBROOK
CROUCH, Rita, NORTHAMPTON
DOWARD, Roy & Edna, PRESCOT, LANCS.
DUNKLEY, Margaret Ann, DUSTON
EL-BAYATI, Mustafa, NORTHAMPTON
ENGLISH, A., NORTHAMPTON
EVANS, Horace, CRANFIELD
FOSTER, T., WELLINGBOROUGH
FOWLER, Alan & Doris, CHESTERFIELD
FOWLER, Harry & Edna, CHESTERFIELD
FOWLER, Tom & Lynn, FAR COTTON
FOWLER, Tom & Katie, FAR COTTON
GARDNER, Councillor John J., KINGSTHORPE
GRANDE, Dustine & Tracey, KINGSLEY
GRANDE, Georgia, KINGSLEY
GRAVER, Bill, SYWELL
HAKES, John, HACKLETON
HANNETT, Ian & Lesley, HUNSBURY
HAWKINS, L. J., BRIXWORTH
HAYWARD, George & Pat, PRESCOT, LANCS.
HAYWARD, Keith & Nora, NEWARK
HAYWARD, Keith, WEST SUSSEX
HEMMINGS, Calvin, THE MALTINGS
HENNELL, Clive, FAR COTTON
HERBERT, Dave, KINGSTHORPE
HERRITY, Joyce & Bob, St. HELENS, LANCS.
HOLDEN, Matt, NORTHAMPTON
HOUGHTON, D. R., RAUNDS
INGRAM, Martyn & Tom, SOUTHAMPTON
Janet & Jeffrey, AUSTRALIA

JOHNSON, Bob, DERBY
JOHNSON, Ian, St. JAMES
JOHNSON, Lee, DUSTON
JONES, Bob, DUSTON
JOYCE, Syd, FAR COTTON
KENNEDY, Martin, KINGSLEY
KINGSTON, A. C., NORTHAMPTON
LAMBERTON, Clive, FAR COTTON
LAVELLE, John, GRANTHAM
LINSDELL, Ron, St. DAVID'S
LOEBELL, John, CHERRY LODGE
LOVE, Trevor, NORTHAMPTON
MARLBOROUGH, T, FAR COTTON
McNEELA, Pat, WELLINGBOROUGH
MUNNS, Glen, FAR COTTON
NASH, Tony, MILTON KEYNES
O'DELL, Fred & Raymond, RAUNDS
OLD WHITE HART SOCIAL CLUB, FAR COTTON
ONLEY, Graham & Andrew, BRIXWORTH
O'REILLY, T. P., MOULTON
PAGE, Graham, KINGSLEY
PARKER, Barry & Jenny, COLLINGTREE PARK
PATERSON, Iain, ABINGTON
PLATT, A. C., PARKLANDS
POWELL, Glenn, DUSTON
POWELL, Jim, EASTBOURNE
Rachael, DUSTON
RICH, Bill, HUDDERSFIELD
RICHARDS, Dave, NORTHAMPTON
ROBERTS, Andy, NORTHAMPTON
RODHOUSE, Ben & Amy, ABINGTON VALE
RODHOUSE, Graham, ABINGTON VALE
RODHOUSE, Terry, ABINGTON VALE
ROWE, John, EASTFIELD
SHERIDAN, Ralph, NOTTINGHAM
SIMMONDS, Martin, DUSTON
STOCK, Clive, DORSET
TACK, Mick, PARKLANDS
TAYLOR, Helen, RAUNDS
TAYLOR, Mike, WESTON FAVELL
TETT, Dave, BRIXWORTH
TITLEY, Michael,ABINGTON
TOMPKINS, Bob, DUSTON
TOMPKINS, Graham, DUSTON
TOWNLEY, Will, N. T. F. C.
TURNOCK, Ian, KINGSLEY
WADE, Mick, FAR COTTON
WALL, Louise & Peter, ROSS-ON-WYE
WALL, Nicky & Susan,ROSS-ON-WYE
WALTON, Roy, DUSTON
WALTON, Peter, WEST HADDON
WARREN, Jeff, ABINGTON

WATSON, John, DUSTON
WEBSTER, Brian, BRIXWORTH
WELLS, Miss. K. J., NEWPORT PAGNELLl
WEST, Keith, DELAPRE
WHITE, Gloria, DUSTON
YORK, Malcolm, RAUNDS